A
HISTORY OF ORNAMENT

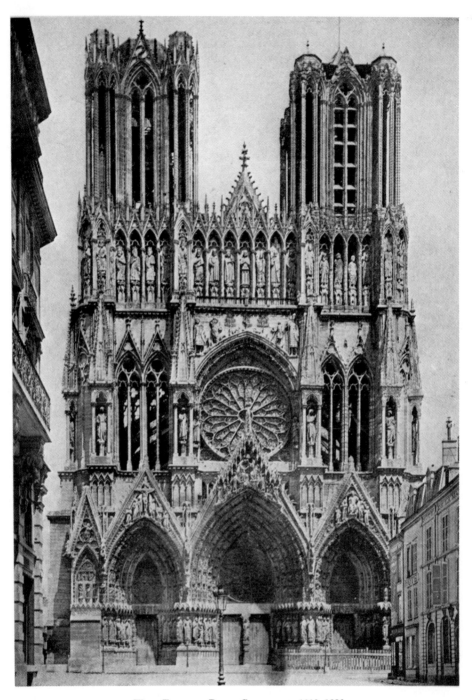

WEST FRONT OF REIMS CATHEDRAL, 1208–1380

A
HISTORY OF ORNAMENT

ANCIENT AND MEDIEVAL

BY

A. D. F. HAMLIN, A.M., L.H.D., A.I.A.

Professor of The History of Architecture in
Columbia University

WITH 400 ILLUSTRATIONS

NEW YORK
COOPER SQUARE PUBLISHERS, INC.
1973

Originally Published 1916
Reprinted by Permission of Genevieve Karr Hamlin
Published 1973 by Cooper Square Publishers, Inc.
59 Fourth Avenue, New York, New York 10003
International Standard Book Number 0-8154-0450-6
Library of Congress Catalog Card Number 72-92374

Printed in the United States of America

TO

MY STUDENTS

IN GRATEFUL RECOGNITION
OF THEIR INTEREST AND DE-
VOTION WHICH FOR THIRTY-
THREE YEARS PAST HAVE
MADE TEACHING FOR ME
A CONTINUOUS PLEASURE

PREFACE

Books on ornament are so many that to add to their number may seem at first sight a wholly superfluous task. Yet in all the long lists of the bibliographies of the subject there appears a singular lack of systematic treatises on the history of the various styles which have marked the growth and progress of decorative .art. Elaborate compendiums of ornament grouped by styles or by other categories are not wanting; the splendid "Grammar of Ornament" of Owen Jones, and "Ornament polychrome" of Racinet; the "Ornamentenschatz" of Dolmetsch, the "Handbook of Ornament" of Franz Sales Meyer, Speltz's "Styles of Ornament," and the excellent plates of "Historic Ornament" published by the Prang Educational Company, are examples of such collections of ornament, all meritorious in various ways, and all highly serviceable to students and decorators. But in the whole catalogue of the Avery Library of Columbia University—the richest collection in this country of works on architecture and the allied arts—I have found but two titles of systematic histories of ornament, one in French and one in German; neither available for those who read only English, and neither of them, even for those who can read French or German, exactly suited to the needs of the average English or American student of architecture or decoration.

I have for years felt the need of some such text-book

PREFACE

for students in my own courses in Columbia University in the History of Ornament. Of the many works in English, French or German, mentioned above, which to any extent recognize the historical element in the styles of ornament, some are too expensive for student use; some are too brief or too superficial in their text, some inadequate in their illustrations. In response to many appeals from teachers in other institutions, from their students and from my own, and with a view of meeting my own needs in teaching, I have ventured on the task of attempting such a systematic history of ornament. This volume represents the first half of the work which I hope to complete by a second volume, if this one shall meet with the favor of the public. It is, however, complete in itself, as it covers the ancient and medieval styles, leaving the styles of the Renaissance, of modern times and of the Orient, for the second volume.

The predominance of illustrations from architecture is due not merely to the fact that these chapters are based on lectures to architects; but also to the fact that the styles are most clearly exhibited in the progress of architecture as the "mistress art." It is hoped that the "Books Recommended" will enable the reader to supply for himself the illustrations from the other arts which he finds lacking in this work.

With regard to the illustrations, I may say that the majority are either from my own drawings or reproduced directly from photographs. As they are presented purely to illustrate the subject and not as models of draftsmanship, I trust they will not be too severely criticised on the technical side. The extreme smallness of many of them has been made necessary by the desire to keep the volume within modest limits of size and price. For the same reason the number of plates in color had to be restricted. Larger plates, larger cuts and more of them, would have made the book bulky and costly beyond measure, at least for student use.

I beg herewith to make my acknowledgments to all who have helped me in preparing these illustrations: especially to a number of my students, whose names will be found in the List of Illustrations; to Messrs. Chapman and Hall for the use of several illustrations from Ward's "Historic Ornament"; to Messrs. Longmans, Green & Co. for the use of a cut of capitals from my "History of Architecture"; to the Prang Educational Company, for the use of a number of illustrations in color from their "Plates of Historic Ornament"; to the publishers of the "Architectural Record" for several cuts from various issues; to the "American Architect" for permission to use a number of my own illustrations in various issues between 1898 and 1901; to the Metropolitan Museum of Art, New York, for permission to reproduce a number of the Museum's official photographs of casts and models in the Willard Architectural Collection; to the house of Bruno Hessling for permission to reproduce a number of illustrations from Meyer's Handbook of Ornament, and my Fig. 332 from Speltz, *Styles of Ornament;* to my daughter Genevieve for two drawings; and to the officers of the Avery Library for much valuable assistance cheerfully rendered. I have tried to give credit, in my List of Illustrations, for all such assistance, and to indicate the sources of the illustrations as far as possible. Some of them, however, were drawn so long ago, or have come into my possession from sources so long forgotten, that I have not been able in every case to do this. I trust I have not trespassed on any one's proprietary rights in any case. Many of my own drawings are re-interpretations of subjects appearing in other works; in such cases I have, where possible, indicated the source by the words "after" so-and-so.

There are two classes of figures besides the Plates I to XXII: those in the text, and those gathered into pages distributed through the text. To aid the reader in finding the references to illustrations, I have in the text referred to all of the first class,—those in the text— by the abbreviation "Fig." or "Figs."; while the word "Figure" refers always to illustrations grouped in pages; the page-reference is sometimes added.

I desire to express my appreciation of the cordial and generous coöperation of The Century Co. in the preparation of this work.

I commend this fruit of my labors to the kind consideration of teachers and students of architecture and decorative design, and to designers generally, with the hope that it will be found to meet their needs and prove useful both in the class-room and the studio.

A. D. F. HAMLIN.

Christmas Cove, Maine,
   August 14, 1916

CONTENTS

xi

LIST OF ILLUSTRATIONS

In the following List, the sources of the illustrations are indicated wherever possible. A number of them, however, have been made from drawings, tracings or engravings in the Author's possession from sources he has been unable to identify. All illustrations not otherwise designated are from original drawings by the Author. Wherever these have been based on or suggested by illustrations in other works, the fact is expressed by "A. after" followed by the source from which the drawing has been derived or on which it is based. Many cuts are from drawings by students of Columbia University; these are indicated by the initials C. U., followed in some cases by the student's name. It has not been possible to trace the source of all these drawings. Other abbreviations and references are as follows: A. = Author; A. C. H. = Haddon, *Evolution in Art;* A. M. N. H. = American Museum of Natural History, New York; Arch. Rec. = *Architectural Record* (N. Y.); A. p. T. = *L'Art pour Tous;* Bond = *Introduction to English Church Architecture;* Colling = *Gothic Foliage, Gothic Ornaments;* F. & L. = Furtwängler und Löschke, *Mykenische Vasen;* F. P. = Flinders-Petrie, *Egyptian Decorative Art;* Hauser = *Styllehre der architektonischen Formen des Mittelalters;* Loftus = *Researches in Chaldœa,* etc.; Met. Mus. = Metropolitan Museum of Art, New York; Meyer = *Meyer's Ornamentale Formenlehre;* O. J. = Owen Jones, *Grammar of Ornament;* P. d'A. = Prisse d'Avennes, *L'Art Egyptien;* P. & C. = Perrot et Chipiez, *Histoire de l'art dans l'antiquité;* Pho. = Photograph; Rickman = *Attempt to Discriminate the Styles,* etc.; Ward = J. Ward, Historic Ornament; W. H. G. = W. H. Goodyear, *Grammar of the Lotus* and articles in *Architectural Record.*

In the text of this work, references to cuts intercalated in the printed page are indicated by the abbreviation "Fig." or "Figs." followed by the number. The word "Figure" in full followed by a number refers to illustrations grouped in full pages.

LIST OF ILLUSTRATIONS

LIST OF ILLUSTRATIONS

LIST OF ILLUSTRATIONS

xvi

LIST OF ILLUSTRATIONS

LIST OF ILLUSTRATIONS

xviii

LIST OF ILLUSTRATIONS

LIST OF ILLUSTRATIONS

LIST OF ILLUSTRATIONS

LIST OF ILLUSTRATIONS

LIST OF ILLUSTRATIONS

xxiii

LIST OF ILLUSTRATIONS

A HISTORY OF ORNAMENT
ANCIENT AND MEDIEVAL

A HISTORY OF ORNAMENT
ANCIENT AND MEDIEVAL

CHAPTER I

INTRODUCTORY

Definitions.

The history of ornament is the record of the origins and progressive developments of decorative design. By *decoration* is meant the adornment or embellishment of an object by purposed modifications of its form or color. When decoration is effected by the repetition or combination of specific form-elements according to a predetermined scheme, the form-elements are called *motives.* Collectively they are denominated *ornament,* and when combined or repeated according to some definite geometric system, they are said to form a *pattern.* Thus on page 9, Figure 1 is an ornament; so is Figure 2, which shows a geometric pattern formed with the motive *aa.* *Pure ornament* is that in which the decorative purpose wholly dominates the design, as distinguished from decorative painting and decorative sculpture, in which the decorative purpose is subordinate to the pictorial or sculptural representation of a fact, event or idea.

3

Thus in the Parthenon the sculptured pediments, metopes and frieze, representing episodes and scenes from Greek mythology and legend, are examples of decorative sculpture; while the triglyphs, antefixæ and painted moldings are examples of pure ornament.

There is a large field of decorative design which partakes somewhat of the character of both pure ornament and pictorial or sculptural representation. Such are symbolical and grotesque figures, masks, lions' heads and much floral ornament, all of which are at once decorative and representative. Each example of such decoration must be classified according to its predominant purpose. Thus, although Figure 1 plainly pictures a grapevine, its formally artificial arrangement shows it to be intended as an ornament and not a picture. There are, however, many cases in which the purposes of representation and decoration are so evenly balanced that they may be with equal propriety assigned to either category.

Classifications.

Pure ornament may be classified according to any of several principles: *e.g.,* according to—

    A.   Its way of covering space.

    B.   The manner and means of its production.

    C.   The method or principle of its design.

    D.   The object to which it is applied.

    E.   Its relation to structure.

    A.   According to the *way in which ornament covers space* it may be divided into *linear, all-over,* and *radiating* ornament. Each of these may be subdivided into *continuous* and *discontinuous* ornament. In linear ornament the motives are arranged in sequence along a single line, to form bands or borders, as in Figure 3, in which *a* and *b* are continuous linear patterns, and *c* discontinuous. In "all-over" patterns the units are arranged along two or more intersecting systems of lines so as to cover a broad surface (Figures 2, 5, 8). In radiating patterns the surface is covered by units radiating from a central point (Figures 6, 7). In each of these cases the ornament may be continuous, each unit being connected with its neighbors (Figures 3, *a, b;* Figure 18, page 23) or discontinuous as in Figure 3, *c* or Figure 5. Continuous "all-overs" forming a mesh of two sets of intersecting lines are called *quarries* (from the French *carré* = square). Discontinuous all-overs are called *powderings;* more rarely they are said to be *spangled* (Figure 5). When isolated units are powdered or spangled in the meshes of a quarry, the combination is called a *diaper.* Figure 5 is a powdering; 2 is a quarry; 8 a diaper pattern.

B. According to the *means by which the ornament is produced,* it is classified as *plastic* or *chromatic.* Plastic ornament is such as depends on light-and-shade for its effect, being produced by raising or depressing the surface in various ways, as by molding, carving, hammering, stamping, etc. (Figures 4, 6, 9). Chromatic ornament is all such as depends on color (including black and white) for its effect, as in Figure 10 representing a painted band. Certain classes of textile ornament, like lace and embroidery, in which open-work and relief are depended on to produce the pattern, are included under plastic ornament. Chromatic ornament comprises all painted ornament, enamel, inlay, stained glass and mosaic, and all such textile ornament as depends upon effects of color, whether produced by weaving, printing, needle work, or otherwise.

C. According to the *source and principle of its design,* ornament is divisible into the three categories of *conventional, naturalistic,* and *conventionalized-natural* ornament. Conventional ornament is in general that which is the product of fancy or definite rule working upon pure form, and is for the most part geometric in character. Zigzags, frets, spirals and all geometric patterns fall under this head (Figures 3, 7). Naturalistic ornament comprises all decorative forms derived from Nature directly and with little or no change, such as flower and leaf forms, lion's heads, and the like, as in Figures 1, 10. When, however, natural forms are subjected to purposed modifications to adapt them to decorative effect, they are said to be conventionalized; and this class of ornament constitutes more than half of all the ornament of nearly all the historic styles. The acanthus leaf (Fig. 174), and a whole world of floral motives in both classic and medieval art, belong in this category (Figures 4, 6, 9, 10, on page 9, and 16 *b*, 20, 28 on page 23). The nature-form is subjected to one or more of the operations of *regularization* of details that in nature occur irregularly or unsymmetrically; suppression or *abstraction* of features that occur in nature but are repugnant to the desired decorative effect; *exaggeration* of minor details; *multiplication* of what occurs only once or at rare intervals in the natural object; and *combination,* or the union in one design of elements that do not in Nature occur together.

D. According to the *object to which it is applied,* ornament is divided into *architectural* ornament, applied to or executed in or upon fixed structures, and *industrial* ornament, which adorns movable objects. Capitals of columns, friezes, gargoyles, finials, cornices, and balustrades are examples of architectural ornament; vase-decorations, furniture-carving, silverware, jewelry, laces, book-covers belong technically in the field of industrial ornament. There is a large class of decorative works that may be placed in either category, such as pulpits, choir-stalls, monumental candelabra and the like.

E. Ornament may again be divided into two categories according to its *relation to structure.* *Structural* ornament is that which belongs to, grows out of, or strongly suggests, the structural framework and constitution of the object ornamented: such are capitals, cornices, balustrades, window-trims, tracery, moldings, paneling, metal scroll-work and the like. Applied ornament is that which is added to an object already complete structurally; such as painted ornament, mosaic, inlay, paper-hangings, tapestries, etc.

Significance of Classifications.

All these classifications are devices for convenience in the discussion and criticism of ornament, and are important only as they serve this purpose. They correspond to real differences of design, process and purpose, but there is always a wide borderland in which classification is not easy, and perhaps not important. Each classification covers the entire field of ornament, so that any decorative design may be assigned its place in all five classifications. Thus the carving in the spandrels of Westminster Abbey (Fig. 367) would be (A) a diaper, (B) plastic ornament of (C) conventionalized-natural flowers, (D) architectural and (E) either structural or applied, as one may prefer to consider it. A fret-border embroidered on an altar-cloth or painted on a vase, would be a linear, chromatic, conventional, industrial, applied ornament. These classifications depend upon one's critical judgment, especially in C, D and E, so that differences in the classifications of the same ornament by different writers are frequent and unimportant, especially where a design combines elements from different categories of the same class, as when carving and color are combined, or natural forms blended with purely geometric or conventional elements.

Meaning of History.

Decorative design appears at first sight to be so entirely a matter of the designer's unhampered fancy, that a history of the art might seem an impossibility; for how can there be a history of millions of independent, unrelated fancies? But as a matter of fact no designer is or ever has been wholly free. In the first place, he knows but an infinitesimal fraction of the world of possible decorative forms—those, in short, which he has been taught or has seen, or has learned by experiment. He is hampered by the traditions of his art, by the taste of his age and the demands of the market, by the

8

Fig.1 Grapevine Border

Fig.2. All-over Pattern: Quarry.

Fig.3. Linear Patterns

Fig.4 Carving: Doge's Palace.

Fig.5 All-over Pattern: Powdering.

Fig.6. Gothic Rosette

Fig.7 Moorish Star Pattern

Fig.9 Carved Conventional Vine

Fig.8 All-over: Diaper.

Fig.11. Persistence of Lotus Motive

Fig.13. Anthemions etc

Fig.10. Painted Plaster

Fig.12 Convergence and Reversion

Fig.14. Fortuitous Resemblance.

9

tools and materials he uses, by his own mental and artistic limitations. By reason of common limitations and environment, the designers of any one place and time tend to work alike in certain respects, and those characteristics which are common to their work constitute the *style* of that time and region. The history of ornament is, then, the record of the origin, growth, decay, succession and inter-relation of the various styles of decorative design.

The Historic Styles.

"Style" is distinctive character or quality. The *historic styles* of ornament are the distinctive ways, methods and systems of decorative design which have prevailed in different countries at different times, and are designated usually by the names of the peoples who have practised them and by the age, century, period or reign in which they have flourished: as, for example, the Roman Imperial Style, the French Gothic, Italian Early Renaissance and American Colonial Style, etc.

Each historic style is seen to have passed through the successive stages of infancy and early growth, maturity and decline, after which it disappears, usually giving place to a new style, either derived from some other civilization, or growing up out of the declining style by the introduction of some new germinant principle of design. Of the great variety of ornament-forms produced in any one period, a few find favor and are constantly repeated, while the others disappear. A tendency thus asserts itself in a given direction, and by countless infinitesimal changes of these familiar forms along the line of this tendency the style is developed and then gradually transformed. The historic styles are phenomena of growth, of racial and epochal environments, not suddenly occurring phases due to chance. No man and no coterie of men can create a real and living style; for style depends not alone upon the designer, but also on his inheritance and environment.

The "Biology" of Styles.

The development of styles presents many analogies to biological phenomena. Transmission by inheritance, persistence of type, occasional reversions towards the primitive type, exceptional forms analogous to the "sports" that occur in Nature—all these are met with in the history of ornament, as well as the constant evolutionary progress from simple to complex, from the rudimentary to the highly organized. There is also observable in the development of ornament a phenomenon which may be called *convergence,* in which two lines of development from different sources approach each other and finally coalesce. The resulting form or pattern resembles somewhat both its ancestors, though constituting a new type in itself. It is therefore often impossible to assign a single origin to an ornament-type; and much of the discussion and controversy about disputed origins might be avoided by recognizing the ornament in question as derived by convergence from both or all of the several sources to which the disputants assign it.

In Figure 11, page 9, *a, b* and *c* suggest the possible evolution of the "trilobe lotus," *c* from its simplest

11

painted form, *a* in Egyptian ornament, while *d, e* and *f* illustrate the persistence of this motive in Greek, Roman and Gothic ornament respectively, the whole covering a period of nearly 3000 years. In Figure 12 a Greek vase ornament of anthemions is shown at *a,* followed by a Roman derivative modified by acanthus-leaf details. The three lower examples are Byzantine acanthus leaves which have *converged* towards the anthemion type to such an extent that they may with equal propriety be called anthemions or acanthus leaves. Figure 13 (in which *b* is an enlargement of *c* in Figure 12) further illustrates this convergence of the Byzantine acanthus towards the Greek anthemion-type, though this latter was probably quite unknown to most Byzantine artists. In Figure 14 we have a curious example of accidental reversion towards an ancient type: the left-hand form *a* being an Egyptian representation of some water-plant, while the two anthemion-like forms at the right, *b,* are late Byzantine conventional representations of the funereal cypress tree!

Prehistoric, Primitive and Savage Ornament.

It remains to consider briefly the relation to historic art of those early forms of ornament which were produced before the dawn of the historic cultures, as well as of the ornament of savage and barbarous peoples that have remained outside the currents of modern civilization. So far as the arts of the cavemen of the palæolithic and neolithic ages are concerned, there is no traceable connection between them and the earliest historic civilizations—those of Egypt and Chaldea: the intermediate links have perished absolutely. With regard to savage ornament, the fact that it is contemporaneous with civilized and even modern cultures, makes possible an influence from the latter upon the savage art which establishes certain occasioned resemblances between the two. But there is no evidence as yet discoverable of the unaided development of savage art into civilized and progressive art. The essential character of savage art is that of arrested development. It is often interesting and effective, but seems incapable of further progress. It is sterile, and as a subject of study, quite outside the field of the historic styles.

Primitive ornament, on the other hand, is ornament in the earliest stages of its development. The term may therefore be applied to the beginnings of historic art or of particular styles, as well as to that of the Stone Age and prehistoric times. Primitive ornament is frequently uncouth, while savage ornament is often highly elaborated (see Plates I and II); but the latter has ceased to advance, while primitive ornament often reveals the promise and potency of indefinite life and growth. The one is a dwarf, the other an infant.

Six Propositions.

The history of art seems to bear out the following propositions:

I. The earliest known historic ornament belongs to civilizations already well advanced.

II. The primitive origins of this earliest known historic ornament have yet to be discovered and identified.

Prehistoric remains in Egypt are being studied, and

have thrown some light upon the earliest stages of art in that most ancient of known civilizations; but the problem has not yet been by any means fully solved.

III. Savage or aboriginal ornament has never yet been known to develop unaided into a civilized and progressive art.

IV. The ornament of every historic style is found to be chiefly derived from that of some older civilization, until we reach back to the earliest historic art of Egypt and Chaldea, beyond which its sources have not yet been traced.

V. Each historic culture has imposed upon the decorative art thus inherited or borrowed a development and form of its own, either by blending with the borrowed forms others of its own invention, or by progressive modifications of detail, or by both together.

VI. In these modifications of the imported or inherited ornament-forms, their original use and significance are in time lost sight of or ignored. Magical forms become mere symbols, symbolic forms mere ornament; and structural forms are applied where the construction does not demand them, so that they become in time motives of architectural decoration pure and simple.

Value of the Study of Ornament Styles.

The importance of this study lies in its value not only to the designer, in enabling him to design consistently, either by following a given style closely or by diverging from it intelligently; but also to the archeologist and the student of history. For the style of a work of decoration is frequently a more reliable index of its date than written documents, which have more than once been proved to be incorrect or to have been misinterpreted, by the evidence of decorative style in the work under discussion. The character and relations of the ornament of different countries, peoples and times have often afforded valuable suggestions, confirmations or corrections as to the historic movements and relations of these peoples, and an index of their advancement in civilization. The history of ornament is thus an important division of the general history of civilization.

Method of this History.

The history of ornament may be treated according to either of two methods. By one of these the origin and development of the dominant motives of ornament are taken up in succession, each of these being traced through all of the styles in which it is formed.[1] By the other, which is followed in this volume, attention is directed to the origin and development of the historic styles of ornament, all the various motives, kinds and types of ornament of each country and period being considered in discussing the style of that time and region. In this volume we shall treat of the styles of ancient and medieval art, leaving the Oriental and modern styles to be treated in another volume.

Summary of the Sequence of Styles.

Geographically as well as chronologically, this study

[1] This is the method followed by Mr. G. A. T. Middleton in his "Motives of Ornament" (New York, 1914) and by myself in a series of papers on the "Development of Decorative Motives" in the "American Architect," 1898–1901.

begins with Egyptian art in the Nile Valley. The art of early Chaldea in the valley of the Tigris-Euphrates, though rivaling that of Egypt in its antiquity, is less important in the domain of ornament than the Egyptian, and less important also than that of Assyria, which developed later in the same river basin. Greek art both inherited and borrowed from both these arts; little, perhaps, directly, but much through the intermediate arts of Phenicia and of the early Mediterranean cultures in Crete, Mycenæ, and other Ægean centers. All these borrowed elements were completely transformed in Greek art, whose developed forms passed into Roman art and were again transformed by the Roman genius. Greek and Roman art have tinged that of all subsequent ages among the European and Western nations. The growth of Christianity after the fall of Rome developed new centers of civilization and new conceptions in art, giving rise to Byzantine art in the East and to Romanesque and Gothic art in the West. For a thousand years the forms of Roman art appeared to be forgotten, except for faint reminiscences of them in Italy. Yet like the Egyptian wheat, buried with a mummy but springing to life after a score of centuries in the tomb, the vital elements of Roman art revived with the Renaissance of classic studies in the fifteenth century in Italy, and have largely dominated Western art ever since.

Meanwhile in the Orient other ideals have prevailed, and although the Mohammedan nations have in each case founded their art on that of the Christian peoples they have conquered, they have developed it under the dominion of their own ideals into something quite apart from Western art. China and Japan have also their own independent though related styles of decoration; while the decorative art of the non-Moslem Hindus represents another group of styles remote in character from those of Europe.

The problem of early American art in Peru, Central America and Mexico is one of great uncertainty and the subject of no little controversy. The art of these countries offers one of the richest as well as most difficult fields for architectural exploration and study. The expeditions conducted by Professor Bingham of Yale University have added much to our knowledge of the monuments; but the subject has not yet entered the domain of precise history, and must lie outside the scope of a manual like this.

Books Recommended.

[The bibliography of ornament is so extensive, and includes so many works of doubtful value to the student, that an exhaustive list of books on the subject of each chapter of this work is out of the question. The lists of "Books Recommended" have been made to include the most important works of reference generally available in the larger libraries of cities and educational institutions, as well as text-books and handbooks of a more popular character, in English, French and German (besides a few in Italian and Spanish). In such a selected list it will inevitably happen that some titles will be omitted which, in the reader's judgment, ought to be included, and others included which might well have been omitted; for individual judgments must differ in many cases. The author and the publishers will welcome suggestions for the improvement of these lists in future editions.]

1. On General Theory of Ornament: BOURGOIN: *Théorie de l'ornement* (Paris, 1883).—W. G. COLLINGWOOD: *Philosophy*

of Ornament (Sunnyside, 1883).—H. PFEIFER: *Formenlehre des Ornaments* (Stuttgart, 1906).—GOBLET D'ALVIELLA: *The Migration of Symbols* (Westminster, 1894).—A. C. HADDON: *Evolution in Art* (London, 1895).—A. D. F. HAMLIN: *Development of Decorative Motives* (in *American Architect*, New York, 1898–1901).—J. HAÜSELMANN: *Studien und Ideen über Ursprung, Wesen und Stil des Ornaments* (Zürich, 1889).— F. E. HULME: *Birth and Development of Ornament* (London, 1893).—J. RANKE: *Anfänge der Kunst* (Berlin, 1879).—ALOIS RIEGL: *Stilfragen; Grundlegungen zu einer Geschichte der Ornamentik* (Berlin, 1893).—G. SEMPER: *Der Stil in der technischen Künsten, oder Praktische Aesthetik* (Munich, 1878–79).—G. STURM: *Animals in Ornament* (London, 1895).

2. General Handbooks and Collections. DOLMETSCH: *Der Ornamentenschatz* (Stuttgart, 1889; also an English edition, London, 1912).—EBE: *Die Schmuckformen der Monumentalbauten aus allen Stilepochen* (Leipzig, 1896).—L. GAUCHEREL: *Exemples de décoration appliquée etc.* (Paris, 1857).—R. GLAZIER: *Manual of Historic Ornament* (London, 1906).— GROPIUS und LOHDE: *Archiv für ornamentale Kunst* etc. (Berlin, 1876–79).—E. J. B. GUILLAUME: *Histoire de l'art et de l'ornement* (Paris, 1888).—D. GUILMARD: *La connaissance des styles de l'ornementation* (Paris, 1849).—A German edition of the same under the title *Geschichte der Ornamentik* (Berlin, 1860).—J. HAÜSELMANN: *Die Stylarten des Ornaments in den verschiedenen Kunstepochen* (Zürich, 1882).—J. E. JACOBSTHAL: *Grammatik der Ornamente* (Berlin, 1874; with large wall-plates for class use).—OWEN JONES: *Grammar of Ornament* (London, 1857; new edition, smaller size, London, 1910). —F. K. KLIMSCH: *Ornaments* (London, n. d.).—MÉCHIN: *Dictionnaire de l'art ornemental de tous les styles* (Paris, 1888–91). —F. S. MEYER: *Ornamentale Formenlehre* (Leipzig, 1886): English edition under title *Handbook of Ornament* (New York, 1898?).—R. NEWBERRY: *Gleanings from Ornamental Art of Every Style* (London, 1863).—R. PFNOR: *Ornementation usuelle de toutes les époques* (Paris, 1866–68).—A. RACINET: *L'Ornement polychrome* (Paris, 1869–87).—H. SHAW: *Encyclopædia of Ornament* (London, 1842).—J. B. WARING: *Illustrations of Architecture and Ornament* (London, 1871).—

INTRODUCTORY

J. WARD: *Historic Ornament* (London, 1898). —G. E. WES-
SELY: *Das Ornament und die Kunstindustrie in ihrer geschicht-
liche Entwickelung* (Berlin, 1877).

In the above list the *Grammar of Ornament* of Owen Jones
and *Ornement Polychrome* of Racinet are monumental collections of decorative designs in color, veritable encyclopædias
of ornament of all kinds except the architectural, of which there
are only a few examples in Owen Jones, and none in Racinet.
The Dolmetsch collection, second only to the above two in richness and elegance of presentation, contains a fair proportion
of illustrations from architecture. Meyer's *Handbook of
Ornament* is another standard collection, arranged not by styles
but by topics and categories of subjects. Glazier's *Manual
of Historic Ornament* is excellent as far as it goes, but its
modest size makes impossible a complete presentation of any
of the styles. Speltz's *Styles of Ornament* is the most compre-
hensive of all the smaller collections, covering all the styles
both of architectural and industrial ornament with a wealth
of illustrations in black-and-white. The new edition, revised
by R. Phené Spiers, of London, is especially recommended.
The Prang Educational Company publish an excellent series
of Plates of Historic Ornament, in color, based on a series originally edited by the late Professor W. R. Ware.

CHAPTER II

The Origins.

When and how did decorative art first begin? The question can never receive a final and complete answer, since the oldest extant specimens of ornamental art, dating back to the palæolithic age, betray a skill which points to beginnings in a still more remote past. The dagger-handle of carved reindeer bone in Figure 15, representing a wounded fawn, is a surprisingly skilful adaptation of naturalistic representation to decorative use; it dates from the neolithic period of the Stone Age. Chipped flint knives and remarkably life-like sketches of animals engraved on bone, including the prehistoric mammoth, found in strata of great antiquity, likewise suggest long antecedent periods of training.

The answer to our query is generally sought by anthropologists in the work and processes of modern savage tribes.[1] The most generally accepted theory is that which derives the earliest ornament from primitive superstitions. The savage—and presumably primitive man did likewise—instinctively animates or personifies all the forces and most of the phenomena of Nature.

[1] Consult however the query raised by Dr. Talcott Williams in a paper printed in the "Report of the Smithsonian Institution" for 1896 entitled, "Was Primitive Man a Modern Savage?"

He fails to distinguish clearly between the real and the imagined, the animate and inanimate, and ascribes to fancied resemblances the qualities of the thing resembled. Hence he seeks to portray, imitate or suggest whatever force or thing he wishes to have or control, ascribing to these caricatures the powers of their originals. An eye painted on a canoe gives the canoe and its owner the power to steer a safe course; a bird on the stern gives it speed (see Plate II, 21); a human face with a mouth full of fierce teeth imparts fierceness and courage to the bearer of the weapon or other object on which it is carved or painted. Figure 17, page 23, illustrates the head of a Mangaia (New Zealand) ceremonial spear to be borne by a chief: it represents, inverted, a tongue protruding from a mouth set with sharp teeth beneath two huge eyes. The protruding tongue signifies defiance; the teeth, ferocity; the eyes, keen vision; together they constitute a powerful amulet, magically endowing the chief with bravery, ferocity and far-sightedness. But it will be noted that the entire representation is decoratively effective; indeed, the decorative purpose quite overmasters all idea of naturalistic portrayal. A like purpose is observed in the Papuan "manhood belts" (Figure 18), on which the scratched patterns of human features are fetishes imparting to the wearer the manly qualities they symbolize.

Such a representation is called a *fetish,* and the superstition to which it is due, fetishism. It is one manifestation of what is generically known as *animism,* of which another form is *totemism.* Among certain tribes, as in Alaska, each family or clan has its own animal or other object not merely as a heraldic symbol, but as a possession conferring its qualities on the whole clan: such a symbol is called a *totem*. An Alaskan totem-pole, like the quarterings of a coat-of-arms, portrays the pedigree and relationships of the occupants of the tent or tepee before which it stands. According to the *animistic theory,* therefore, primitive and savage ornament is believed to have grown up out of the carving or painting or weaving of fetishes and totems primarily for the sake of their magical use. This practice in time awakened the rudimentary decorative instinct; and this instinct asserting itself with constantly increasing force has led to the progressive modification of the original semi-naturalistic forms until they are often no longer recognizable as such, as in Figures 17, 18 and 24 (page 23) ; Figure 24 showing patterns derived from the head of the frigate-bird.

The Technic Theory.

Another theory attributes the awakening of the decorative instinct to the processes and results of primitive industries, especially pottery, basketry and weaving. In these industries there occur inevitably certain rhythmical repetitions and alternations of form or color which are in themselves decorative. Thus in grass-weaving and basketry, if grasses of two colors are alternately plaited or woven together a checker pattern results, while simple variations in the plaiting produce plaids, quadrangles, stepped triangles and crosses (Figure 19). The awakened decorative instinct seizes upon these effects and develops them purposefully. It

Fig. 15

a.

Fig. 16

b.

Fig. 20

a

b.

Fig. 19

c.

d.

Fig. 17

Fig. 18

Fig. 21

a

Fig. 22

b

Fig. 23

b

Fig. 24

Fig. 25

c

d

Fig. 26

Fig. 27

Chiriqui Indian Alligator-forms.

Tusayan Jar (Mexico)

Fig. 28

15. Primitive dagger-handle. 16. New Zealand "tiki-tiki" motive. 17. Maori spear-head. 18. Papuan face-motives. 19. Basketry forms. 20, 21. Peruvian animal motives. 22. Maori and Hawaiian carvings. 23 Brazilian grass-cloth patterns. 24. Papuan frigate-bird forms. 25. Maori flute ornament. 26. from Brazil.

then begins to appropriate for decorative use fetish and totem forms (Figures 20, 21, 24, 28) and adds to these other nature forms, which it eventually uses as pure ornament, with little or no regard for magical intent. Figure 16 shows in *a* an apparently conventional ornament thus derived from the New Zealand totem-figures of women shown in *b,* which represent the pedigrees of New Zealand chiefs in the female line. The technic of wood-notching has converted these figures into the ornament known as the tiki-tiki-tangata.

It seems likely that both theories are measurably correct and must be jointly invoked to explain the beginnings of ornament. The discovery and development of motives originating in technical processes and the development of nature-forms through animistic impulses have probably been concurrent. It seems quite clear that nearly all spirals, zigzags, plaids, lozenges, and many other geometric motives, have originated in the

FIG. 29. DETAIL FROM MAORI PADDLE IN PLATE I, 21.

processes of weaving, plaiting and string-lashing. Even the fact that modern savage tribes call these motives by the names of animals, winds, etc., does not prove their animistic origin. Thus in Figure 23 the Indians of Central Brazil call *a* the tunny-fish pattern, *b* the lizard pattern, and *c* and *d* bat-patterns! All four patterns were probably technomorphic in origin, and received these names as afterthought explanations of their origin

24

and meaning. For primitive man is always a myth-maker, who seeks to explain everything by a story or by some theory of magic; and the widely different names given to the same form by different tribes suggest that their several explanations are invented after the fact, not handed down by tradition from still more primitive ages.

Character of Savage Ornament.

Its artistic quality is often of a high order, revealing a keen sense of decorative propriety, a wise choice and proportioning of means to ends, and great skill in space-filling (Plates I and II). In boldness and effectiveness of design it often surpasses the work of more civilized peoples. If lacking in subtlety and the higher graces of line and movement, it is often rich, well distributed, and executed with singular patience and skill. Structural ornament, in the strictest sense, hardly exists at all; nearly all savage ornament is pure surface-decoration. It consists largely of patterns of small motives indefinitely repeated by painting, stamping or weaving, or by surface carving, so as to cover the whole or a major part of the object. (Figures 16, 20, 22, 23–27; Plate I, Nos. 4, 6, 8, 13, 15, 21, 23.) Here and there appears a caricature of the head or body of a bird or beast (Plate II, 19, 20); or even the grotesque head of a man, as in Fig. 30.

The South Sea Islands.

Among the most interesting developments of savage decorative art are those of certain Polynesian peoples, particularly in New Guinea in the north and New Zea-

FIG. 30. WAR-DRUM HEAD, JAVA.

land in the south. Second only to these in interest is the art of the Hawaiian, Friendly or Tonga, Samoan and Fiji Islands. Basketry, weaving and wood-carving are the chief artistic industries of these peoples; their pottery is unimportant. Animism is everywhere in evidence in these products: clubs, spears, paddles, stone-headed adzes, often designed for ceremonial and not practical use, are covered with patterns invested with fetishistic or totemistic meanings. Many of these patterns may, however, have had a technic origin in basketry, wood-notching, etc. (Figure 29; Plate I, 11, 15, 21, 23).

The patterns in Figure 24 (p. 23), are all derived from the frigate-bird's head; they are from the Papuan Gulf of New Guinea. The very similar pattern in Figure 25—a pattern scratched on a Maori (New Zealand) flute—is claimed by Haddon [2] of Cambridge as having a different origin, as the art of New Zealand appears to be wholly disconnected from the northern Polynesian styles, and the frigate-bird does not otherwise figure in Maori patterns. Figure 22 shows a variation of the tiki-tiki pattern from New Zealand, and two narrow borders from Hawaii, both carved in wood. In Plate I, No. 7 is a specimen of New Zealand tattooing, an art

[2] A. C. Haddon, "Evolution in Art," London, 1895.

originating in Polynesia, and carried to high perfection both in New Guinea and New Zealand. Some of the tattoo-patterns appear to be purely decorative, conforming to the facial modeling; others have a definite significance as fetishes or as totems.

Primitive American Ornament.

Basketry, weaving and pottery are the chief industries of the primitive and ancient peoples of South and Central America, Mexico and the southwestern regions of the United States. The pottery of these countries is particularly abundant and interesting. As Peru, Central America and Mexico were the seats of a highly developed civilization centuries before the Spanish conquest, the art of those ages has no place in a discussion of primitive and savage ornament. While the beginnings have been made in the working out of the Mayan and Aztec chronologies, we must await the decipherment of their written records before we can write the history and chronology of the Peruvian, Mexican and Central American art of antiquity, many of whose monuments have long been known, and others more recently discovered by the Yale expeditions under Professor Bingham. Until these problems have been worked out it will be impossible to determine the historical relation of such advanced decorative art as is shown in Plate II, 2, 3 and 7, to the more modern pottery shown on the same plate.

Both the Mexican and the Zuñi and Pueblo pottery show great fondness for the spiral (Figs. 31, 32;

Plate II, 8, 11, 13). According to W. H. Holmes this is due to the derivation of all American pottery from primitive processes of building up the vessel with successive spiral coils of clay "rope," which process in turn is derived from coiled basketry (see Plate II, 12, a Washoe basket-bowl). This theory is borne out by the

FIG. 31. *a*, PUEBLO JAR; *b*, DETAIL FROM PLATE II, 8; *c*, PREHISTORIC JAR FROM BOSNIA.

occurrence of many basketry patterns in Bolivian and other pottery. But the Peruvian spirals in Plate II, 14, may be derived from the coiled snake (II, 16). The spiral is common in Pueblo pottery; Fig. 31 *a* shows an example, which curiously resembles an ancient jar (reversed) from Budmer in Bosnia, illustrated in Hoerner's "Urgeschichte." The spiral *b* is an enlarged detail from the jar in Plate II, 8. In the same plate the illustrations 5 and 8 offer curious analogies to early Greek pottery-ornamentation. Such resemblances, probably wholly fortuitous, have given rise to many speculations as to the origin of the ancient American civilizations.[3]

The modern American Indians, especially those of the

---

[3] All of the illustrations in Plate II are from sketches made in the American Museum of Natural History in New York, which possesses a superb collection, in its Anthropological section, of examples of primitive art, both American and foreign.

Southwest, are clever potters and particularly skilful in basketry. The blankets, baskets and beadwork of many other Indian tribes are rich in decorative suggestion, and will be increasingly valued as these arts tend to disappear with advancing civilization.

The examples shown in these figures and plates can by no means adequately illustrate the richness and variety of savage and primitive ornament; they can only suggest its general character. Every tribe has its own special products and patterns; to some extent they

FIG. 32. MEXICAN JAR.

mingle and overlap through commerce and migration. They seem to have been but little modified in style by the contact of civilization, though this contact is apt to result in the disappearance of the native art and the substitution of manufactured foreign products.

Summary of Characteristics.

The main characteristics of savage art may be briefly summarized as follows:

I. Geometric ideals control generally both the distribution and details of the decoration.

II. Natural forms are invariably of magical significance. They converge towards the technomorphic treatment because the savage cares nothing for accuracy of representation, provided the type is recognizable; and

29

exaggeration and caricature resulting from the influence of materials and tools do not destroy the type. The technomorphic geometrization of details is a natural result of the processes of their production.

III. Of many motives it cannot be determined whether the origin is animistic or technomorphic. Native identifications and explanations of form are by no means always trustworthy.

IV. The zigzag, quadrilateral, fret and spiral appear in nearly all savage styles, though the coil and spiral are wanting in certain defined districts in the South Seas.

V. Savage ornament is almost wholly surface ornament, in which general effect is the chief concern and is produced by a disposition of parts almost always judicious and artistic. It is usually composed of minute motives, more or less crowded. The higher qualities of grace, refined curvature and rhythmic movement, and highly organized and complex composition, are generally wanting. In short, the pursuit of an unattained ideal and the progress that results from it, do not appear in savage art, which remains content with its past which it reproduces with variations but without consistent advance.

Books Recommended.

As before, the general collections of Dolmetsch, Glazier, Owen Jones, Racinet and Speltz.—Also, H. BALFOUR: *The Evolution of Decorative Art* (London, 1893).—A. C. HADDON: *Evolution in Art* (especially for Polynesian art: London, 1895).—J. RANKE: *Anfänge der Kunst* (Berlin, 1879).—H. STOLPE: *Evolution in the Ornamental Art of Savage Peoples*

PRIMITIVE AND SAVAGE ORNAMENT

(Trans. Rochdale Literary and Scientific Society, 1891); *Studier i americansk Ornamentik* (Stockholm, 1896).—E. B. TYLOR: *Primitive Culture* (London).—Consult also W. H. HOLMES: *Origin and Development of Form and Ornament in Ceramic Art* in Fourth Annual Report, Bureau of Ethnology (Washington, 1886).

CHAPTER III

"Egypt is the oldest daughter of civilization"; [1] "a lighthouse in the profound darkness of remote antiquity." [2]

Land and People.

The valley of the Nile was the birthplace of historic civilization, so far, at least, as extant evidence can determine it. The history of Chaldea carries us back, it is true, six or seven thousand years, but the oldest monuments of Egypt point to a long precedent development, the beginnings of which are lost in the mists of antiquity. It is, however, outside of our purpose to study this twilight age of Egyptian art. Of the thirty dynasties enumerated by Manetho, the first reigned in Memphis in Lower Egypt at a date variously estimated at from 3600 to 4500 years B.C., over a well organized kingdom possessed of cities, a priesthood, established grades of society, and other features of a developed civilization. Hemmed in between the wall-like cliffs of the Nile valley, this kingdom flourished for some thousands of years the one civilized nation in a vast world of barbarous nations, developing unaided her own arts and supported

[1] Perrot & Chipiez, "History of Ancient Art"; vol. I, page 1.
[2] Rénan, quoted by Perrot & Chipiez; *ibid.*, page 19.

32

by the inexhaustible fertility of the Nile mud. Herodotus rightly called Egypt "the gift of the Nile," which became to the Egyptians a source of endless symbols and cosmic-religious ideas.

Within this valley the Egyptians were long untouched by foreign influences, and the apparent changelessness of Egyptian art is one of its most striking characteristics.

The government of Egypt was an autocracy, and society was divided into castes, with the priest-caste at its head. To this caste belonged the king, who was deified after death. The religion, grossly idolatrous in its lowest popular form, and polytheistic in its highest phases as understood by the educated priest-caste, possessed many lofty spiritual conceptions underlying its externally complex mythology. Particularly important were its solar deities Amen or Ra, identified with the sun; Osiris and his sister-spouse Isis or Hathor, and Horus their son. The ideas of death and immortality were conspicuous, making sepulchral art the most important

Fig. 33. Detail of Sarcophagus of Menkaura.

branch of design next to temple architecture. Primitive fetish-conceptions never wholly disappeared; Maspéro declared that "every Egyptian ornament was a talisman," and symbolism characterized every detail of decorative art. The tombs, designed to be inviolable so far as the intention of their designers was concerned, and hermetically sealed against the entrance of the living, were internally decorated with pictures of scenes, objects and pursuits which, it was believed, would become realities to the *Ka,* the shadowy "double" or half-spirit of the deceased, who could thus enjoy the pleasures of feasting and the chase while imprisoned in the tomb, awaiting final release by the judgment of Osiris and his forty assessors. It is from these tombs and from the sarcophagi (Fig. 33) and mummy-cases found in them that a large part of our knowledge of Egyptian life and decorative art have been derived.

Influence of Climate.

Except during the short rainy season the Egyptian sky is cloudless, the sun intensely brilliant. Mists, half-lights, soft gray tones and delicate tints such as northern lands and artists know and love, are here unknown. In the blazing sun and black shadows delicate relief and subtle modulations of surface would be lost. Hence strong and bold relief are necessary out of doors: while both there and in the dim interiors color is essential for decorative effectiveness. Egyptian ornament is pre-eminently an ornament of color. The dryness of the air and the absence of frost result in a permanence which cannot be secured in other climates. Wood and cloth seem in Egypt as imperishable as stone and bronze. Hence an influence towards slowness of change, towards permanence both of types and details, which exists nowhere else.

Materials.

There is almost no timber in Egypt, and where stone was lacking, or was unsuitable or too costly, mud or clay served as the building material, often with a framework of reeds or stiff papyrus-stalks bound together to form posts and beams. The palm was the principal tree, with the sycamore for occasional use in cabinet-work. The painted representations of framed woodwork always show long and narrow panels, such as could be framed with long thin pieces from the palm-trunk (Fig. 33). Marvelous was the decorative art which grew up under these limitations. Pottery, glass, enamel and metal-work in copper, bronze and gold were all known to the Egyptians from an early age, and weaving of "fine twined linen," embroidery and the tanning of leather were also practised.

Historic Periods.

Without going into details, we may divide the history of Egyptian art into six periods. I, The Prehistoric Age. II, the Old or First Empire, comprising the first ten dynasties; this is the age of the Great Pyramids and of the earliest tombs, from 3400 B.C. [3] to 2160 B.C. III, The Middle or First Theban Empire, two dynasties,

[3] These dates are those of Breasted. Some other authorities assign much earlier dates to the Old Empire.

2160 to 1788 B.C. IV, The New or Second Theban Empire, the 18th–20th dynasties inclusive, 1588–1150 B.C. This is the great age of Egyptian history, the most splendid in its temples and tombs, as well as in war and conquest. It followed a period of two centuries of artistic sterility under five foreign dynasties called the Hyksos or Shepherd Kings. V, the Saitic and Persian Period, comprising the dynasties 21 to 26 inclusive, and the Persian rule which began in 525 B.C.: from 1150 to 324 B.C. VI, the Revival or Ptolemaic Period, under the Macedonian Ptolemies and the Roman dominion: 324 B.C. to 330 A.D. The first half of this period was one of revived artistic activity after a long decline.

Prehistoric Ornament.

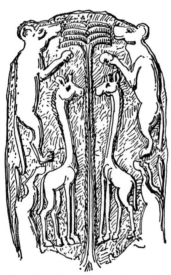

FIG. 34. PREHISTORIC SLATE PALETTE IN THE LOUVRE.

It is only within recent years that the pre-Pharaonic art of Egypt has become known by a sufficient number of examples to permit of assigning any dates or sequences of style. Discoveries at Koptos, Nagada and Abydos since 1893 have unearthed the products of long ages before the first dynasty— crude painted statuettes of earthenware, ivory pins and combs, spoons and rings, flint knives with ivory gold-plated handles, vases of pot-

36

tery and slate palettes or ink-mixers (Fig. 34). In none of these is there evidence of a developed decorative style, zigzags and a few crude patterns derived from basketry being almost the only pure ornaments. There is, however, considerable imitation of Nature, more and more realistic and correct as one approaches historic times. Religion and magic account for much of this naturalism. The slate palette from the Louvre shown in Fig. 34 is in its motive so like many "Sacred Tree" compositions from Assyria in which a tree is flanked by erect monsters or human figures, that some authorities refer it to prehistoric Chaldean influence. On the other hand, the entire Asiatic series of figures of beasts facing a central tree or shaft may have originated in Egypt. On the whole these finds throw little light on the origins and early development of the historic ornament of Egypt.

Historic Ornament; General Survey.

The historic ornament of Egypt may be dated as extending from about 3500 B.C., the date of the earliest examples in the collections, down to the Christian era. From the Old Empire the remains are almost wholly of sepulchral and industrial art—scarabs (Fig. 53), mummy-cases, jewelry, furniture and tomb decorations. The Middle Empire has bequeathed us a few examples of its architecture, but the great architectural age is that of the New Empire, though the Ptolemaic is also rich in this field. The Middle and New Empire periods have also left us many examples of sepulchral art. This entire body of decorative art, covering a period of between three and four thousand years, shows an extraordinary continuity and uniformity of character and spirit, in spite of the progress observable when it is closely studied. Egyptian art is marked by a highly developed decorative sense which rarely fails to employ both form and color in the most effective and appropriate manner. The influence of symbolism and of surviving traditions of magic is everywhere observable, though the symbolic significance of the forms used was probably by no means always a controlling influence in the design. In many cases it may not have been at all consciously present in the mind of the designer.

Sources and Motives.

The Egyptians employed both geometric and natural forms, the latter always more or less conventionalized. The geometric motives were no doubt chiefly of technic origin, the natural forms magical or symbolic. The conventionalizing tendency was always strong, even in purely pictorial and representative painting and sculpture, largely from the influence of heiratic formulæ and traditions in sepulchral and temple decoration. In ornament there is rarely any attempt to picture natural objects realistically. Thus the lotus (Figure 36, page 47), which appears in Nature as at *a,* is usually depicted in side-elevation, greatly simplified, as at *b* and *c;* and a dish of fruit is shown partly in plan and partly in elevation, the two combined in one representation (Fig. 35). Human figures are drawn

FIG. 35.
A DISH OF FRUIT.

with the head in profile, the shoulders in front view, and the legs and feet in side view, both feet planted squarely on the ground, one behind the other.

Besides the classes of ornament above described, there is the important category of architectural ornament. This consists largely of conventionalized Nature-forms, with only a comparatively limited list of really structural motives.

General Character.

Egyptian ornament is characterized by a certain rigidity and formality of character, which permitted of only a very slow and gradual evolution; there is no such marked change of style, previous at least to the Ptolemaic age, as marks for instance the development of Greek or of Gothic ornament. But there is an extraordinary variety of detail in the treatment of a somewhat limited stock of fundamental motives. It is predominantly an art of surface-decoration by color: the range of structural and architectural forms is very narrow. Color was largely depended upon for the decoration of buildings as well as of movable objects, and color was used with admirable judgment for decorative effects. The colors chiefly used were red, yellow, blue and green, with black and white occasionally as foils; these colors are seldom the pure colors of the spectrum or their nearest pigment analogies, but "reduced" tones or shades, the red verging towards the red-brown; the yellow a warm tone such as is produced by tinging yellow ochre with burnt-sienna; the blue commonly of a dark shade, the green ranging from a sap-green to a dark olive. There are of course exceptions, especially in enamels and glass, but they only emphasize the prevailing sobriety and richness of the color in other works. The use of gold in decoration was very sparing.

Nature Forms.

Both plant and animal forms were used in Egyptian ornament. The animal forms—chiefly the vulture or hawk, and the uræus or cobra, together with wings and feathers—were almost invariably religious or symbolic. So also was probably the lotus and perhaps also the papyrus among vegetable forms; most of the other plants and flowers that occur seem to have been used for purely decorative reasons.

The Lotus.

This has been called the sacred flower [4] of Egypt (Figure 36); it was the largest and most beautiful of flowers known to that land, and figured prominently in both royal and religious ceremonies. As a product of the life-giving, wealth-bestowing Nile it was symbolic both of that river and of the solar divinities which ruled the river's inundations and imparted to it its fertility and life-renewing powers. It is shown in the hands of kings and gods; laid as an offering on altars and tied to the tops of posts and columns. It figures in the capitals of columns and is made the basis of endlessly varied borders and all-over patterns. Professor Goodyear in

[4] Flinders Petrie, however, denies its sacred and symbolic significance ("Egyptian Decorative Art," page 106).

40

his "Grammar of the Lotus" has endeavored to prove that all Egyptian ornament is based on the lotus and that since all classic ornament can be traced back ultimately to Egypt, and most later styles to the classic, the lotus must be considered to be the parent of nearly all historic ornament. This is surely carrying the thesis too far, but it is undeniable that a very considerable part of Egyptian ornament is of lotus origin, while many forms not lotuses at all, converged towards the lotus type, so that the lotus influence is traceable far beyond the area of actual lotus derivations.

The Egyptian lotuses used in decoration were the *nymphœa lotus* and the *nymphœa cerulœa*—respectively the white and blue lotus. The rose lotus (*nelumbium*) was probably not known till a late date. The Nile lotus is a large water-lily, with four green sepals and a corolla of white or blue petals surrounding the yellow central group of stamens and pistils (Figure 36, *a*). It was represented usually in side-elevation, showing three sepals and usually six petals. The bud was shown with only two sepals visible, and sometimes with no division of sepals at all. The outline of the open flower was either trumpet-shaped, bell-shaped or rectilinear. A derived form was the *trilobe,* in which the petals were omitted, and the two lateral sepals curled over into volutes; but by a decorative inconsistency, a second set of sepals frequently adorned the trilobe (Fig. 37, *c, e*).

As a border ornament, the lotus was alternated with the bud, usually in a pendant position, perhaps in imitation of, or convergence towards, fringes of tassels; and with these alternating forms were combined round dots, loops and other details whose meaning is not obvious (Figure 38). In late work the lotus-bud is often replaced by bunches of grapes or by nondescript forms generally recalling the oval outline of the bud (Figures 38, 39).

The lotus was also frequently used as an isolated

FIG. 37. LOTUS FORMS; *a*, FULL FLOWER; *b-e*, TRILOBE FORMS.

motive, as on paddles, vases and other objects; and as a terminal ornament, *e.g.*, to adorn the prow or stern of a boat (Figure 36, *c*), or to form the capital of a column (Plate III, 10, 19). Many writers consider Egyptian rosettes in general to be representations in plan of the open lotus, or even of the seed vessel of the flower, but Flinders-Petrie has shown [5] that many rosettes are plainly representations of other flowers, and that others are probably of technic origin. Some rosettes are, however, unmistakably lotus rosettes (Figure 40, page 47).

The lotus figures in many all-over patterns in association with the spiral (Figure 41, page 47). The architectural uses of the lotus are discussed later.

[5] "Egyptian Decorative Art," page 58.

Other Plant Forms.

The papyrus (Fig. 42) is the most important of these. Its straight, stiff triangular stem with four root-leaves wrapping its slightly swelling base, is imitated in the clustered shafts of many columns (Plate III, 11), and painted as a decoration on walls and on bell-capitals, often alternating with conventional lotuses (Figures 43, 45, Fig. 46). The stem bears a bunch of tiny flowers, forming with their stems a group of green filaments with reddish tops, growing out of a calyx of four leaves

Fig. 42. The Papyrus in Nature.

Fig. 46. Campaniform Capital, Karnak.

or bracts. These supply the suggestion for many bell-shaped forms in ornament (Figure 47), including the great campaniform capitals of huge columns like those of the Karnak hypostyle hall (Figure 43; Plate III, 10).[6]

The daisy, convolvulus, grapes, and thistle occur in ornament; also other plant forms not always recognizable. Many rosette and leaf forms are probably mere conventional ornament types, not intended to portray particular plants. The spiked ornament of Figure 44

[6] In the "Grammar of the Lotus," Prof. Goodyear claims as lotus-forms a host of ornament motives and pictorial representations plainly derived from the papyrus. There are, it is true, many forms in which, by convergence, the two types are blended in one.

is identified by Flinders-Petrie as well as Goodyear, as a lotus with the central sepal exaggerated. This does not seem convincing: it is too persistent and uniform a motive in late art, and too unlike the lotus to warrant this explanation without strong proof, and may represent some aquatic plant not now existent in the Nile valley. The palm appears in capitals during and after the XVIIIth dynasty, and is frequent in Ptolemaic and Roman work (Fig. 64, *c,* page 50; Plate III, 17).

Animal Forms.

The *vulture,* with widespread wings, symbolizing protection and maternal care, is a frequent and a splendid decoration of temple ceilings, and appears in many other applications (Figure 57; Plate III, 20, 23). The wings alone, with the sun-disk significant of Ra, are still more frequent, especially over the gateways or entrances of temples (Figure 58). The *uræus* or cobra is a symbol of death, hence of the royal power of life and death, and hence of royalty itself. It decorates the winged disk (Figure 58), the royal head-dress, and the cornices of certain buildings; especially in the Ptolemaic age, of the front screen-walls of the hypostyle

halls (Figure 59). The *scarabæus* or beetle is rarely a purely ornamental motive, but appears isolated on mummy-cases and elsewhere, as a symbol of creation and life, and was the commonest of amulets (Fig. 53). It is occasionally found in late all-overs, as in Plate III A. The *head of Hathor* was used as a sym-

Fig. 53. *Scarabæus Amulet* (Reverse).

44

bolic decoration on columns, especially in the Ptolemaic age (Plate III, 9). The *sphinx,* a symbolic compound of lion's body with human head (*androsphinx*) or a sculptured ram (*criosphinx*), was employed to line the *dromos* or avenue leading to a temple, and is occasionally found executed in bronze, basalt or diorite, of small size, perhaps as an amulet. But the sphinx belongs rather to sculpture than to ornament. *Feathers* appear not only in representations of great fans or royal insignia, but in the form of scale-like ornament

FIG. 61. ZIGZAGS; *b,* IMBRICATIONS; *c,* CHEVRONS.

or imbrications (Fig. 61, *b;* Plate III, 21, 22), which may be derived from the actual use of feathers in clothing. Figure 60 may represent fans, or highly conventional lotus forms.

Conventional or Geometric Motives.

These are of the greatest variety, and are used with consummate skill, sometimes alone, very often in combination with flower-forms, especially the lotus. Fig. 61 *a* illustrates one of many effective examples of the decorative use of simple straight lines. The *zigzag* occurs with great frequency; it is used often to represent water on the Nile, but may not always have had this significance. Associated with the zigzag is the *chevron* (Fig. 61, *c*). Opposed zigzags produce lozenges or diamonds, and occur in simple all-over patterns (Figure 50). It is quite likely that all these are primarily of technic origin, from basketwork and weaving. Plaids and check-patterns are undoubtedly technomorphs. In the tombs of Ti and of Ptah Hotep at Sakkarah, mattings of plaited rushes or straw are plainly represented as filling the panels of the walls, with patterns of great variety in checks, quarries and zigzags.

The *circle* was the basis of a great number of patterns, and intersecting circles forming four-petaled flowers or stars are very common (Figure 52; Plate III, 16, 18). *Rosettes* are found in unlimited variety. It is impossible to affirm in every case whether they are purely geometric and conventional, or floral, or technomorphic: nor is their origin important except as affecting theories of esthetics and psychology. In many designs they are clearly floral: a beautiful rosette is formed by four spreading lotuses alternating with lotus buds about a common center (Figure 40).

The *spiral,* though not as important in Egyptian ornament as later it became in Greek art, was much used both in linear and all-over patterns. Its earliest occurrence is on scarabs or seals of the very early dynasties, where it appears merely as a decorative space-filler (Fig. 53) or border. It is not frequent on large objects until the XVIIIth dynasty; it is one of the commonest decorative motives thenceforward until the Decline. It appears occasionally as a current scroll or "Greek wave" (Figure 51). Its most frequent use is in all-over patterns on textiles (or painted representations of them), and on ceilings in the tombs. Quarries are formed by four (rarely three) lines winding spirally about each of a series of dots arranged in diagonally

46

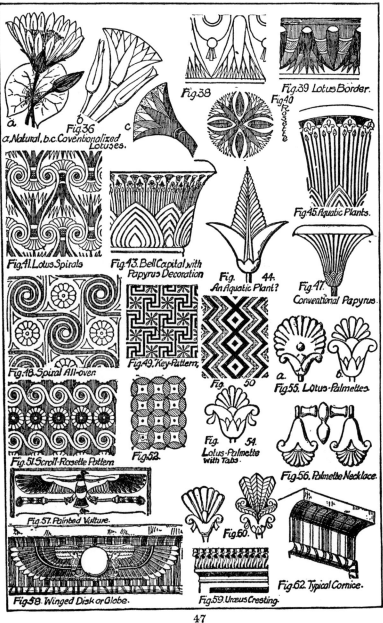

Fig. 38

Fig. 39 Lotus Border.

Fig. 40 Rosette

Fig. 36

a, Natural, b, c, Conventionalized Lotuses.

Fig. 41. Lotus Spirals

Fig. 43. Bell Capital with Papyrus Decoration

Fig. 44. An Aquatic Plant?

Fig. 45. Aquatic Plants.

Fig. 47. Conventional Papyrus.

Fig. 48. Spiral All-over.

Fig. 49. Key-Pattern.

Fig. 50

Fig. 55. Lotus-Palmettes

Fig. 54. Lotus-Palmette with Tabs.

Fig. 51. Scroll-Rosette Pattern

Fig. 52.

Fig. 56. Palmette Necklace.

Fig. 57. Painted Vulture.

Fig. 60.

Fig. 58. Winged Disk or Globe.

Fig. 59. Uræus Cresting.

Fig. 62. Typical Cornice.

47

intersecting rows. The angles are often filled with lotus-blossoms, and the quadrilateral spaces with rosettes, lozenges or other motives (Figures 41, 48; Plate III, 7, 8). A variant pattern is formed by series of C-shaped links or volutes in horizontal and vertical pairs. Another variant is seen in patterns of opposed vertical rows of S-scrolls forming lyre-shaped spaces as in Figure 41 and Plate III, 8.

Fret patterns are the angular or rectilinear counterparts of spiral patterns, though the quadruple convergence on the points of a mesh is rare (Figure 49, which is the counterpart of Figure 48). The fret is but rarely met with as a border-pattern. It will be noted that the pattern in Figure 49 is formed by two intersecting line-motives, and that it produces a series of "swastikas." There is no evidence, however, that the swastika, as a separate motive or as a symbol was used or even known in Egypt. Its occurrence in these patterns is purely fortuitous (Plate III, 12, 14).

The Palmette.

This is the name given to an ornament which occurs in Egyptian, Assyrian, Phenician, Cypriote and Greek art, in almost countless variations, and of which the Greek anthemion is the direct derivative. It consists (Figures 54, 55, 56) of a group of diverging leaves or petals springing from between two spirals; it is predominantly used as an isolated or terminal motive in Egyptian art. An early example is a gold jewel from the IVth dynasty (Figure 55, *a*); later examples are shown in Figures 55, *b,* 56. The origin and significance of this ornament are not fully determined. All authorities agree that it is a lotus-motive, but how the particular combination of a species of semi-rosette with a trilobe lotus came about and what it meant are not wholly clear. One theory makes it a half-plan of the flower above an elevation of the same [7] (see *ante*, Fig. 35); another sees in it the symbol of the rising sun or Horus, over the lotus or Nile. The spiked flower-motive in Figure 44 may perhaps be a variation of the palmette rather than of the lotus or of an unknown aquatic plant. It is not to be confounded with representations of ceremonial royal fans, though somewhat resembling them. Peculiar horn-like volutes in some examples (Figure 60) are probably representations of the third and fourth sepals of the lotus-calyx. The oval or semicircular object nesting between the voluted front sepals is probably the core-body or pericarp of the flower seen between its sepals; it becomes an essential feature of all the later and derivative forms persisting through Greek art and, indeed, through all the ages to our own.

Architectural Forms: Piers, Columns and Cornices.

The architectural forms of Egyptian ornament were comparatively few and simple. There was no system of uniform orders like the Greek and Roman; but one type of cornice, the cavetto cornice, was universal (Figure 62; Plate III, 9, 11). This was usually ornamented with vertical flutings, perhaps as reminiscences of primitive papyrus-stalk framing, and with a torus at

[7] F. P., *op. cit.,* page 70; also Goodyear, "Grammar of the Lotus," *passim.*

its base, plainly derived from a bundle of reeds bound together. This torus was frequently carried down the corners of pylons and other enclosing walls. A

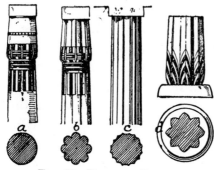

winged disk invariably adorned the central part of the cornice over all temple doorways (Fig. 58).

Columns had shafts of three types: the circular or cylindrical, the clustered, and the polygonal or proto-

FIG. 63. TYPES OF COLUMNS.

doric (Plate III, 10, 11; Fig. 63, *a, b, c*). The fisrt two tapered upward in most cases, and sometimes had a slight swelling or convexity at the base (Fig. 63, *d*). The clustered shafts consisted of four or eight members (or rarely even more), which were sometimes cylindrical, sometimes formed with an arris or edge (Fig. 63, *d*). The so-called "proto-doric" columns had from eight to thirty-two sides, flat or slightly concaved; they are chiefly found in rock-cut tombs and a few scanty temple-ruins of the Middle Empire (Fig. 63, *c*).

The *Capitals* of columns were of the greatest variety, but divisible into a few main groups: the *bud* capital, single or clustered (Fig. 63, *a, b;* Plate III, 11); the

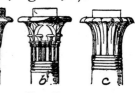

FIG. 64.

bell-shaped or *campaniform,* single or compound (Fig. 64, *a, b;* also Figure 46 and Figure 43; Plate

III, 9, 10) ; the *palmiform* (Fig. 64, *c;* Plate III, 17) ; and the *Hathoric* (Plate III, 9'). The bud-capital was the most common; the campaniform appears chiefly in the central aisles of hypostyle halls, as at Karnak and the Ramesseum; the compound campaniform, the palmiform and the Hathoric belong chiefly to the Ptolemaic age, which produced also various exceptional forms of which those in Plate III, 15 and 19 are ex-amples. The bell capital was adorned with painted petals around its lower part, and with rows of flowers on erect green stalks. These are apparently survivals or elaborations of the green filaments of the papyrus-head from which this type of capital is probably derived [8] (Figures 43, 45, 47; Fig. 46; Plate III, 10). Indeed, many other features of the Egyptian columns point to the influence of papyrus origins. Every shaft, even when cylindrical, is bound by five or more bands at the top, a detail evidently derived from the binding of clustered supports such as bundles of papyrus stalks; the clustered

FIG. 65. OSIRID PIER, LUXOR.

shafts often have an edge or arris, like the triangular stem of the papyrus; the slight swelling at the base, swathed in leaves, with the upward taper, is a marked characteristic of the papyrus stalk (see Fig. 42) ; the

[8] Prof. Goodyear in his "Grammar of the Lotus" and elsewhere sharply dis-putes this view, contending that this capital is derived from the seed-vessel of the rose-lotus. His authority is weighty, but his arguments not convinc-ing. See *ante,* page 43, Note.

bound stalks of the bundle-molding plainly point to the structural use of papyrus stalks in primitive times; and the bell-shaped cap, striped with green vertical lines rising from a calyx of leaves, and with its red lip, is the appropriate architectural interpretation in stone of the spreading papyrus-head of green filaments rising from a pseudo-calyx of leaves, and bearing small reddish tops or heads. The combination of all these features is more easily and naturally explained by the papyrus origin than by any other theory. But there is probably convergence towards familiar lotus-types: it is always dangerous to attempt any narrow and exclusive assignment of origins to decorative forms.

The shafts of simple cylindrical columns were generally covered with bands of incised and painted hieroglyphics and pictures, serving both to adorn them and to give scale to their simple masses (Plate III, 10).

Osirid Piers.

Besides the columns there occur in several temples square or rectangular piers, often fronted with colossal sculptured figures of Osirid holding a scourge and a "Nile key" or "key of life" (Fig. 65).

FIG. 66. PAINTED PECTORAL ON A MUMMY-CASE.

Industrial Arts.

The Egyptians practised the arts of the goldsmith and jeweler; not only have we in our museums gold jewelry of very great antiquity—rings, bracelets, pendants, brooches and necklaces (Figures 55, *a*, 56;—but we have on mummy-cases and in pictures representations of necklaces and pectorals of great splendor (Figure 66). In all these the lotus, bud, and palmette are constantly recurring motives. The art of enameling was understood and practised with skill, especially for amulets. Glass was known, was used for vials and small objects, and was highly prized. Small objects like spoons and perfume-boxes were carved in wood, often in highly artistic designs (Fig. 67; Plate III, 25). Textile art was highly developed, linen being the chief material. The figured stuffs, hangings, etc., have perished, but the tomb paintings show us the designs once employed: some of these have already been illustrated (Figures 41, 48, 52; Plate III, 6–8, 12–14. Pottery and earthenware were produced in large quantities, and were

FIG. 67. CARVED WOODEN SPOON.

articles of export, but the product did not compare either in grace of form or in decoration with the later ceramic work of the Greeks. Enameled earthenware was used for the finer bowls, platters, etc., and enameled tiles were early used in architecture, as around a door in the stepped pyramid of Sakkarah, but apparently not in buildings after the Hyksos period. Amulets and small ornaments were made of enameled earthenware, of cloisonné enamel on metal (gold or copper), of bronze, and of diorite and other hard stones. Of these amulets the *scarabæi* are the most numerous; one side being modeled to represent the scarabæus beetle (an emblem of life after death), the other side, flat, having incised hieroglyphs and spiral or scroll ornaments.

Not much furniture has been preserved, but the few extant examples, of sycamore wood, and the very numerous sarcophagi and mummy-wraps and *cartonnages,* furnish almost countless examples of painted ornament. Carved spoons and perfume holders were often highly elaborate (Fig. 67; Plate III, 25).

Books Recommended:

FLINDERS-PETRIE: *Egyptian Decorative Art* (London, 1895). —W. H. GOODYEAR: *Grammar of the Lotus* (London, 1891).— PERROT and CHIPIEZ: *Histoire de l'art dans l'antiquité: Egypte* (Paris, 1884); also English edition, *History of Ancient Art in Egypt,* trans. W. Armstrong (New York, 1885).—PRISSE D'AVENNES: *L'Art Egyptien* (Paris, 1878).—ROSELLINI: *I Monumenti del Egitto e della Nubia* (Pisa, 1832–1844).

CHAPTER IV

The valley of the Tigris and Euphrates rivers was the cradle of a civilization second only to that of Egypt in antiquity. Indeed, it is believed by some scholars to reach as far back as that of the Nile Valley, though its origins are buried in obscurity. The two civilizations early came into contact with each other, and there are traces of reciprocal influences between them. The material remains of Chaldean art are far less rich and important than those of Egyptian art, and the most important among them, from the point of view of decorative design, belong to a period when Egyptian art was already in its decline. Early Chaldean art lasted from a date reaching back 3000 or 4000 years B.C. to 1250 B.C., when the Assyrian power attained the ascendancy. The Assyrian empire was overthrown 606 B.C. by the second Chaldean or Babylonian empire, and this in turn succumbed to the Persians 525 B.C. The most important monumental art of these three periods is that of the Sargonidæ of Assyria, from 900 to 606 B.C. Recent excavations by the Germans at Babylon have brought to light many remains of both the earlier and later Chaldean empire: but our chief concern is with the products of the Assyrian dominion.

Land and Materials.

From the high table-lands and hills of Northern Mesopotamia to the Persian Gulf, the country is almost flat, a vast alluvial plain, abounding in clay, extremely fertile under irrigation, but lacking both stone and timber. All building was consequently of brick, either sun-baked or kiln-burned, and chiefly the former. Timber from the distant mountains or from Syria was costly and was used but sparingly; fuel was expensive and burned brick therefore also expensive. Thin slabs of alabaster or of limestone were the only forms in which stone could be used, except in rare instances. These limitations made all architectural art based on stone construction impossible, and confined decorative art within narrow limits. Ceramics in the form of bricks and enameled tiles and pottery; textiles, especially rugs and hangings, and bronze in small amounts, were the principal media of artistic expression, although sculpture, chiefly in the form of carving in low relief on alabaster, was also practised with a skill which is remarkable when one considers the scarcity and costliness of stone. Of wood carving there are hardly any examples.

Early Chaldean Art.

The remains of decorative art from ancient Chaldea are not numerous. Abundant cylinders and inscribed bricks, ruins of temples and palaces, a few statues of kings or deities carved in stone obtained from abroad, some pottery and a few objects in bronze, make up the bulk of the product of the excavations carried on in Niffer (Nippur) the sacred city, in Warka, Mugheir, in Babylon, and in other places belonging to this empire. The plastic arts were apparently not in general highly developed. The most ancient examples of its architectural ornament known are the walls of Warka (Erech), formed with vertical reedings and

FIG. 68. WALL-MOSAIC, WARKA.

panels, and covered with a simple mosaic (Fig. 68) formed of cones of terra cotta driven into their sun-dried brick facings. The flat exposed bases of these cones, enameled in various colors, form patterns of lozenges and zigzags, apparently derived from familiar mattting-patterns. Flat tiles may have been used in other cases, but they have all perished.

Assyrian Ornament: Origins and Motives.

Assyrian decoration depended largely on naturalistic representation: human figures, bulls, lions and other animals appear frequently, not merely in the great sculptured pictures on the alabaster wainscot of palace halls, but in the subordinate decoration of buildings and in the ornament of minor objects. There was also a large group of motives derived from Egyptian art, greatly modified oftentimes in treatment but still recog-

FIG. 69. ASSYRIAN ORNAMENT MOTIVES.

nizably Egyptian. Another class of motives are in dispute, but two facts seem clear: first, that the Assyrians originated little in the way of decorative motives; and, secondly, that whatever they borrowed underwent a transformation into something that is purely Assyrian in character.

The lotus (Fig. 69, *a*); lotus-palmette (*b*), and

winged disk or globe (e) are undeniably derived from Egypt. The rosette (Fig. 69, c) and the guilloche (f) are common to both Egyptian and Assyrian ornament, but it is not demonstrated that they were not independently invented by the Chaldeans from whom the Assyrians probably received them.

The chevron (Fig. 69, g) and imbricated or scale ornaments (d) are peculiarly Assyrian, but as they are also found in Egyptian art, they belong with the rosette and guilloche in the doubtful class as to origin. The so-called "pomegranate" (Fig. 69, h, i) is probably Chaldean. The pine cone (Fig. 70, a) is an Assyrian form, but as it conforms in outline and in its occurrence to the lotus-bud, it may be claimed as a lotus derivative. The stepped-pyramid, used as a parapet ornament, seems to be purely Chaldean.

But if the Assyrians borrowed freely from Egypt [1] they as freely modified what they borrowed. The lotus was carved in low relief with sharply pointed, gracefully curved petals and sepals (Figs. 69, a, 70, a), and was given a wholly new calyx, the three sepals being evidently looked upon as petals; the bud was likewise given an extra calyx and carved sometimes with three instead of two sepals showing (Fig. 70, b). It was alternated with buds and with pine-cones, and combined into elab-

[1] Prof. Goodyear quotes Oppert for proof that under Gudea (3000 B. C.?), the Chaldeans imported stone from Egypt during the Fourth Dynasty; points out ·that under the XVIIIth Dynasty Assyria was a province of Egypt, and calls attention to the later Assyrian conquests in Egypt and Syria and to the importance of Phenician commerce between Assyria and both Egypt and Syria ("Grammar of the Lotus," page 177, note). It must be remembered that the Phenicians not only carried Egyptian products to Asia, but themselves counterfeited or imitated them, so that Egyptian forms and motives were greatly multiplied and widely disseminated.

orate rosettes (Plate IV, 8). The lotus-palmette (Fig. 69, b) was often substituted for the lotus (Plate IV, 1) and used in borders; as an isolated terminal

ornament (Fig. 72, a); as the chief detail of the Sacred Tree (Fig. 70, c; Plate IV, 2), and in many other ways, carved in alabaster-relief, painted on plaster, enameled on bricks, cast or engraved in bronze. In all borders, the units were connected by voluted bands, often curved into semi-circles or semi-ellipses (Figs. 69, a, 70) and frequently fastened together by links. This is a purely Assyrian device, and the organic linking of the units—no

Fig. 70. a, b. Pine and Lotus Border; c, Detail of Sacred Tree.

longer merely strung along a straight line as in most Egyptian examples—marks a decided decorative advance. Whether the frequent use of branching and opposed double volutes (Fig. 71), so common in Assyrian decoration, was derived from the volutes of the Egyptian trilobe lotus and lotus-palmette, or from the curled-over ends of the linked bands, is not clear and perhaps not important. The discussion as to whether the palmette in Assyrian art "is" a lotus or a palm-tree also becomes unimportant if one simply admits that the decorative motive was derived from or suggested by the Egyptian lotus-palmette, but was treated in detail by the Assyrians in a manner plainly suggesting a conventional palm-tree (Fig. 72); an example of decorative convergence which has scores of parallels in the history of ornament motives and symbols. In the singular "sacred tree" which so often occurs in Assyrian reliefs (Fig. 70, c), the intention is unquestionably to represent or symbolize the palm; in that sense the palmettes which compose it "are" palm-tree forms, while in decorative type and origin they "are" lotus-palmettes. The so-called pine-cones referred to above may represent, as believed by E. B. Tylor, the inflorescence of the male date-palm, or it may be what it appears to be, a pine-cone.

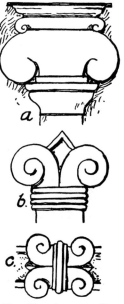

FIG. 71. ASSYRIAN VOLUTES.

The rosette is used with such frequency as to deserve to be called the Assyrian motive *par excellence*. It appears in every branch of Assyrian decoration, and in every possible material. The pomegranate is more exclusively Assyrian but less conspicuous by its frequency. All-over patterns are rare; of architectural or at least of genuine structural forms there are very few. Columns appear only in the form of colonnettes; a few bases and capitals have been found, and the reliefs from the palaces show how they were used, as mullions and as supports for pavilions. In these, as also in furniture, coupled volutes are favorite devices, and undoubtedly furnish the first step in the development of the Ionic capital (Fig. 71).

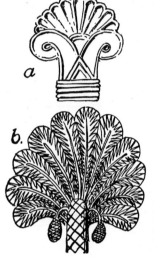

Living Forms.

The human figure, grotesques or monsters, part man and part beast, and representations of animals, all play a large part in Assyrian decorative art; not merely in the great pictures in low relief which wainscoted the lower parts of the interior walls, but in more purely ornamental and symbolic compositions, sometimes carved in relief in alabaster, sometimes in flat color on

FIG. 72. *a*, TERMINAL PALM-ETTE; *b*, PALM-TREE, FROM A RELIEF.

tiles or plaster. The huge symbolic "portal guardians" —winged monsters with human heads and bodies of bulls—that flanked the arched gateways of the palaces and fortifications, are genuine decorative compositions of extraordinary power and remarkable execution. The details are highly conventionalized; five legs are shown, two appearing in front elevation and four in the side view; the hair and beard are curled into closely coiled spirals and the muscles exaggerated (Plate IV, 7). The winged lion and winged bull, as well as winged human figures representing deities, appear frequently in enameled earthenware tiles. The griffin (Fig. 73), a monster with a lion's or panther's body and the head and wings of an eagle, plays an important part in this decorative system of religious symbolism. It probably originated in Chaldea, and spread thence through Western Asia, to appear in Greek and Roman art in later

FIG. 73. GRIFFIN OR MONSTER, FROM A RELIEF.

years. In naturalistic pictures the forms and action of animals were rendered often with surprising realism; but these belong in the field of pictorial relief sculpture rather than of ornament.

Colors and Technic.

The Assyrian technic in the representation of nature never fell into the absolute rigidity of hieratic convention observed in Egypt. Within its far narrower field, it was excellent in execution, but less rich in variety of motive and pattern of ornament. The gamut of color was restricted: green, blue, yellow, black and dark red were the colors chiefly employed. The use of black in chevrons as a detail of the decoration is particularly noticeable (Fig. 69, *b, c, g, h*). Not many examples of painted ornament have been preserved; a few fragments of plaster show patterns like those of the enameled tiles. Bronze was used for jars and bowls, for furniture and probably also for covering gates and sometimes other architectural features; but very few examples of this application of bronze to architecture have been preserved. The gates of Balawat in the British Museum, dating from the time of Shalmaneser II (9th century B.C.) were decorated with strips or bands of sheet bronze bearing *repoussé* reliefs of the campaigns of that king. The recent German excavations in Babylon have uncovered the palace with its Gate of Ishtar, whose towers were adorned with plates of bronze which have disappeared. In these excavations it was also found that the Babylonians, lacking stone and alabaster, faced their gateways with enameled bricks bearing large compositions in color, each brick being separately molded and colored to produce its own small fraction of the design. This style of decoration was later adopted in Persia: it is probable that Babylonian artists were imported to Susa to execute the Persian bricks and to teach the art to the Persians, among whom decorative ceramics have been an important art ever since.

Books Recommended.

BOTTA and FLANDIN: *Monument de Ninive* (Paris, 1849–50). —PERROT and CHIPIEZ: *Histoire de l'art dans l'antiquité: Chaldeé et Assyrie* (Paris, 1883); also English translation by W. Armstrong, *History of Art in Chaldæa and Assyria* (London, 1884).—PLACE: *Ninive et l'Assyrie* (Paris, 1867–70).

CHAPTER V

WEST ASIATIC ORNAMENT

PHRYGIA, LYDIA AND PERSIA

The northern half of Asia Minor, west of the river
Halys, was occupied, during the centuries from the
tenth to the sixth B.C., by the Phrygians, originally from

FIG. 74. *a,* PART OF FAÇADE OF "TOMB OF MIDAS"; *b,* DETAIL FROM TOMB AT
DOGHANLOU.

Thrace; whose empire was overthrown early in the sixth
century by the Lydians of the extreme western littoral.
Along the Asiatic shore south of Lydia were the Cary-
ans and Lycians. In all of these several domains there

developed a material civilization which has left numerous remains, chiefly of tombs, though excavations now being made at Sardis and others that are still in the future may supply us with products of other arts as well as of architecture. The principal examples of ornament thus far to hand occur in the rock-cut tomb-façades, some of which, like the so-called Tomb of Midas (Fig. 74, *a*) and a tomb at Doghanlou (*b*) suggest textile design. This region has from great antiquity been noted for the weaving of rugs; other ornaments are clearly derived from wood-construction, while others again show Assyrian, Persian and Ægean influences.

FIG. 75. CAPITAL FROM NEANDREIA.

Several capitals and fragments of capitals (Fig. 75) found in Asia Minor, with branching volutes and with recurved petals, furnish the probable prototypes of the Greek Ionic capital and of certain details of the Persian capitals.

Persian Ornament.

The art of Asia Minor bears no comparison in splendor and variety with that of the great Medo-Persian empire of the Achæmenid kings—Cyrus, Cambyses, Darius, Xerxes and their successors. This empire, which began its conquering career in 608 under the Mede Cyaxares, and fifty years later attained greatness under Cyrus (559–529) and his successors, developed a grandiose architecture of palaces, halls, gates and tombs in which Egyptian and Assyrian motives were blended with others derived from wooden construction and from the early art of the Ionian Greeks of Asia Minor. This brilliant and showy art expired with the fall of Persia before the Macedonian armies of Alexander (330 B.C.); but the art instinct of Persia, though under an eclipse for several centuries, was destined to revive under the Sassanian rule, and in still later centuries to affect profoundly the development of Mohammedan decorative art.

Architectural Ornament.

The ruins of Persepolis, Pasargadæ and Susa reveal a remarkable development of columnar architecture of stone with wooden ceilings and roofs. The walls were of stone, or of brick with stone dressings to the doors and windows. These have banded architraves with papyrus-bundle moldings and cavetto cornices, evidently derived from Egypt (Figs. 76, 77, *a*).

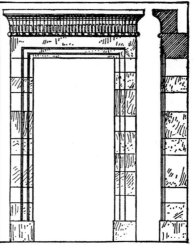

FIG. 76. DOORWAY, PERSEPOLIS.

Stone was used for embankment walls and stairs, for the great palace terraces, for the window-dressings just mentioned, and for the columns; the walls were chiefly of sun-dried brick, though at Susa enameled bricks were used with extraordinary effect, to produce huge wall-pictures in low rounded relief, and bands of elaborate decoration, all in rich colors enameled or fused upon the surface of the bricks (Plate IV, 14, 15). Decorative relief-sculpture in stone was employed, based primarily on Assyrian models, but treated in a taste peculiar to the Persians, and always highly decorative.

The most striking feature of Persian architecture was the columns with forked capitals representing the fore parts of bulls set upon an elaborate composition of double scrolls, upright and inverted bells, and carved beads (Plate IV, 9, 10). These are typical of Persian eclecticism; one recognizes the Egyptian bell capital (see Fig. 46); the Assyrian and Phenician double scrolls (Fig. 71); the Asia Minor recurved leafage (note the astagal or necking in Fig. 75); and the primitive wooden forked post which has been used from immemorial antiquity, in Media and Phrygia, to support the timber roofs of peasant huts.

The shafts were finely fluted, and rested on elaborate molded bases, often bell-shaped (Fig. 77, d; Plate IV, 9) carved with elaborate leaf-patterns. The slender proportions of the shafts, their small flutings and molded bases, all point to a common origin with that of the Greek Ionic column which came to its full development a century later than the Persian column. Both probably had their origin in Asia Minor, though the remains of their prototypes thus far discovered are scanty.

The same is true of the banded architrave and the

dentils of the Ionic order; they are found both in Persian (see Fig. 77, *a*) and Lycian architecture, in both of which they plainly reveal their origin in timber construction.

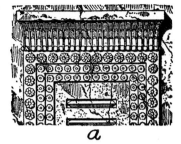

a

Persian Ornament Motives.

These were chiefly derived from Egypt and Mesopotamia; the lotus, lotus-palmette and rosette are those most frequently employed, but treated with details which differentiate them clearly from the Egyptian, Assyrian or Chaldean forms. In linear bands of lotus-palmettes and buds the units are connected by nearly semicircular loops instead of the flattened links of the Assyrian style (Plate IV, 14). Plate IV, 12, and Fig. 77, *b*, show the lotus palmette on a stem like that of some palms which grow by successive pairs of leaves rising one out of the

FIG. 77. PERSIAN DETAILS.

a, Architrave and Cornice from a Tomb; *b*, Rosettes and Palm; *c*, Stair Parapet; *d*, Column-Base, Persepolis.

69

other; evidently, therefore, not intended at all for a lotus, but as a purely conventional plant-form, perhaps even a palm-tree. Spiral and voluted forms are also common, both in flat ornament (see Plate IV) and in the mighty grouped vertical volutes of the capitals of columns (Fig. 78). The Assyrian stepped parapet also appears in the decoration of the platforms and stairs of Persepolis (Fig. 77, c). From Egypt were derived the fluted cavetto cornice (Fig. 77, a) and the winged disk, converted into a winged ring encircling the figure of a god, Ahuri-Mazda (Fig. 79). The sculptural representations of warriors, winged lions and winged bulls were based on Assyrian prototypes. The wood-constructions of Media and Asia Minor gave the

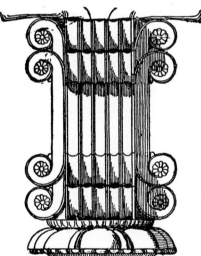

suggestions for the forked capital, the banded architrave and the dentil. The leaf ornaments on the bases (Fig. 77, d) and the shorter leaf-ornaments resembling eggs and darts (Fig. 77, c) are possibly remote derivatives from the lotus bud and from lotus bands; more directly, however, derived from Assyria, as is also the stepped-pyramid para-

FIG. 78.   VOLUTES OF A CAPITAL, PERSEPOLIS.

pet. The bead-and-reel molding, which occurs in some

capitals, is possibly derived from the papyrus-bundle molding. The torus, which appears in the column bases, the bead-and-reel, the shaft-fluting, the decorated column-base, the banded architrave, were all destined to become important elements in the architectural decoration

FIG. 79. AHURI-MAZDA FROM A RELIEF.

of the Greeks. Whether their origination is to be credited to the Persians, or, as is more likely, to the Ionian and other races of Asia Minor, is not clear; but the Persian was the earliest developed architecture in which they were systematically employed.

Persian ornament is of interest partly on account of its own splendor, partly on account of its relations on the one hand to the Semitic art of Mesopotamia and on the other to the Aryan art of Greece. It stands intermediate between the two, alike in time, place and character. It is an eclectic style, borrowing freely from every source, but profoundly modifying whatever it adopted, and displaying a genuine creative originality, as well as a remarkable power of ingenious adaptation,

A HISTORY OF ORNAMENT

in its use and development of what it borrowed to new purposes and in new combinations.

Books Recommended.

DIEULAFOY: *L'Art antique de la Perse* (Paris, 1883).— FELLOWS: *Account of Discoveries in Lycia* (London, 1841).— FLANDIN and COSTE: *Voyage en Perse* (Paris, 1843–54).—PERROT and CHIPIEZ: *Histoire de l'art dans l'antiquité: Perse; Phrygie, Lydie, Carie et Lycie; Sardaigne et Judée* (Paris, 1885–1890).—The same in English: *History of Art in Persia; History of Art in Phrygia, Lydia, Caria and Lycia; History of Art in Sardinia and Judæa* (London, 1886–1891).—TEXIER: *Description del' Arménie et la Perse* (Paris, 1842-52).

CHAPTER VI

Intermediate between the art of Egypt and Mesopotamia on the one hand, and the distinctively Occi-
dental art of Greece on the other, stands the group of
styles that developed in the islands and along the shores
of the Ægean and the Mediterranean Seas during a
period of thirteen to fifteen hundred years previous to
the first Olympiad (776 B.C.). The cradle of the civilization represented by these styles was the island of
Crete—Crete "of the hundred cities," as it is called in the
Homeric poems. The Cretan civilization, as made
known to us by the discoveries of Evans and others at
Knossos, Phæstos and in other parts of the island,
beginning in a remote past in the third millennium B.C.,
had attained a high development by the end of the XXth
century B.C., and reached its culmination in the XVIth
and XVth centuries. This progress was interrupted
by repeated catastrophes which mark its division into
periods,[1] and was finally overwhelmed, about 1400 B.C.,
by a foreign invasion, perhaps of Pelasgi or Achæans
from Greece.

[1] First, Middle and Late Minoan eras, each subdivided into periods. The
name Minoan is derived from that of the more or less legendary King Minos.

The influence of the Cretan culture—which though contemporary with the Middle and New Empires in Egypt seems to have borrowed but little from that country,—dominated that of prehistoric Greece and Asia Minor. Out of this influence was developed the art of Mycenæ, Tiryns and Troy (Ilios, Ilion), commonly called Mycenæan, which flourished from 1500 to 1300 B.C., and after two centuries of decline was in turn extinguished by the Dorian migration of 1104 B.C. Artistic activity, however, continued in certain islands like Melos and Rhodes, while Assyrian art was flourishing in Asia (1100–600 B.C.), and while the Phenicians were distributing and imitating the art-products of both Egypt and Assyria and making them known throughout the whole Mediterranean basin. On the island of Cyprus all these various currents of art-influence converged into a singularly mixed product, which partakes by turns of the characteristics of each of its components, and in its later phases also reflects the influence of early Greek art.

Cretan Ornament.

The excavations at Knossos, Phæstos, Hagia Triada and other Cretan sites have disclosed the remains of a well-developed civilization with an art vigorous and full of character, which strongly influenced that of the whole Ægean and eastern Mediterranean. Of its architecture nothing is left but foundations of extensive palaces and fortifications, fragments of a few columns and architraves, and bits of painted plastering on walls. The columns (Fig. 80) tapered downward and bore simple heavy torus capitals. A notable architectural motive, frequently recurring in Mycenæan art, is that shown in Figure 81 (page 76) composed of a pair of semi-rosettes flanking a vertical rectangle. Its significance and origin are uncertain. On plaster and on pottery the circle, rosette and spiral wave or "Vitruvian scroll" are frequent, in various combinations (Figure 82); also a heart-shaped motive which was carried into Mycenæan decoration. The elaborate "key" or fret-pattern of Figure 83 is from a plastered wall at Knossos.

FIG. 80.
COLUMN FROM
KNOSSOS.

Of Cretan pottery comparatively little has survived, but the elaborate late Minoan vase from Knossos shown in Fig. 84 reveals a highly developed pattern of conventional leaf-forms. Fig. 85 from a sarcophagus found near Gortyna, shows a curiously conventionalized portrayal of marine plant-life. Figure 86 shows two all-over patterns from a large pottery ossuary; one resembles a common Egyptian pattern (see Figure 52); the other is peculiarly Cretan. The interior of the same ossuary is decorated with representations of waves, fishes and shells.

Mycenæan Ornament.

The art-products of the Mycenæan culture include those from Tiryns, Troy, Argos,

FIG. 84. LATE MINOAN VASE. Nauplia, Menidi and other sites,

75

Fig.81. Cretan Frieze Ornament

Fig.82. Cretan Painted Orn!

Fig.85. Marine Plants: Cretan

Fig.83. Fret Pattern, Knossos.

Fig.88. Mycenæan Bowl.

Fig.86. Cretan All-over Patterns.

Fig.87. Mycenæ. Column

Fig.89. Mycenæan Frieze Ornam!

Fig 90. Marine Life, Mycenæan Pottery.

Cuttle Fish

Fig. 92

Fig.93. Scale Ornament. Tiryns.

Fig. 94. Mycenæan Motives.

76

as well as from Mycenæ proper, besides specimens found in Rhodes, Cyprus and other islands, which were obviously imported from Mycenæan centers. This culture was especially proficient in the minor arts, in pottery, goldsmith's work and bronze. It was less notable relatively in its architecture, although the great tomb known as the Tholos of Atreus, and the Lion Gate, both at Mycenæ, attest the power to produce a certain amount of architectural splendor. The ruins of Troy, Tiryns and Mycenæ show extensive stone structures of a somewhat primitive character. Figure 87 shows the upper part of one of the columns of the Tholos doorway, with a capital and downward-tapering shaft evidently derived from Cretan prototypes.

Of sculpture there is very little, no free statues having come down to us; but the so-called "island stones" or carved gems exhibit a high degree of artistic skill, and there are fragmentary reliefs showing intelligent study of nature.

Mycenæan ornament displays many motives from Cretan art (*e.g.,* that in Figure 89 from a frieze), and is itself continued in many works of Cypriote, Rhodian and Phenician art. Each has its own characteristic forms, but connected more or less by common motives. Pottery and metal work were the fields most successfully cultivated, and the ruins of Tiryns have also revealed much clever decoration on plaster. Primarily growing out of Cretan art, Mycenæan ornament displays frequent traces of Egyptian influence, and in addition exhibits a considerable amount of indigenous design, both naturalistic and technomorphic. The example in

FIG. 91. MYCENÆAN POTTERY, SPIRALS.

Figure 88 shows patterns derived from basketry, singularly like many found on South American pottery; while in Figure 90, *a, b, c,* and Fig. 97, the representations of marine plants and animals reveal an instinct for the observation and imitation of Nature, of which traces are found in Cretan art, and which later, in Greek art, flowered into the superb sculpture of the Periclean age.

Besides the architectural forms already referred to, the motives characteristic of Mycenæan ornament are the zig-zag (Figure 87), spiral (Fig. 91); the running scroll; a heart-shaped motive (Figure 94) perhaps converging towards the cuttlefish (Figure 92); the rosette, both carved and painted (see Figure 89); the double-branched volute recalling the lotus trilobe (Figure 94, *c*); a peculiar variant of the guilloche (or the current scroll?) shown in Fig. 95, *a* and in the detail of Figure 89; and a number of unnamed motives, *e.g.,* the imbricated pattern from Tiryns in Figure 93.

FIG. 95. *a,* CURRENT SCROLL, TIRYNS; *b,* VASE ORNAMENT, MYCENÆ.

A somewhat similar motive in a linear repetition on vases, suggests an inverted egg-and-dart (Figure 95, *b*).

78

Figs. 96 and 97 show various Nature-forms, apparently derived from marine life; Fig. 97 is a vase from Ialyssos bearing a squid as its chief ornament. The cuttlefish squid, dolphin (?), and sea-weed are common, besides many forms like those in Figure 90, *d,* Figs. 96 and 97, impossible to identify. On the so-called "Mycenæ buttons" —thin plates of gold stamped or *repoussé* in low relief, appears the peculiarly Mycenæan motive of a band winding in and out around small eyes or round dots, with excellent decorative effect (Fig. 98).

FIG. 96. PLANT - FORMS, MYCENÆ POTTERY.

The lotus and the multiple scroll, so common in Egyp-

FIG. 97. SQUIDS, ON MYCENÆAN VASES.

tian decoration, appear frequently, as in a slab from a tomb-ceiling in Orchomenos,[2] in the band from a wall-

[2] Figured in P. & C., "Histoire de l'Art"; Sturgis, "History of Architecture," vol. I, 125; Tarbell, "A History of Greek Art," page 55; Marquand, "Greek Architecture," page 155.

painting in Tiryns (Figure 99), the ornament from a Mycenæan sword shown in Figure 100, *a,* and the

Mycenæan stele *b.* The spiral also appears in other forms, as in Figure 101, page 81, on the base *a* and in the bronze work detail *b* (from a tripod in Athens; its Mycenæan origin is problematic).

FIG. 98. A MY-CENÆ BUTTON.

In Figure 103 we have rosettes from Tiryns and Mycenæ obviously derived from Cretan prototypes like those in Figure 82. Figure 102 shows a Mycenæan double-rosette frieze ornament in alabaster very similar to the Tirynthian example of Figure 88, both being nearly identical with the Cretan example in Figure 81. Figures 104, 105 and 107 exhibit other Mycenæan nature-forms. In Figure 104, *a* is a common Mycenæan plant form (see also Fig. 96) which it is interesting to compare with the Egyptian lotus-palmette *b.*

Phenician Ornament.

During the decline of Ægean art, from 1500 B.C. on, the Phenicians were developing and extending their commerce and industries. This presumably Semitic people, occupying a narrow strip of the Syrian coast, north of Palestine, were the mercantile carriers of the ancient world, with prosperous colonies along the

FIG. 99. PAINTED WALL-PATTERN, TIRYNS.

Mediterranean shores, of which Carthage became the chief. They were traders and imitators rather than

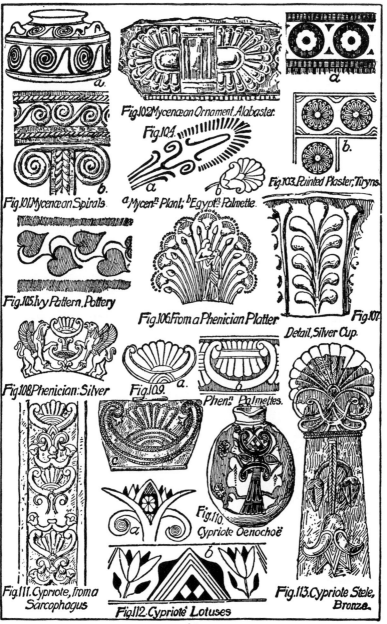

Fig. 102 Mycenæan Ornament. Alabaster.

Fig. 104.

Fig. 103. Painted Plaster, Tiryns.

Fig. 101 Mycenæan Spirals.

a. Mycen^{n.} Plant; b. Egypt^{n.} Palmette.

Fig. 105. Ivy Pattern. Pottery

Fig. 106. From a Phenician Platter

Fig. 107. Detail, Silver Cup.

Fig. 108 Phenician: Silver

Fig. 109. a. b. Phen^{n.} Palmettes.

Fig. 110. Cypriote Oenochoë

Fig. 111. Cypriote, from a Sarcophagus

Fig. 112. Cypriote Lotuses

Fig. 113. Cypriote Stele, Bronze.

81

originators in art; they carried and exchanged, and freely counterfeited, Egyptian and Assyrian or Babylonian wares and stuffs. The detail from a silver

FIG. 100. MYCENÆ SPIRAL ALL-OVERS; a, GOLD INLAY ON SWORD; b, BRONZE STELE.

platter in Figure 106 is plainly an imitation of Egyptian work. Sidon was for a long period under Egyptian rule. The Phenicians were skilful weavers, dyers and bronzeworkers. Solomon's temple at Jerusalem was largely of Phenician workmanship, and the accounts in I Kings, vii, 13–45 and I Chronicles iii, 15–iv, 17 prove the Phenicians of 1000 B.C. to have been capable of casting large objects of "brass" (bronze), such as the columns "Jachin" and "Boaz" and the huge "laver" borne on twelve oxen.

FIG. 114. CYPRIOTE STONE STELE.

Distinctive Phenician ornament motives are few.

The most characteristic is a species of palmette springing

FIG. 115. CYPRIOTE LOTUS, FROM VASE.

from the concave side of a voluted crescent (Figures 108, 109, *a, c*), derived from the Assyrian palmette with horns, converging with the Phenician crescent, symbol of the goddess Astarte. It persists into Greek art of the fifth century B.C. appearing as a vase band-motive (Figure 109, *b*).

Cypriote Ornament.

Cyprus was an important *entrepôt* of Phenician commerce, and its art is peculiarly interesting because of the mingling of Egyptian, Ægean, Phenician and early Greek influences which it betrays. In general character it resembles sometimes the Mycenæan, sometimes the Phenician. Its principal motives are the lotus, almost grotesquely transformed from the Egyptian type (Figure 112, also Fig. 115); the lotus palmette in several variant forms, one the Phenician palmette with upturned volutes (Figure 111), and others such as those in Figure 113 and Figure 114, used as finials or cap for steles and pilasters. A curious de-

FIG. 116. CYPRIOTE ORNAMENTS ON VASES.

sign, compounded of palmettes, trilobes and horns is that in Figure 111 from a sarcophagus in the Metropolitan Museum in New York, from Amathus; in a variant form which may be a lotus and not a palmette, it ap-

A HISTORY OF ORNAMENT

FIG. 117. PHENICIAN VASE FROM JERUSALEM.

pears also in Figure 110, apparently related to the Assyrian Sacred Tree (see Fig. 70, *c*). It will be observed that this entire composition recalls the primitive Egyptian design of Fig. 34. The type constantly reappears in Asiatic art. Rectangles, lozenges, and checkerings applied even to the central sepal of the lotus betray the persistent influence of primitive basketry patterns (Fig. 115, in which note also the swastikas). The lotus is always ungraceful in Cypriote art. The recurved or voluted sepals in Figure 112 and Fig. 115 are closely related to the branching volutes in Fig. 116, the lower ornament in which— a four-petaled flower —is probably, like the checkers, lozenge and triangle of Fig. 115 and Figure 112, a reminiscence of

FIG. 118. DETAIL FROM CYPRIOTE VASE FROM ORMIDIA (MET. MUSEUM, N. Y.).

primitive pottery and basketry (see Chapter II).

84

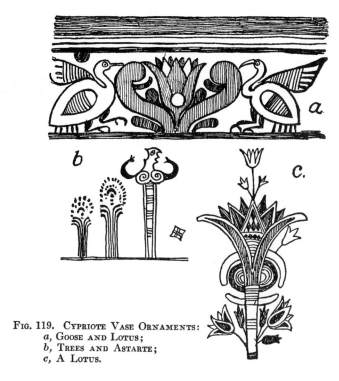

Fig. 119. Cypriote Vase Ornaments:
a, Goose and Lotus;
b, Trees and Astarte;
c, A Lotus.

This survival appears also in the splendid Phenician vase from Jerusalem (Fig. 117) and the Cypriote vase from Ormidia (Fig. 118)—the latter in the New York Metropolitan Museum.   Animals, human figures and plant forms appear on vases—the horse, goose (Fig. 119, a) and bull, and caricatures of the human form (Fig. 119, b).[3] The swastika or fylfot appears occasionally as a minor detail, probably as a solar symbol, as in Fig. 115. The affronting

[3] Compare the queer plants beside the figure (is this Astarte?) with those from Mycenæ, in Fig. 96 and Figure 104.

of two opposed birds or beasts on either side of a central shaft or column, as in Figure 110, preserves

or repeats a common Asiatic (Assyrian, Mycenæan, Hittite, Phenician) symbolic motive, of which probably the earliest examples is the prehistoric Egyptian slate-carving shown in Fig. 34. Whether the goose, horse, swastika, etc., are solar symbols, is a question not

FIG. 120. LOTUS-AND-BIRD BORDERS ON RHODIAN AND MELIAN VASES.

yet certainly answered. Fig. 119, *c,* from a Cypriote œnochoë in the Metropolitan Museum, illustrates the singular mixture of lotus and other forms frequently met with in Cypriote art.

The ornament of Rhodes (Kameiros, Ialyssos, etc.) and of Melos, is a later development from the Mycenæan, less mixed with Egyptian and Assyrian forms than the Cypriote. It is found chiefly in pottery remains, covering the period from the ninth century B.C. down to historic Greek art, thus supplying a connecting link, though a slight one, between the Hellenic and pre-Hellenic cultures. Examples are shown in Fig. 120 of a Rhodian lotus-band (above) and a Melian (below), the latter an almost exact duplicate of that on the Cypriote vase from Ormidia shown in Fig. 118. Comparison of both with the Mycenæan jars of Figure 88 and Fig. 117 sufficiently demonstrates the interrelation of these three phases of pre-Hellenic art.

ÆGEAN AND ASIATIC

Books Recommended.

A. P. DI CESNOLA: *Salaminia, Cyprus* (London, 1884).—M. COLLIGNON: *Archéologie grecque* (Paris, 1887), also an English edition.—FÜRTWÄNGLER and LÖSCHKE: *Mykenische Vasen* (Berlin, 1886).—MITCHELL: *History of Ancient Sculpture* (New York, 1883).—PERROT AND CHIPIEZ: *Histoire de l'art dans l'antiquité, la grèce archaïque* (Paris, 1903).—H. SCHLIEMANN: *Mycenæ and Ilios* (New York, 1881).

CHAPTER VII

Introductory.

The Hellenic peoples were gifted with an especial endowment of the artistic faculty. While their geographical situation brought them early into contact with the older civilizations of Egypt, the Mediterranean basin and Mesopotamia, their own esthetic aptitudes enabled them to assimilate all that they borrowed, and in transforming it, to endow it with a wholly new elegance and refinement. Two characteristics are conspicuous in all their intellectual and artistic activity:— their attitude of persistent inquiry in the presence of every fact and phenomenon of their experience; and their recognition and pursuit of ideals. The Greek asked Why? Whence? How? where other peoples had simply acquiesced unquestioningly in Nature's order or the teachings of tradition, and he strove unceasingly after unrealized perfections in every undertaking. The progress of Greek civilization stands therefore in sharpest contrast with the slow advance and slow decline of Egyptian art bound by ancient and sacred traditions, and with the stagnation of Assyrian art. It was from the earliest stages progressive, and in this respect breathes the modern spirit and appeals to modern tastes.

88

FIG. 121.—GREEK VASE, "FINE" PERIOD.   (NAPLES MUSEUM)

FIG. 121A.—ANTHEMION BAND AND CAP MOLDINGS, FROM THE ERECHTHEION

GREEK ORNAMENT, I

Greek art in its keen observation of Nature, its vivacity, charm and grace, its refinement of proportion, its delicacy combined with vigor, and its artistic restraint, is not only vastly superior to the arts that preceded it, but at its best, and within certain clear limitations, unsurpassed by any that have succeeded it.

The People.

The Greeks were not a nation, but a group of small states, bound together by a common language and religion, and by certain common ethnic traditions. Greece proper was the center and focus of their culture, but Greek colonies established themselves in Southern Italy, Crete, Cyprus, Rhodes, the Ægean islands, while a large part of Asia Minor was inhabited by Ionian Greeks. In spite of this division into small states, often rivals and even enemies in war, the Greek culture was fundamentally one: all Greeks called themselves Hellenes, and the rest of the world Barbarians, and all the states took part in the quadrennial Olympic games. The Dorians and Ionians were the leaders in the development of Greek art, and their names have been given to the two principal "orders"—originally distinct styles—of Greek architecture.[1] The other two chief constituent races of the Hellenes were the Achæans and Æolians.

Periods of Greek Art History.

Between pre-Homeric art, discussed in the last chap-

[1] For a concise summary of the historical beginnings and race movements of the Greeks, consult W. M. West's "Ancient History," §§ 80–100 (Allyn & Bacon, Boston).

ter, and that of historic Greece there is a noticeable
hiatus. Dörpfeld, it is true, derives the Doric style of
architecture directly from the palace architecture of
Mycenæ and Tiryns, but there are grounds for ques-
tioning this derivation. In any case, the ornament of
that age seems to have died with the civilization to which
it belonged, and historic Greek art differs in quality and
spirit as well as in its forms from that of the Ægean
culture.

Dated Greek history begins with the first Olympiad,
776 B.C. It is customary for convenience to divide the
history of Greek art into six periods. The first or
Archaic may be considered as lasting from the first
Olympiad—or from 650 B.C. when the earliest Doric
temples known to us were begun—to 500 B.C. (Some
writers prefer to specify an early and a late Archaic
Period, divided at 550 B.C. and lasting until 480 B.C.,
the date of the Persian invasion.) The next or Transitional Period, beginning at 500 (or at 480) B.C., lasts
until the middle of the fifth century, and ushers in the
great age of Greek art, commonly called the Periclean,
which followed the final victories over the Persians in
466 B.C. This occupied the second half or the last two-
thirds of the fifth century B.C., and was followed by the
Decline of the first half of the fourth century. A brilliant revival manifested itself during the last half, which
constitutes the Alexandrian age. A further decline en-
sued, more rapid and complete, lasting until the Roman
conquest in 146 B.C.: this we may designate as the Post-
Alexandrian Period. But even in its decline Greek art
produced many noble and beautiful works; while after

the Roman conquest, Greek artists wrought for Roman masters and infused a new artistic element into the Roman taste and art; so that a complete sketch of Greek ornament must take into account works produced as late even as the time of the Antonines.

All these periods are but vaguely defined, for historic Greek art was continuously progressive; the change of style was gradual and constant. Hence they are to be considered merely as arbitrary devices for facilitating the grouping and classifying of the works of different times and styles, and for marking certain well-defined stages of development.

Some General Characteristics.

Whereas in Egyptian ornament color predominates over form, it plays a subordinate part in Greek orna- ment, in which *plastic form, as expressed and revealed by outline and light and shade, is the controlling element.* The Greeks seem to have been the first people to delight in pure beauty of form and of line-movement apart from symbolism and representation, and it was their constant reaching out after an ideal perfection of form that gave to their works their immortal freshness of beauty and vitality of interest.

The Greeks cared little for mere patterning; there is no characteristic Greek all-over ornament. But in every work of Greek decoration the *idea of structure* is present; not necessarily of the structural framework of the object decorated, though this is generally recognized; but an organic and logical relation between the object and its decoration, and between the various parts of the

Fig. 122. Greek Palmettes, from a Vase

Fig. 123 Greek and Assyrian Ornament-Links

Fig. 131 Greek Frets

Fig. 127 Carved Rinceau from Miletus. (Late).

Fig. 141. Scroll, Apulian Vase

Fig. 135. Varieties of Anthemion Motive

Fig. 137 Greek Vine Pattern

Fig. 132. Guilloche

Fig. 138. Elementary Rinceau on Vase

Fig. 136 Varieties of Lotiform Motive

94

decoration. This quality also appears in the way in which the ornament itself is designed and its elements put together; they are never merely strung together; they are organically united into a coherent design (Figure 122). This structural quality is by no means confined to architectural ornament, though it is there most conspicuously in evidence; it appears in the painting of a vase or the composition of an anthemion band as truly as in the ornament of the Erechtheion. Compare, for example, the monotonous and inorganic stringing together of lotuses and buds in Egyptian bands, or even the stiff linking of Assyrian forms, with the organic structural combination of alternating motives in the Greek anthemion bands figured in Plate V and Figure 123.

Another unfailing quality of Greek ornament is its *artistic restraint*. The Greek artist knew when to hold his hand, when to leave a surface plain, when not to elaborate a motive or pattern.

These qualities of plastic beauty, grace and vivacity of rhythmic movement, structural fitness and artistic reserve, impart to Greek ornament a distinction which sets it apart from all other decorative styles, unless it be that of the early Gothic period in France.

The examples of Greek decorative art that have come down to us consist chiefly of two classes: architectural ornament, for the most part carved, though often enhanced by added color; and pottery, for the most part painted. But so marked is the architectural feeling in the vase decoration, that many motives were carried from pottery into the architecture; while not a few of the architectural details were executed in terra-cotta and painted, much like the vases.

The Motives.

These constitute an alphabet of only moderate extent.

FIG. 124. GEOMETRIC ELEMENTS.

The greatness of Greek ornament lies in the variety and originality of the combinations of these few fundamental forms, and the elegance of the results, rather than in the number of the primary motives. So nearly endless are the variations of these, that instances of exact reduplication of any ornament on different objects are almost unknown. Even such forms as the Doric capital, or the egg-and-dart molding, are never exactly alike on two different buildings.

In framing any list of motives, it is difficult to draw the line between related forms and to determine when it is proper to distinguish them as really separate motives, and when not. With regard to certain nature-forms, also, there may be differences of judgment as to whether they should be accounted as ornament or as sculpture or painting. We

FIG. 125. NATURE-FORMS.

group the motives listed below into three groups— geometric, natural and structural.

The *geometric motives* (omitting simple dots, circles and parallel lines) are six: the *fret* or meander; the wave or Vitruvian scroll; the spiral, both single and branched; the S-curve or " line of beauty"; the rosette [2] and the *guilloche* (Fig. 24).

The principal *natural forms* are: the *lotus and lotus-bud,* the *palmette or anthemion,* the *vine,* and the *acanthus leaf,* from the vegetable world (Fig. 125); and from the animal kingdom *human heads* or masks, *heads of animals,* paws, wings, *griffins* or chimeras and *sphinxes* (Plate VI, 25, 26, 29, 35). *Festoons* of flowers and fruit (called the "swag" in English books), *ox-skulls* (bucrania) and fluttering *ribbons* also occur in late Greek art, usually on altars, with symbolic signifi-cance. Purely pictorial representations of men, horses and beasts, whether painted or carved, are ex-cluded from the list, as belonging to pictorial art rather than to pure orna-ment.

The chief *architectural motives* not included above are seven (Fig.

FIG. 126. ARCHITECTURAL ELEMENTS.

126): *moldings; flutings* or channelings; *dentils;* the *egg-and-dart* and its derivatives; the *bead-and-reel;*

---

[2] The *star* which occurs in rare instances may be considered as a variant of the rosette.

scales and imbrications (also used in painted ornament; not shown in the figure), and the rinceau or branching scroll (Figure 127).

The *swastika* or fylfot has been omitted from these lists, although occurring on early vases, because it is there used rather as a symbol than as a systematic ornament, and was early dropped from Greek art. The *guttæ* of the Doric order might perhaps be added, though their use is very restricted, and they do not form a motive capable of variation and combination into manifold patterns.

Of all these motives three, the lotus (bud and blossom), the palmette, and the egg-and-dart, are clearly traceable to Egyptian origins. Four others, the fret, guilloche, rosette and wave, occur in Egyptian ornament, but it cannot be proved that they came into Greek art from Egypt, though this may quite possibly be the fact. The spiral has been the common property of all decorating races, and it was the Greeks who first discovered the real beauty of its combination with the S-curve and developed it into the most important single contribution to the art of pattern-design made by any people since the Egyptians first discovered and exploited the value of contrasted alternation in their lotus-and-bud bands. In the adaptation of the acanthus leaf to carved ornament they further increased the debt of subsequent ages to Greek art. The *rinceau* (Figure 127), which is a combination of the S-line, the spiral, the vine-motive and the acanthus leaf, was developed during the Alexandrian age into an ornament which has contributed a most important element to the splendor of Roman, medieval and modern art.

Pottery Decoration.

A brief sketch of the historic development of Greek pottery is essential for the intelligent discussion of its decoration.

The potter's art was transmitted from the pre-Homeric to the post-Homeric civilization without interruption, and practised in various centers of which Rhodes, Melos, Athens, Corinth, Cœre in Etruria (though the majority of the vases found in Etruscan tombs were of Greek and not local manufacture), and in the post-Alexandrian period Apulia and Campania in Southern Italy, were the most important. Burnt clay, though fragile, is an almost imperishable material, and tens of thousands of vases have been preserved to our day, for the most part in ancient tombs, from as far back as the seventh century B.C., and covering the entire period from that time to the Christian Era. All these vessels were made on the wheel [3] and painted, chiefly in black and red. Very few of these were modeled in relief, notwithstanding the Greek predilection for sculpture. The Greek potters preferred the simplicity of a pure and refined silhouette to the more complex effects of relief-modeling (Figure 121, Fig. 128). The same reserve was shown in their long-time preference of the simple black-and-red decoration, with

[3] Note that the dates given above exclude from consideration the archaic Mycenæan and other pre-Homeric pottery, of which some of the earlier examples are crude vessels molded free-hand and not turned on a wheel.

only occasional and sparing use of other colors, to the more showy effects possible with a varied palette, such as became fashionable to a limited degree in and after the Alexandrian age. Thus their pottery decoration was in sober colors, while in their architectural ornament they employed brilliant reds, blues, green and gold. This is in striking contrast to the modern taste which prefers sobriety of coloring in its architecture and brilliant tones for pottery and porcelains.

Changes of Style.

The earliest pottery was of a light red color, with decorations in black and dark red or brown. In the sixth century B.C. the color of the earthenware of the vases was often a yellow-red, nearly orange, and the decorations almost exclusively in black, while the forms were more refined, profiled with more subtle curves than formerly. In the early fifth century or second archaic period, the ware was of a darker red, and the black slip employed in the decoration—really a black paint covered with a thin slip or glaze—became very perfect and was used as a solid background, the decorations being left of the natural dark red of the ware. This change of technic led to a complete change in the character of the ornament, as will later be shown. During the fourth century a further change occurred; the ornament became complex and overcharged, varied colors were added to the black and red to brighten the effect; the vase-profiles lost their earlier refinement, and modeling of figures and details in relief became more or less common, especially in Apulian and other Italo-

Greek vases, which were often of great size. The art declined rapidly under Roman rule; as bronze, marble,

FIG. 128. TYPES OF GREEK VASES: *a*, ARYBALLUS; *b*, LEKYTHOS; *c*, RHYTON; *d*, ALABASTRON; *e*, *g*, AMPHORA; *f*, KRATER; *h*, OINTMENT BOX; *i*, HYDRIA; *k*, KYLIX; *l*, HYDRIA.

alabaster, glass, gold and silver came more and more into use for the finer vessels, the plain clay earthenware ceased to be a medium for artistic expression.

The grace and beauty of the Greek vases of the 6th–

4th centuries B.C. are due, first to the innate artistic spirit of the people; and secondly to the use of terra cotta vases as gifts and prizes. They were regarded as works of art, and the painters who decorated them were proud to sign their works. The decoration of these vases was executed with a bold, free hand which the published illustrations generally fail to reproduce. Special care and attention were bestowed upon the form, proportions and silhouette of these vases, in spite of their humble material. A singular elegance of shape characterizes nearly all of the Greek pottery; the profiles are composed of exquisitely subtle curves harmoniously blended. The chief among many types are the *amphora,* a tall two-handled (or three-handled) jar for wine

(Fig. 128, *e, g*); the *œnochoë,* a large-bodied wine-vessel; the *hydria* (*i, l*), a wide-mouthed water-jar; the *lekythos* (*b*), a small slender-necked vase for perfumes or for votive and funereal uses; the somewhat similar *alabastron,* usually of alabaster (*d*); the *krater* (*f*); a cup or jar with a spreading mouth; the *kylix* (*k*), a broad, dish-like ves-

FIG. 129. GEOMETRIC VASE, SÈVRES.

sel (these two types merge into one another); the *rhyton* (*c*), a drinking horn, shaped often like an animal's head; the *aryballos* (*a*), and various other forms.

Development of Motives.

In an important group of early archaic vases the decoration consists of successive bands alternately of ornament and pictures (*e.g.,* the Dodwell vase, *a* in Fig. 128). Another group, in the so-called "geometric" style,[4] are adorned with bands of parallel lines, zigzags, curious frets, concentric circles, stars or flowers, swastikas irregularly disposed, and checkered patterns imitated from basketry or textiles (Fig. 129). In others, mostly from the islands or from Asiatic Greek factories, Oriental influences are evident; lions, sphinxes and gazelles, horses and the solar goose are pictured upon them, and in the ornament proper the lotus and lotus-palmette are common (Fig. 130; this may possibly be a Rhodian vase).

As the potter's art advances, the fret, wave and anthemion are increasingly used and developed into the greatest possible variety of forms. The fret occurs in several varying types; the *simple fret* as in Figure 131, *a* (page 94), the *compound fret,* formed by two intersecting lines of alternate "keys" and "humps"

Fig. 130. Early Vase; Rhodian?

crossing to form a series of swastika motives (*ib., b*); the *rosetted fret* in which the key-motive alternates with

---
[4] Called also "Dipylon style," "Dipylon vases," because of the number of vases in this style exhumed near the Dipylon gate in Athens.

103

a square or round rosette (Plate VI, 5, 9); the *oblique fret,* and the *double fret* (Figure 131, *c*). All these were drawn free-hand, usually in such manner as to

FIG. 132A.

make the black stroke and red background of, about equal thickness.

The spiral wave was not, as has been frequently asserted, a representation of water, and hence always placed at the foot of the vase: it was used as a border alike above and below the picture or vase-painting, as a variant of the fret, from which it was probably derived (Plate VI, 1, 3; Fig. 132 A).

The Anthemion.

The *anthemion* is the most important and most beautiful of all Greek ornament motives. Its origin can be clearly traced back through Phenician and Assyrian forms to the Egyptian lotus and lotus-palmette.[5] Its resemblance to the blossoms of the honeysuckle, recognized by the Greeks in its name ἀνθέμιον, is a fortuitous resemblance or an afterthought, more noticeable in the late examples than the earlier, and is not an explanation of its origin. In the Assyrian lotus-and-palmette borders (see Plate IV), the units are connected by linked voluted bands; the Greeks substituted for these the double-curved or S-scroll (Figure 123), introducing thereby a wholly new element of grace and rhythmic movement into the composition (see Plates V and VI). They also curved the "petals" of the palmette in vari-

[5] For an exhaustive discussion of this derivation, cf. Goodyear, "Grammar of the Lotus" (London, 1891).

ous ways, elaborated the connecting scrolls, and refined their forms and combinations in an extraordinary variety of ways, creating out of the somewhat monotonous and lifeless Oriental pal-mette an entirely new and exquisitely beauti-ful ornament (Figs. 133, 134). Fig. 134 represents diagram-matically a few of the principal types of

FIG. 133. ANTHEMION WITH VOLUTED SCROLLS; FROM A VASE.

Greek anthemion bands—single and double, opposite and alternate, vertical and oblique; the anthemion *open* as in *a, c, d* or *framed* as in *b, e,* almost always alternating with a contrasting motive derived from the lotus,

FIG. 134. TYPES OF ANTHEMION PATTERNS.

105

which we may call the *lotiform* motive (Figure 136). Figure 135 illustrates a number of typical treatments in detail of the anthemion proper, which springs from a triangular-shaped spot or *nucleus* (or rarely a simple dot) set between opposed spirals or volutes. In Figure 136 are shown a few of the variants of the lotiform motive. Very admirable is always the skill with which the ornament is distributed and the spaces occupied.

The change in the fifth century from the black-on-red to the red-on-black technic led to a change in the character of the anthemion patterns. To economize the labor of painting-in the black background, the spaces between the leaves or other elements of the design were reduced, the ornament became more crowded and richer in effect, and the hair-like lines of the black-on-red type were omitted or replaced by broader lines of red (Figure 135, *e*). Some of the anthemion patterns of the late fifth and of the fourth centuries are remarkably rich and elaborate; they were made in the later vases to cover large areas on the body of the vase, taking the place of a picture on one side of the vase, especially in the Apulian pottery (Plate V).

Next to the fret and anthemion, the *vine* is the most important motive in pottery decoration (Figure 137; also Plates V and VI). It occurs sometimes with a straight stem, sometimes with a wavy stem, and may represent in different examples the laurel, ivy or grape-vine. The laurel crown of victory in athletic and literary contests is symbolized by the laurel "vines" on vases intended as prizes or honorary awards; while the ivy and the grapevine were both sacred to Dionysos, and naturally figured on vases for wine as well as on those presented as gifts in token of good fellowship.

The type of vine in which a wavy stem throws out its leaves alternately on either side to fill the hollows of the waves (Figure 137), furnished one of the most important elements in the development of the *rinceau*. The substitution of branching scrolls (already common as a subordinate detail of certain anthemion patterns in the Periclean period, see Fig. 133) in place of the leaves and berries, produced the elementary *rinceau* of Figure 138.

The Guilloche.

This is found in its simplest form in both Egyptian and Assyrian ornament (see Fig. 69, *f*); but was developed by the Greeks into a richer band-pattern by doubling and even trebling the rows of "eyes" and braided interlacings. Only the simpler forms are, however, common on pottery (Figure 132).

Other Forms.

The "egg-and-dart" appears frequently on the lips of vases, and both it and other U-shaped and scale-like imbrications (Plate VI) are used on the bodies. These related forms are probably derived from the lotus-and-bud, as suggested in Fig. 139;[6] but it is equally likely that the scale-ornament was derived from the use of feathers, scales in armor, or other like industrial imbrications.

[6] This derivation was first pointed out in "Comptes-rendus de la Société Centrale d'Architectes" for 1875, and later elaborated by Professor W. H. Goodyear.

Spirals and branching scrolls are common in the details of pottery-decoration, especially the spirals of the wave or Vitruvian scroll; but the branching scroll as

FIG. 139. EVOLUTION OF EGG-AND-DART.

an independent motive is never used except in late *rinceaux*. The scrolls of anthemion frames and links sometimes branch twice or even three times, as in Fig. 133, but never more than this.

Alexandrian and Apulian Pottery.

The Alexandrian age brought in a new taste for magnificence in all branches of art, and the pottery of the late fourth and early third centuries reflects this changed spirit in the excessive elaboration of the decoration. The coloring was enriched and varied, all parts of the vase were covered with pictures and ornament, in which branching scrolls played an important part. Simplicity and grace of movement were lost in the complexity of multiplied spirals and fantastic details. The potter's art was developed in new manufacturing centers in southern Italy (Apulia and Campania), which became celebrated for the size and splendor of the vases they produced. The handles were made especially impor-

tant, and modeled heads and figures were often introduced into the decoration. Fig. 140 illustrates one
of these Italo-Greek vases, and
in Plate VI and Figure 141
(page 94) are shown some of
the complicated details common in this pottery.

Architectural Ceramics.

Painted terra-cotta orna-
ments were long used on buildings of stone or wood, though
stone and marble displaced
them on the more important
buildings from a very early
date. Moldings, especially
crown-moldings on cornices,
antefixæ, acroteria and ridge-

Fig. 140. Apulian Vase;
Sèvres Museum.

tiles were the chief of these ceramic ornaments. They
display many of the motives and patterns of pottery-
decoration, in modified form and richer coloring, in which
green and yellow were used as well as red and black:
frets, anthemions, the egg-and-dart, guilloche and scale-
motive are the commonest decorations. Similar ornaments were later painted on marble and formed an important element in Greek architectural ornament.

Books Recommended:
List follows next Chapter.

CHAPTER VIII

Architectural Decoration.

In the application of the arts of decoration to architecture, the Greeks attained an extraordinary degree of perfection within a comparatively narrow field. The artistic reserve was even more noticeable in their architecture than in their pottery. Accordingly we find a sparing use of ornament upon their buildings, but its scale and distribution were determined by the most judicious taste, and its execution was as nearly perfect as the artist's utmost skill would permit. In the Doric buildings the ornament proper is chiefly painted and confined to certain well-defined members—ceiling-panels, moldings, capitals and the like (Plate VI, 32–35). The most important decorative effects depended not upon the ornament but upon sculpture—pediment groups, metopes and friezes. The plastic ornament of Doric buildings, as distinguished from the sculpture and the painted details, consisted chiefly of the moldings, triglyphs, mutules and guttæ, the antefixæ ranged along the edge of the cornice, the lions' heads serving as spouts at each end of the long horizontal lateral cornices, acroteria at the angles of the pediments, and the flutings and very simple capitals of the columns. Most of these are shown in the lower part of Plate VI. Of the bronze gates, grilles, lamps and other adjuncts of these buildings we have no remains.

The painted ornament of architecture comprised (*a*) molding ornaments (Figure 142, page 113); (*b*) ceiling-panels (Fig. 143); (*c*) solid color applied to triglyphs (blue), metopes (red) (Plate VI, 33), and sometimes to walls and possibly columns; (*d*) the painting of the woodwork of the interior ceilings; (*e*) mural pictures on the interior walls. Of *d* and *e* no remains are extant. We do not certainly know

FIG. 143. PAINTED PANEL, CEILING OF PLEROMA, PARTHENON.

the exact tones of the colors used in *a, b* and *c,* owing to the faded condition of such vestiges of color as still exist. Modern restorers usually represent them as somewhat brilliant (Plate VI, 33–35): perhaps they were less intense than these representations would indicate.

With the development of the Ionic style in the sixth and fifth centuries, carved ornament assumed greater importance and took on increased richness and variety, which reached the highest point of splendor in the Alexandrian age, especially in Asia Minor, and gave birth in the fourth century to a variant form, the Corinthian, in which the capital of the column was the most important and ornate feature (Plate VII, 14). The carved egg-and-dart and "water-leaf" molding ornaments

A HISTORY OF ORNAMENT

(Figure 144; Plate VII, 8, 11), the carved anthemion-band (Figure 121 A), rosette and guilloche, the acanthus-leaf and rinceau, and the splendid carved stele-heads of the fourth century (Plate VII, 13, 15), were all important fruits of this development.

Style History.

The earliest architecture of "historic" Greece, *i.e.*, subsequent to the first Olympiad (776 B.C.), was of the Doric style. It was characterized by massive columns with 16 to 20 shallow channels meeting in sharp arrises, set directly upon the stylobate (the stepped platform supporting the building) without bases, capped by simple capitals, and bearing an entablature consisting of a plain architrave, a frieze divided into square panels or metopes by triglyphs, and a simple cornice with mutules under the overhanging cornice (Plate VI, 33–35; VII, 6). A triangular pediment filled with sculpture framed between the horizontal and raking cornices, marked the gable-ends of the low-pitched roof. Carved ornament was almost wholly lacking. This style was employed for six hundred years or more, varying only in its proportions and minor details. It reached its culmination in the Parthenon (438 B.C.), and was the style chiefly used for temple architecture in European Greece, including Magna Græcia (Southern Italy and Sicily).

Towards the end of the sixth century the Ionic style, originating in Asia Minor, began to dispute the supremacy of the Doric, and became the dominant style in the Greek cities of Asia Minor. Its slender proportions

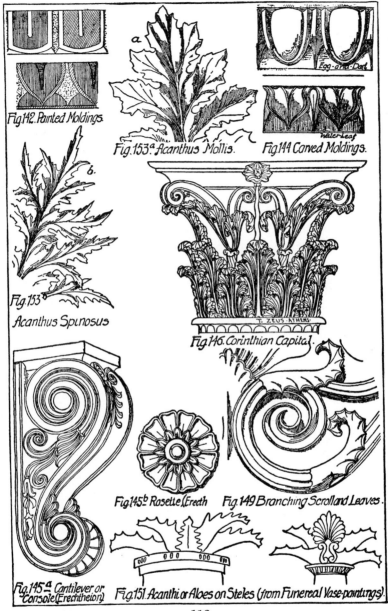

Fig.142. Painted Moldings.

Fig.153.ª Acanthus Mollis.

Egg-and-Dart

Water Leaf

Fig.144 Carved Moldings.

b.

Fig.153 Acanthus Spinosus

T. ZEUS ATHENS

Fig.146. Corinthian Capital.

Fig.145.ᵇ Rosette.(Erecth

Fig.149 Branching Scroll and Leaves.

Fig.145.ª Cantilever or Console (Erechtheion)

Fig.151. Acanthi or Aloes on Steles (from Funereal Vase-paintings)

113

and some of its details betray the influence of early prototypes in wood. Its distinguishing features are the slender columns adorned with twenty-four flutings separated by narrow fillets and standing on molded bases, bearing capitals formed by spiral volutes connected by a horizontal band; the doubly or triply banded architrave, unbroken frieze, and cornice without mutules, often (especially in Asia Minor) adorned with dentils and invariably crowned by a cymatium (Plate VII, 9). As already remarked, carved ornament took the place of painted ornament on the moldings and on other parts, although color was still used as a subordinate element to enhance the decorative effect. The carved anthemion was used with fine effect both on flat bands and on the high cymatia of the cornices (Plate VII, 5, 11). Carved rosettes, "cantilevers" or brackets (Figure 145) and other enrichments also occur. The style reached its highest magnificence in such splendid Asiatic monuments of the fourth century as the Apollo Temple at Didyme near Miletus, the Artemision (temple of Diana) at Ephesus and the Mausoleum at Halicarnassus.

In the variant form known as the Corinthian, which was in time, especially under the Romans, developed into a distinct order, the column was made still more slender, and the capital, more than a diameter in height, was composed of one or two rows of acanthus leaves under coupled volutes which supported the corners or horns of a molded abacus (Figure 146, page 113; Plate VII, 12, 14). Employed at first only for small decorative structures like the Choragic Monument of Lysicrates, it was later applied to propylæas (Eleusis), shrines or treasuries (Epidaurus), and later even to the colossal temple of Zeus at Athens (170 B.C.). Carved ornament was in these buildings carried to the furthest limit of elaboration known in Greek art, as in the three-branched finial of the Lysicrates Monument (330 B.C.), shown in Plate VII, 3; the capitals from Eleusis (240 B.C.), the rinceaux on column-bases at Didyme (Fig. 127, page 94), and later under Roman rule, the frieze and cornice of the Temple of Zeus at Aizanoi.

Painted Details.

In the decoration of moldings with color, the object in view was to emphasize the profile by means of repeated motives of the general character of the egg-and-dart or U-motive, modified in outline to suit the profile (Figure 142). Flat surfaces, such as the corona of a cornice or the edge of a Doric abacus, were often painted with a fret, though the wave, the guilloche and the anthemion-band were also often used, both on terra-cotta and on marble (Plate VI, 28, 32). The anthemion also figures in beautiful symmetrical patterns in gold on a blue ground in the ceiling-panels or cofferings of the pteroma or peristyle of the Parthenon and other buildings (Fig. 143), recalling by their grace and freedom of line the finest of the black-on-red vase decorations. Acroteria, antefixæ and stele-heads were in the earlier examples painted, in the later ones carved; the anthemion was the almost exclusive ornament used on all these, sometimes combined with the acanthus-leaf as a subordinate detail (Plate VII, 1, 13, 15).

A HISTORY OF ORNAMENT

Carved Details.

In nearly all the carved ornament we may trace the imitation and elaboration of painted ornament derived primarily from pottery-decoration. Let us first consider the moldings. Five chief motives occur in their decoration by carving: the bead-and-reel for small bead-moldings; the egg-and-dart on convex profiles; the "water-leaf" on cyma-reversa moldings; the guilloche on torus moldings (Fig. 147); and the anthemion on the high Ionic cymatium or crownmolding. All but

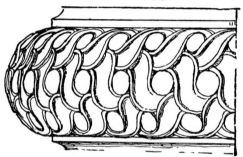

FIG. 147. CARVED TRIPLE GUILLOCHE ON TORUS OF IONIC BASE.

the first and fourth are carved elaborations of the painted molding ornaments described above as themselves derived from pottery-motives, or from pottery directly; the bead-and-reel is an importation from Asia Minor and may have been derived, *via* Asia Minor and Persia, from the Egyptian papyrus-bundle molding. All these carved ornaments were designed and executed with extraordinary skill and care, and their beauty and perfection have seldom been approached and never surpassed in later ages. Apart from the beauty of their decoration, moreover, the Greek moldings are remarkable for the refinement of their profiles, composed of curves as subtle and delicate as the silhouettes of the

116

Greek vases. It was the Greeks, indeed, who first discovered and developed the artistic possibilities of moldings in architecture. The unvarying Egyptian combination of the bundle-torus and cavetto or gorge was effective but monotonous, and neither in Assyrian nor in Persian architecture is there apparent any sense of the beauty of effect inherent in moldings of varied profile artistically combined.

The Ionic Capital.

The origin of this peculiar architectural feature, with its twin spiral volutes and lateral "bolsters," set above a carved echinus and supporting a molded abacus, has been a subject of much controversy.[1] As in so many other cases, it was probably the result of convergence of more than one line of development. The volutes can be traced back to the branching voluted forms of Assyrian (see *ante,* Fig. 7) and Ægean art, and finally to the trefoil-lotus of Egypt. This seems to have blended with reminiscences of primitive "bracket" caps used on Asiatic wooden columns, and a wooden origin is further suggested by the slender proportions of the shaft and its setting on a well-marked base. The oblong voluted bracket cap was apparently combined with what seems to have been originally an independent form of capital—a crown of one or two rows or rings of leaves like "oves," clearly derived from nature and not from the egg-and-dart motive, toward which, however, it con-

---

[1] Cf. W. H. Goodyear, "Grammar of the Lotus," and his article in the "Architectural Record," vol. III, No. 3, "The Lotiform origin of the Ionic Capital." Also in Perrot and Chipiez, "Histoire de l'art dans l'antiqueté," vol. VII, 618 *seq.*

verged to form the carved echinus of the Ionic capital. One form of this foliated capital, shown in Fig. 148, is probably a prototype of the high bell or basket of the later-developed Corinthian capital.

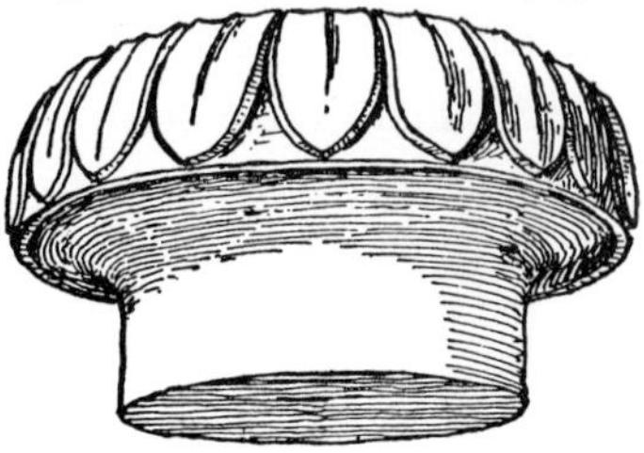

The fully developed capitals of the Erechtheion are among the most elegant forms in classic architecture, and were executed with extraordinary perfection of detail. The high necking adorned with a carved anthemion is peculiar to this one building (Plate VII, 7).

FIG. 148. CAP FROM AEGÆ.

The Carved Anthemion.

This was, next to the capitals, the most characteristic motive in Ionic decoration. Its origin in the anthemion bands of painted vases has already been explained. The technic of carving brought about a number of modifications of detail, such as the ridging and furrowing of the stems, leaves and scrolls, the elaboration of the "lotiform" motive (Plate VII, 4), and the introduction of the acanthus leaf (or in some cases apparently the leaf of a thistle or aloe) to mask the junction of fluted scrolls where they branch (Figure 149). The most celebrated example of the carved anthemion is that which adorned the north and west sides of the Erechtheion, and which is much like that on the neckings of the columns (Figure 121 A; Plate VII, 11).

The commonest application of the carved anthemion band was to the high cymatium of the Ionic cornices.

There are many fragments of such carved cymatia of great beauty. One of these on the Acropolis at Athens shows a bird perched upon its scrolls—an almost isolated instance in Greek art of a purely naturalistic representation in the midst of a bit of formal ornament.

Another and quite a different use of the carved anthemion is found in carved marble antifixæ and acroteria which replaced the earlier painted terra-cotta and painted marble. Plate VII, 1, illustrates a marble antefix (or possibly a ridge-cresting unit) from the Parthenon, which may be compared with Fig. 150, a painted acroterium or antefix of terra-cotta, and the stele-heads in Plate VII.

Stele-heads.

Closely related to the acroteria and antefixæ are the stele-heads, *i.e.,* the upper ends or finials of memorial, sepulchral or votive stones. Apparently the earliest sepulchral steles were topped with a gable-formed finish suggesting the end of a sarcophagus, and adorned with a painted anthemion springing from a nest of acanthus leaves. This combination perhaps recalled an ancient practice of planting an acanthus or similar plant

FIG. 150. PAINTED TERRA-COTTA ANTEFIX.

119

(aloe?) on the flat top of a square or round stele (Figure 151, page 113). With the increased vogue of carved decoration the painted stele-heads disappeared and the carved type was elaborated into a remarkably beautiful design, especially in the fourth century, to which belong the fine examples in Plate VII, 13, 15.

The Acanthus.

The acanthus is a common plant in Greece and Italy, related to the common burdock (Fig. 152). The

variety known as the acanthus spinosus offers, by its formally regular growth and its crisp, crinkly and prickly leaves, excellent suggestions for decorative conventionalization (Figure 153, b). The date of its first appearance in Greek ornament is uncertain; it began to be quite frequently used, however, by the latter part of the fifth century B. C., as a covering leaf to mask the branching scrolls of carved anthemions, as in the example from the Erechtheion (Figure 149). These earlier examples suggest the thistle and the aloe quite as much as the acanthus; but this may be merely fortuitous resemblance. Another early example is shown in Fig. 154, probably the earliest type of the Corinthian capital—found in the ruins of the Apollo temple at Phigalæa

FIG. 152. ACANTHUS LEAF (above); BURDOCK (below).

(Bassæ) in Attica, but now lost. With the development of carved ornament the leaf was more and more highly elaborated, almost always in association with volutes or spiral scrolls, chiefly applied to one or another of four decorative uses: the anthemion-band, the Corinthian capital, carved stele-heads, and the carved rinceau. The last three were executed with especial richness of detail in the Alexandrian age.

The Corinthian Capital.

This, the richest of all capital-types, developed only gradually into the final form which the Romans adopted

FIG. 154. EARLY CORINTHIAN CAPITAL FIG. 155. CAPITAL FROM "TOWER OF
FROM BASSÆ.   THE WINDS," ATHENS.

and made their own. Contemporary with the overelaborate "Lysicrates" example in Plate VII, 14, we find the much simpler form from the "Tower of the Winds" shown in Fig. 155. A capital from the Tholos of Epidauros shows an approach towards the later form from the Temple of Zeus at Athens (Figure 146), which dates from 170 B.C., and furnished the prototype for the

121

Roman Corinthian. In this, sixteen volutes spring in branching pairs from eight caulicoli or leaf-nests, to meet in pairs under the centers and corners respectively of the hollow-curved and molded abacus, each caulicolus rising from between two upright acanthus leaves of the upper or second of two rows of eight leaves each which encircle the bell or core of the capital. The plain bell-type of Fig. 155 suggests a possible imitation of Egyptian palm-capitals; but its late date makes this explanation of its form less probable than that of derivation by simplification from the more elaborate contemporary type of Epidaurus or the Lysicrates monument. Very complicated variations were produced in Eleusis, while at Didyme near Miletus, at Priene, and in some other examples, piers or pilasters were capped with the curious form shown in Plate VII, 10.

The Greeks never developed any type of modillion cornice for the Corinthian entablature, which remained essentially Ionic in character.

The Rinceau.

The foliated scroll known by this French name does not appear, at least in carving, until the Alexandrian age. Its origin in painted ornament has already been suggested (see *ante,* page 98); in carved ornament it appears to be an extension of the branching scrolls which accompanied the anthemion on some Ionic cymatia, on the anthemion band of the Erechtheion (Plate VII, 11) and on the more elaborate types of stele-heads (Fig. 150; Plate VII, 13, 15). In these examples the scrolls branch only twice or thrice in diminishing repetitions.

GREEK ORNAMENT, II

On the gable of one of the splendid sarcophagi from Sidon in the Museum at Constantinople, twin scrolls branch symmetrically from the center to form not a subordinate feature, but the entire decoration, of the pediment (Plate VII, 1). The Choragic Monument of Lysicrates was capped by a superb finial of triple branching and interlaced scrolls, springing from three scroll-arms which spanned the flattened dome of the roof, and supporting presumably the prize tripod awarded to the choir-leader Lysicrates (Plate VII, 3). It was an easy and natural step from these to a continuous line or band of equal branching scrolls, with an acanthus-leaf wrapping and partially masking the several branchings. The base of one of the colossal columns of the Didymæon near Miletus (the Temple of the Didymæan Apollo) bears a superb carved rinceau, the earliest and almost the only example of a complete continuous rinceau in Greek architecture (Figure 127, page 94). The Greek rinceau generally lacks the reversed calyx or cup-flower at each branching that characterizes the Roman type; the acanthus-leaf is simple, thick and rather flat; the scrolls end in a sharp point instead of a rosette or flower, and are formed by deeply channeled bands and not by round stems like the Roman. It was reserved for the Romans to develop and elaborate this type, as will appear in a later chapter. But although the rinceau as a continuous band-motive is rare in Greek carved ornament, it appears frequently as a limited motive after Alexander's time, and several elaborate examples of its use are in the British Museum from Eleusis.

Other Carved Motives.

Carved scales representing tiles adorned the dome-like roof of the Monument of Lysicrates, and the gabled cover of the great "Alexander" sarcophagus (so-called) from Sidon, now at Constantinople. The latter also has a finely executed frieze of a grapevine with a continuous waving stem. The carved fret appears occasionally, as on a marble funereal monument in the form of a vase, in Athens. Lions' heads are carved to decorate the spouts for discharging roof-water through the cymatium, as on the Parthenon (Plate VII, 29, 35), the Temple of Apollo at Delos and other examples. The griffin was carved in the round as an acroterium ornament, and in relief on either side of a central tree or vertical motive—an Oriental device already referred to (see *ante,* page 86). Beautifully executed examples of these grotesques or monsters adorned many of the capitals of the Temple of Apollo at Didyme. The fine marble table-supports found in Pompeii were very probably of Greek workmanship, but will be noticed later under the head of Pompeiian ornament (see page 186).

Relation to Roman Ornament.

Greek ornament may be said to have finally passed over into and been absorbed by Roman art. With the conquest of the Greek states, Greek artists became the servants of Roman wealth and power with all the Roman love of magnificence, and contributed greatly to the decorative beauty and refinement which are so often

GREEK ORNAMENT, II

present in Roman works. In Asia Minor the Greeks retained in considerable measure their independence of taste under Roman rule; the remarkable crocket ornament from the frieze of the Temple of Zeus at Aizanoi, of the time of the Antonines, as well as many other details of this and other temples and tombs in Asia Minor, exhibits the Greek originality of design. The capitals of pilasters of the Arch of Hadrian at Athens (cir. 120 A.D.) reveal something of the same originality, crispness and independence of the Imperial formalism. Southern Italy and Sicily abounded in works and products more Greek in style than Roman; and the entire decorative system of Pompeii, in all its branches, displays a Grecian delicacy, fancifulness and charm, which are due either to the employment of Greek artists, or to the large element of Greek blood in the population of all Magna Græcia. Doubtless the walls of Pompeii represent the last corruscation of the Greek mural painter's art, and they are the only examples which have come down to us.

Books Recommended:

ANDERSON AND SPIERS: *Architecture of Greece and Rome* (London, 1907).—BAUMEISTER: *Denkmäler des klassischen Altertums* (Berlin, 1881–89).—BÖTTICHER: *Die Tektonik der Hellenen* (Berlin, 1874–81).—CHIPIEZ: *Histoire critique des orders grecs* (Paris, 1876).—DURM: *Antike Baukunst* (in *Handbuch der Architektur* series, Darmstadt, 1885).—L. FENGER: *Dorische Polychromie* (Berlin, 1886).—A. FLASCH: *Die Polychromie der griechischen Vasenbilder* (Würzburg, 1875). —FURTWÄNGLER AND REICHHOLD: *Griechische Vasenmalereien* (Munich, 1900).—J. I. HITTORFF: *Restitution du Temple d'Empédocle à Sélinonte, ou L'Architecture polychrome chez les Grecs* (Paris, 1851).—G. KACHEL: *Kunstgewerbliche Vorbilder*

A HISTORY OF ORNAMENT

aus dem Alterthum (Karlsruhe, 1881).—A. MARQUAND: *Greek Architecture* (New York, 1909).—LAU: *Die griechischen Vasen* (Leipzig, 1877).—M. MEURER: *Die Ursprungsformen des griechischen Akanthusornamentes,* etc. (Berlin, 1896).—STUART AND REVETT: *Antiquities of Athens* (London, 1762); also French and German editions of the same.—TARBELL: *History of Greek Art* (New York, 1902).—L. VULLIAMY: *Examples of Ornamental Sculpture in Architecture . . . Greece, Asia Minor and Italy* (London, 1824).—W. R. WARE: *Greek Ornament* (Boston, 1878).—J. C. WATT: *Examples of Greek and Pompeiian Decorative Work* (London, 1897).—J. R. WHEELER AND H. N. FOWLER: *Handbook on Greek Archæology* (New York, 1909).

CHAPTER IX

The Roman Genius.

With Roman ornament we enter upon a new chapter of the history of art. Roman art grew up under conditions almost the opposite of those under which Greek art developed. Instead of a group of rival and frequently hostile states, allied only by race, religion and language, we have in the case of the Romans a single state comprising peoples of many races, languages and religions, welded together into a powerful and highly organized military empire. Lacking the prevailing artistic and philosophical instincts of the Greeks, the Romans possessed on the other hand a remarkable genius for organization and administration, and a spirit at once practical and progressive. With the growing wealth and power which followed upon their long career of conquest, the Romans developed, somewhat late in their national life, a taste for luxury and splendor. The arts which flourished under the direction of these tastes were chiefly of foreign origin, though they took on in time a distinctively Roman character. The Romans became a nation of mighty builders and engineers, and architectural decoration and all the decorative arts that are concerned with personal comfort and luxury were car-

127

FIG. 156. ETRUSCAN TERRA-COTTA CRESTING.

ried to a remarkable, and in some cases an extraordinary, degree of elaboration and splendor. Sculpture, on the other hand, was never a characteristic medium for the

FIG. 157. ETRUSCAN DETAILS.

128

expression of the Roman genius. Roman ornament lacked somewhat of the refinement and restraint of the Greek, but was more varied and more flexible. It was eminently adapted to the purposes which it had to serve, and is well worthy of study for its elegance and versatility of design.

Etruscan Ornament.

Before the conquest of the Greek states introduced Greek art into Roman life, the Romans depended mainly upon the Etruscans for such forms of art as their modest requirements called for. This singular people, whose race-origin and early history are still shrouded in obscurity, possessed an architecture of their own betraying a certain remote kinship with the Greek, but crude and undeveloped artistically. Their frequent use of the arch, and the character of their ornament, so far as it appears in their works in bronze and gold, suggest an Asiatic influence, chiefly Phenician, possibly *via* Carthage. Their ceramic art, especially in its later phases, was based on Greek models. The Campana collection of terra-cotta reliefs in the Louvre, belonging to the first century B.C., show much technical cleverness in adapting Greek pictorial subjects, and even the painted scroll ornaments on late Greek and Campanian vases, to modeling in relief. The ornamental borders

FIGS. 158 AND 159. ETRUSCAN TERRA-COTTA BORDERS.

129

FIG. 160. DETAIL OF A PILASTER.

of these reliefs retain a curiously Asiatic character (Fig. 159). In Figs. 156–160 a number of typical Etruscan forms are shown. Painted terra-cotta ornaments, such as were used on the wooden superstructures of their temples, are preserved in the museums of Italy; they strongly resemble others found in Pompeii and southern Italy, which are very likely of Etruscan workmanship. These represent the highest development of Etruscan architectural decoration, but plainly exhibit their Greek derivation. The cap shown in Fig. 161 illustrates the crudity of native Etruscan details and

FIG. 161. ETRUSCAN PILASTER CAP.

strongly suggests a Phenician or Oriental influence.

The Etruscans were skilful bronze-founders, and appear to have practised also at an early period the art of *spheirelaton* or sheet-metal hammered into relief on a base of carved wood. The fine bronze chariot in the Metropolitan Museum at New York appears to be a product of Etruscan work of this sort of the seventh century B.C.

Etruscan jewelry and filigree were often of great beauty—brooches, pendants, chains, etc., of gold sometimes set with gems. Some of it is possibly, however, of Greek manufacture (Fig. 162).

The pottery of Etruria was unimportant compared with that of Greece. The most interesting of its products were black vases

FIG. 162.

131

modeled in relief (*bucchero nero*), but these display little pure ornament except flutings on the body. It appears to have no relations with the prehistoric black pottery of the so-called *Terramare* and Villanova periods.

The Greek Conquests.

The conquest and absorption of the Greek colonies in southern Italy and Sicily in the late third century B.C., and of the states of Greece proper, ending, with the fall of Corinth (146 B.C.), in the establishment of the Greek province of Achaia, not only made the Roman campaigners familiar with the marble magnificence of the Greek cities and the beauty of Greek art, but brought to Rome itself countless treasures of that art and hosts of Greek artists and artisans. Roman architecture underwent a gradual transformation, which accompanied and expressed the change in the Roman taste. Mummius, the conqueror of Corinth, was in all matters of art a boorish ignoramus; Sulla, who sixty years later captured Athens in the course of his final campaign against Mithridates, was a cultivated admirer of literature and art. As a result of this process of education and growth in refinement of taste, the Etruscan city of Rome, built of brick, terra-cotta and timber, was transformed into a Greco-Roman city of stone and marble. The Greek orders, radically modified in detail, were adapted to new uses, in combination with Etruscan forms of column and Etruscan types of plan and the Etruscan arch and Asiatic vault, and entirely new decorative forms and effects devised in connection with new constructive ma-

132

terials and processes. Sculpture, mostly by Greek artists, received new decorative applications; the arts of the bronze-founder, the modeler in stucco and the mural painter were developed rapidly to a high pitch of excellence; and the modest alphabet of Greek ornament-forms was expanded into a remarkably rich and varied system of decorative devices. In all these arts it is not always possible to distinguish between true Greek handiwork and that of the Roman imitators, who were probably in many cases Etruscan by race.

The Decorative System.

The Romans created for architecture wholly new requirements, applications and uses. To meet these they devised equally new methods and processes of construction, employing combinations of brick, rubble, cement, concrete, stone and marble never known before. The Roman genius for organization and system asserted itself in the erection, by means of the vast armies of unskilled labor at their disposal, of ingenious and stupendous structures, massively built of coarse materials, and producing novel effects of scale and grandeur made possible for the first time by the use of the arch and vault. This massive construction of coarse materials required a decorative skin or dress, both internally and externally, of finer material, such as stucco, mosaic, marble wainscot or veneer, or facings of cut stone, with moldings, panels, friezes, cornices, carving, sculpture and the like, besides such structural features and adjuncts as columns, porticoes and porches, which must be wholly made of the finer materials. This system was funda-

133

mentally different from that of Egyptian or Greek architecture, in which stone or marble was the only material, and temples the chief subjects of architectural design. In these the decoration, other than painting and free sculpture, was of necessity an integral part of the construction, or at least incorporated in it or executed directly upon it. With the Roman system, a large part of the ornament was, equally of necessity, ap-

FIG. 163. TEPIDARIUM, BATHS OF CARACALLA.

plied ornament, executed after the completion of the massive structural frame or core of the building (Fig. 163). This is the system which has prevailed, and must prevail, in all styles and in all regions in which the chief building-materials are coarse or undecorative in themselves, or in which, even where stone and marble abound, the exigencies of building require the use of the commoner and coarser materials for the main fabric of the edifice. It is the system in general use in modern practice, and is entirely reasonable and artistically proper, in spite of the objections raised against it by certain critics who assail it as "false" and "illogical," because the construction is not identical with the decoration but is concealed by it. But solid masonry of cut stone or of brick and terra-cotta, and in some cases wooden or steel construction, afford the only opportunities for the Greek or Gothic system in which construction and decoration are, or may be made, inseparable; and even with these the interior must in most cases be concealed by plaster, wainscot, tiles, ceilings and the like. The analogy of the skin of human beings and animals affords a justification from Nature, of the Roman, Byzantine and modern system, in its decorative concealment of the internal organism and construction, revealing only the general masses of the structure.

By the Roman system, the unskilled labor of hordes of slaves, soldiers and peasants could be turned to account in the heavier work of construction, and great numbers of vast buildings be erected with comparative rapidity, leaving the decorative work to be later executed by artists and artisans, upon this structural core. The Roman genius for organization and adaptation, guiding and directing these artists, who were chiefly foreigners, at least in the earlier periods, developed new forms of decoration, in which conventional ornament took the place of figure sculpture.

The principal types of decorative work thus developed were: (1) the decorative use of architectural features, such as columns, entablatures, pediments, moldings, panels and ceiling-coffers; (2) carved ornament in extraordinary variety; (3) figure-sculpture, such as groups in pediments, free statues on columns or entablatures in certain classes of structures, and reliefs in panels, spandrels and other defined spaces; (4) the chromatic effects of colored marbles and granites in columns, wainscoting and pavements; (5) mosaic of glass or marble in floors and ceilings; (6) stucco-relief in delicate patterns, often combined with (7) mural painting in brilliant colors, and (8) bronze work on ceilings, in grilles and doors, and in decorative adjuncts like tripods and candelabra.

Plan of Front Face of Arch.

FIG. 164. ROMAN ARCH (ARCH OF TITUS).

Architectural Features.

The remarkable variety of the Roman buildings and structural devices lent itself to a corresponding variety of decorative effects in which the purely decorative use of various structural features played a prominent part. Pilasters and engaged columns with their entablatures, pediments over doors, windows and niches, recessed arches and deep ceiling-panels were the chief elements of this pseudo-structural decoration. The combination

136

of the arch—adorned with its archivolt and keystone
—with engaged columns carrying entablatures (Fig.
164) was the most important of these decorative devices, and has been in more or less constant use ever
since Roman times. In the later Imperial age, and
particularly in the provinces, as at Spalato in Dalmatia

FIG. 165. NICHE-CAP, BAALBEK.

and in Syria at Baalbek and Palmyra, there was, under
the Antonines and later emperors, a remarkable increase
in the variety of these decorative applications of architectural features. Curved and broken pediments,
colonnettes on brackets, spirally fluted columns, and
niches with shell hoods are among the features most
widely used. Some of these works have a singularly
modern look, as if of the Palladian Renaissance, which,
indeed, independently re-invented many of these devices
thirteen hundred years later [1] (Fig. 165).

[1] This use of structural forms as mere decoration has been condemned
as "sham" and "false" design by certain purist critics, who contrast it un-
favorably with the "truthful" architecture of the Greek and Gothic builders.

Conventional Ornament.

In developing the details of this system the Romans were obliged to employ Greek artists and to begin with Greek models for the most part. The Greek orders, the Greek fret and anthemion, molding-ornaments, rosette, acanthus-leaf and rinceau, were appropriated, but not without radical modifications. With such stupendous

Fig. 166. Fragment from Temple of Vespasian, in Villa Aldobrandini.

aggregations of buildings as the Romans raised in their cities both in Italy and abroad—structures often many-storied and of vast dimensions—figure-sculpture was out of the question as the chief decoration, not so much on account of its enormous cost as because it would have been wasted and ineffective. Carved conventional ornament, on the other hand, with its repeated units, (Fig. 166) enriches such buildings without requiring

But even in Greek architecture there are analogous "shams," like the pseudo-structural paneling of the Greek pteroma-ceilings, while the useless false gables and the rich wall-traceries of Gothic art are perfect examples of the purely ornamental use of forms primarily structural. The fact is that in all advanced stages of art the structural forms of earlier stages have been similarly turned to decorative account.

that semi-isolation and that nearness to the eye which are essential for the best effect of figure sculpture. Plastic ornament was carried by the Romans to the highest perfection of appropriate design, of rich effect, and often of exquisite execution. Moldings were combined and profiled with the greatest care, though the profiles were generally less subtile than those of the Greek moldings. In monumental buildings nearly all

FIG. 167. ROMAN MOLDINGS.
a, SIMPLE WATER LEAF; *b*, ENRICHED WATER LEAF; *c*, *d*, ACANTHUS LEAF ENRICHMENTS.

the moldings were enriched by carving, the ornamentation being more elaborate than in the Greek prototypes —sometimes, indeed, too minute for the best effect, but almost always appropriate and beautiful (Fig. 167).

The general effect of all this decoration was one of great dignity and splendor. The striving for magnificence sometimes led to offenses against good taste, and the execution is occasionally coarse, but such offenses are rare, and beauty, refinement, delicacy and charm frequently characterize even the grandest works.

The Orders.

The most conspicuous adornment of Roman buildings was effected by the use of columns and pilasters with their entablatures, in one or more of the so-called "Five Orders"—the Tuscan, Doric, Ionic, Corinthian and Composite (Plate VIII). In reality there are but

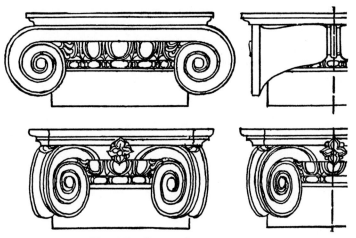

Fig. 168. Roman Ionic Capitals.

three, the Tuscan and Doric being mere variants of one type and the Composite and Corinthian of another. Upon their so-called Doric column, which was really an enriched and refined form of the Etruscan (Tuscan) column, the Romans placed an entablature derived from that of the Greek Doric order, with its triglyphs and mutules. The Ionic was but slightly varied from the Greek Ionic type of Asia Minor. The capital occurs in two forms: one following the Greek model, but with a straight band between the volutes, on the front and

140

rear faces, instead of a depressed curved band (see Plate VIII, 3); and the other with four double volutes at the angles of the abacus, in order to make the four faces of the capital alike; this is sometimes called erroneously the "Scamozzi Ionic" (Fig. 168). The Corinthian, an elaboration of the Greek Corinthian but

FIG. 169. CORINTHIAN CAPITAL, TEMPLE OF MARS ULTOR.

with a special type of cornice, is the really distinctive Roman order. With the Greeks it had been a mere variant of the Ionic; the Romans developed its capital into a type generally recognized as one of the most beautiful ever devised. In its most perfect examples, as in that of the Pantheon, the Temple of Castor and Pollux and the Temple of Faustina, it consists of two rows of erect acanthus-leaves surrounding and concealing the lower two-thirds of a bell-shaped core on which rests a

141

molded abacus with concave sides. The upper part is concealed by sixteen spiral volutes which spring in branching pairs from eight *caulicoli* or leaf-nests, set between the eight leaves of the upper row. These volutes meet in eight pairs under the four corners of the abacus and under rosettes at the centers of its four sides (Fig. 169, Figure 174; Plate VIII, 4, 6). The details of this type are endlessly varied; in late examples animals and human figures sometimes take the place of the

FIG. 172. MODILLION.

corner volutes. The Composite capital, having volutes only at the angles, and larger than in the Corinthian, may be considered an inferior variant of the Corinthian, though sometimes very splendidly carved (Plate VIII, 2, 7; Figure 170). It somewhat resembles a four-faced Ionic capital placed upon the lower part of a Corinthian capital. Pilaster caps show a greater variety of design than capitals of columns (Plate VIII, 8; Figure 171).

To these improvements upon the Greek order they added that of a special type of base, an elaboration of the Attic base, consisting of two tori separated by two

Fig. 170.—Composite Capital (Lateran Museum, Rome)

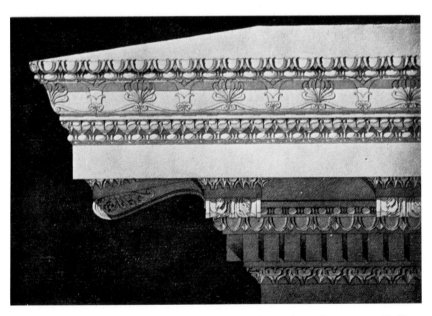

Fig. 173.—Restoration of Cornice, Basilica Æmilia (from Drawing by R. H. Smythe)

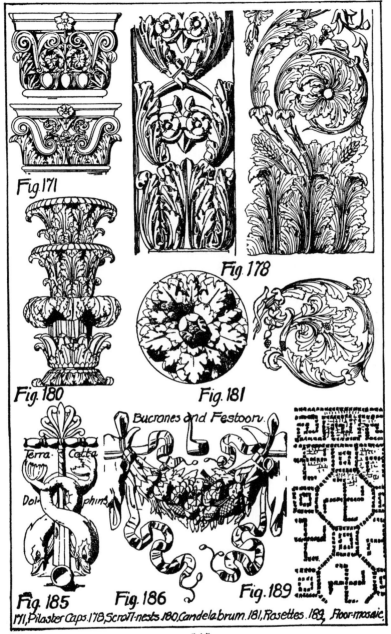

Fig.171

Fig.178

Fig.180

Fig.181

Bucranes and Festoon.

Terra Cotta

Dol phins

Fig.185   Fig.186   Fig.189

171, Pilaster Caps. 178, Scroll-nests. 180, Candelabrum. 181, Rosettes. 189, Floor-mosaic.

scotias and a single or double bead. In late examples these moldings were all carved, reproducing at the base something of the elaborate richness of the capital (Plate VIII, 9, 10, 11).

But the Romans not only perfected the Greek Corinthian capital and base; they developed also a new type of cornice which completed the Corinthian as a distinct order (Figure 174, page 151). This was accomplished by the simple but epoch-making device of introducing modillion brackets beneath the corona and above the bed-mold of the typical Ionic cornice. The modillion (Fig. 172) was a completely new architectural invention. The recently excavated fragments of the Basilica Æmilia (86 B.C.) show a primitive form composed of a mutule decorated on the under side with a reversed scroll (Figure 173).[2] The modillion of the Maison Carrée at Nîmes (4 A.D.) somewhat resembles this type; the more perfect type is shown in Plate VIII, 4.

Variety in the Roman Orders.

It is frequently asserted that the Romans reduced their Orders to a purely mechanical system of mathematically formulated dimensions for each part. This assertion springs from a blind acceptance of the rules laid down by Vitruvius (or of the later formulæ of Vignola and other Italian Renaissance writers) as if they represented the actual historic practice of the Romans. In reality nothing could well be further from the truth. There are *no two examples of any of the*

[2] This appears to have been used over an Ionic order.

orders from different buildings that are alike, either in general proportions or details. The Roman Doric is at least as varied as the Greek Doric, and the variety in Corinthian capitals and entablatures is simply astonishing. There was, no doubt, throughout the Imperial age a tendency towards uniformity in certain general features and proportions, but this never hardened into cast-iron formulæ, and the beauty and vitality of Roman ornament are largely due to the variety and individuality of the designs of different buildings, and of different times and places.

Decorative Uses of the Orders.

In Roman architecture columns were not only used for their original function as true structural supports in porticoes and colonnades, but also, with their entablatures, for decorative purposes, by engaging them in the walls, which were thus architectually divided into bays and stories. In arcaded structures the columns, apparently engaged into the piers between the arches, were in reality parts of the piers themselves, acting to that extent as buttresses; but their chief function in such buildings was esthetic, not structural. They were expressive as well as decorative, emphasizing to the eye the lines of vertical support and of concentrated thrust of the building, while indicating externally the internal structural divisions. At the same time they broke the surface of the edifice into rectangular panels or units, outlined by strong lights and shades, in which the arches were effectively framed.

The Romans also invented the *pilaster,* a flattened

replica of the column, used as a wall-decoration, and as a respond behind free-standing columns, as in triumphal arches and forum walls. Over columns so placed in front of pilasters the entablature was made to project in a salient block, while between the columns it was set back nearly to the wall-face, thus producing the much criticized *ressaut* or "broken entablature." When this projecting block and the column below it together serve as a pedestal for a statue, as in the Arch of Constantine (Figure 175), they serve at least a real esthetic function. In other cases the order thus used becomes a purely factitious decoration, unexplained to the eye, as it supports nothing even in appearance.

The *shafts* of columns and of pilasters were sometimes fluted, sometimes smooth. When monolithic shafts of polished granite or marble were used, as was general in the later Imperial age, the decorative splendor of the colored material took the place of enrichment by fluting, as a characteristic Roman practice.

The use of pedestals, by means of which an order of smaller-scaled parts could be used for a given height of story, was another distinctively Roman device to add to the flexibility of the Orders (Figure 175).

Books Recommended:

See List at end of Chapter X.

Fig. 175.—Restoration of Arch of Constantine, Rome (Model in Metropolitan Museum, New York)

Fig. 174.—Order of Temple of Castor and Pollux, Rome (Cast in Metropolitan Museum, New York)

CHAPTER X

Carved Ornament.

In this field Roman art surpassed all previous styles in the variety and splendor of its achievements, and originated types which have persisted through all the centuries since. The beauty of the Corinthian capital and entablature has already been alluded to, as well as the richness of the Roman carved moldings. Roman

Fig. 176. Typical Acanthus Leaves.

friezes, bands and panels were adorned with a like richness of conventional carving. Practically the whole of this ornament was based on Greek prototypes—the an-

151

themion and rinceau supplying the motives for the greater part of it. If we add to these the rosette, festoon or garland,[1] and the use of symbolic and grotesque forms, and note that the acanthus-leaf in an endless variety of modifications, was worked into every possible detail, we have the key to the greater part of this ornament. But with these few fundamental motives the Roman artists developed a quantity and variety of designs which for richness and appropriateness of effect and extraordinary flexibility of application have never been surpassed. Some of it is heavy and over-wrought; but the beauty and refinement of the great majority of examples entitle them to high praise.

The Acanthus.

This constitutes a type rather than a particular form of leaf. As compared with the Greek type, it is less massive, less pointed, more minutely modeled; it suggests a larger, thinner, more flexible and more complex leaf, with well-developed "eyes" at the bases of the lobes and "pipes" or ribs curving from these to the base of the leaf (Fig. 176). The standing leaves in the figure may be compared with the natural *acanthus mollis* in Figure 153, a (p. 113). There are many leaves in nature which are divided in much

FIG. 177. TYPES OF ACANTHUS.

[1] Or "swag," as it is often called by English writers.

the same way, and the Romans varied the carved type almost *ad infinitum,* so that it recalls various leaves, and modern writers have given them fanciful names accordingly—the "olive," "palm," etc.—though in each case we have a purely conventional variation of the type. Fig. 177 shows a few of these variants.

The acanthus was used (a) as a standing leaf in capitals and on some moldings; (b) as a molding ornament (Fig. 167, *c, d*) ; (c) as a nest or bunch of leaves from which to start a rinceau (Plate IX, 1, 10, 12; Figure 178, Fig. 179); (d) as a *caulicolus* or wrapping-leaf to mask the branching of the scrolls (Plate IX, 10; Figs. 166, 179); (e) as an ornament around the stems of candelabra and the bellies of vases (Plate X, 13; Fig. 180) ; (f) as a conventional plant to alternate with or replace the anthemion (Plate IX, 8), and (g) to form the petals of a rosette (Fig. 181; Plate IX, 9). All these applications may be studied in Plates VIII, IX and X.

The Rinceau.

The origin and development of the *rinceau* have already been traced in Greek ornament (pages 000). The Roman version of it became the most important of all Roman motives, and has been perhaps the most prolific of all historic ornament-forms except the lotus. A round stem, springing from a nest of acanthus-leaves (Figs. 166, 179, 182), branches into scrolls alternately winding upon one and the other side, each terminating, not in a point as in the Greek type, but in an elaborate flower or bunch of leaves (Figure 181, page 143). Each branching is concealed by an elaborate *caulicolus* or wrapping-leaf, which springs from a calyx-like cup-flower at its base. Such spaces as would otherwise be

FIG. 179. RINCEAU, FORUM OF TRAJAN.

left bare are often filled with subordinate scrolls and tendrils, and in rare instances animal life is introduced in the form of birds, mice and insects (Plate IX).

FIG. 182. RINCEAU, FROM TEMPLE OF THE SUN.

While some examples of the rinceau are heavy and overcrowded, as in the example from the Temple of the Sun (Fig. 182), others are remarkable for their deli-

154

cately handled relief and exquisite details (Fig. 179). There is the greatest possible variety of effect both in the composition and detailed treatment.

The rinceau was used (a) for friezes and bands; (b) for pilasters, either single, filling the whole width of the pilaster-panel, or doubled symmetrically on either side of a central axis (Figure 178); (c) on flat surfaces or panels of almost any form symmetrically repeated on either side of a vertical axis. Examples are shown in Plate IX.

The Anthemion.

The preceding examples illustrate the applications of the acanthus listed under *c* and *d* (page 153); Fig. 183 and Plate IX, 8, illustrate a group of forms based on the anthemion. While some examples resemble quite closely the Greek carved anthemion, others depart widely from the type, constituting a new and original ornament form.

Ceiling Decoration.

The wooden ceilings of the basilicas and private houses have perished. Vaulted ceilings were decorated in either two ways: by stucco ornament, modeled in relief and painted, or by paneling in deep "coffers" or "caissons." These were derived originally through Greek architecture from wooden ceilings framed with intersecting beams. In the Pantheon they appear to have been hewn out of the solid brick masonry of the dome, long after its original completion, its 28 rows of panels fitting but indifferently over the eight-fold

divisions of the architecture below. An early and elegant example of vault-paneling is seen in the soffit of the Arch of Titus (80 A.D.). The panels were in most cases simple geometric forms— squares, octagons, "lozenges," etc.; the sides of each caisson were molded and the fields of the panels adorned with splendidly carved rosettes or with mosáic patterns, or else left plain (Fig. 184). Ceiling decoration in stucco is treated in a later paragraph (page 161; see Figures 187 and 201).

Figure Sculpture.

FIG. 183. ROMAN CARVED ANTHEMI-
ONS.

Figure sculpture played a far less important part in the decoration of Roman buildings than in the Greek monuments. The reasons for this have been already touched upon (page 138). Nevertheless the splendid decorative value of the figure was not ignored, but was availed of in many decorative reliefs of high artistic excellence. The Romans were especially successful in the sculpture of symbolic grotesques and of infant figures (genii and *amorini*). By a *grotesque* is meant an artistic combination of heterogeneous Nature-forms, as in Fig. 195, where an infant figure is provided with wings, and terminates in a superb acanthus scroll in place of legs. The festoon or "swag" and garland, bound with fluttering ribbons representing sacrificial

FIG. 184.

fillets (Figure 186; Plate VIII, 3, 6); the *bucrane* or ox-skull, likewise a sacrificial symbol (Plate IX, 7); the dolphin and steering-paddle symbolizing Neptune and water (Figure 185); the Imperial eagle, and trophies of arms and armor, are common in Roman decorative art.

The most beautiful of Roman relief decorations are perhaps the charming reliefs modeled in plaster on the ceilings and walls of houses and thermæ, as noted in a later paragraph.

A HISTORY OF ORNAMENT

Wall Decoration.

Three methods were employed: marble veneer, painting and stucco-relief. Both in the richer private houses and palaces, and in the thermæ, basilicas and temples, the lower part at least of the interior walls was wainscoted with slabs of variegated marble, so set as to produce symmetrical patterns of veining. This practice was probably introduced from Asia Minor, where marble abounds, although it has been contended [2] with a good deal of force, that it came from Alexandria together with the sort of mosaic called Opus Alexandrinum. The origin is less important than the result. A special emporium was established on the Tiber for the traffic in marble, of which enormous quantities were required for columns, wainscots and pavements. The ancient wall-incrustations have mostly disappeared, torn away to supply materials for medieval and even Renaissance buildings. One important example, however, remains; the interior wall of the Pantheon, up to the main cornice, still retains for the most part its original lining, in perfect condition. This style of decoration has survived in the Early Christian basilicas and Byzantine churches (see Chapters XII and XIII).

Stucco Relief.

It was the Romans who first, with the aid, most probably, of Greek artificers, developed the artistic possibilities of work in stucco for interior decorations, especially of vaulted ceilings. This art had evidently reached

[2] See "Transactions of the Royal Institute of British Architects," vol. III, New Series; 1887.

Fig. 187.—Stucco Relief; Tomb on Via Latina

Fig. 188.—Stucco Relief, from a Roman House (in Museo delle Terme)

a high state of perfection by the middle of the first century A.D. The substructions of the Golden House of Nero (who died A.D. 68), and of the Baths of Titus, built in 74 on the same site, together with numerous examples in Pompeii, which was overwhelmed by the eruption of 79 A.D., afford abundant proof of the brilliance, delicacy and originality of the Roman stuccowork of this time. The Roman stucco, made in part with pounded marble and thoroughly slaked lime, was extraordinarily fine and durable. It was applied only as fast as it could be worked into decorative form, and molded partly by mechanical means, partly freehand, while still wet. The area to be decorated was laid off in panels of various geometric forms, outlined by moldings of delicate profile, often enriched with eggs-and-darts, leaves or other ornaments. The panels were then adorned with paintings, with glass-mosaic (as in the Baths of Caracalla), or more frequently, with relief arabesques or figures modeled in the stucco; and it is in these last that the highest skill was manifested. The exquisite charm of this work, its delicacy of low relief, the freedom and dash of its execution indicate artistic ability and taste of a very high order (Figures 187, 188).

Important examples of various handlings of this material are: at Rome, Tombs on the Via Latina, the substructions of the Baths of Titus and of Nero's Golden House, ruins on the Palatine and fragments in the Museo delle Terme from a house uncovered in 1879 near the Villa Farnesina, in excavations for the new Tiber embankments; at Pompeii, the Baths of the Forum (the tepidarium), Stabian Baths and a few examples in private houses. The great majority of these date from the first century A.D., after which a more robust and monumental decoration of walls and ceilings appears to have gradually displaced this charming but minute and intimate form of art.

The ornaments of stucco in low relief were often combined with painting, on walls as well as ceilings. The labyrinth of piers and vaults under the ruins of the Baths of Titus on the Esquiline (part of them belonging to the Golden House of Nero) are doubly interesting because they furnished the models from which Raphael drew his inspiration for his remarkable painted stucco-relief decorations in the Loggie of the Vatican, and less directly, Giulio Romano and Giovanni da Udine for those in the Villa Madama.

Painting.

The above examples, especially those from the house uncovered in 1879, and others in the Villa of Hadrian at Tivoli, and in the so-called Casa di Livia on the Palatine, prove the substantial identity of style of the mural paintings in the Capital with those at Pompeii, with only such differences of quality as one might expect between the Capital and a provincial town, somewhat hastily rebuilt after the earthquake of 63. This phase of Roman ornament will be treated in the next chapter, devoted to Pompeii, on account of the great number and importance of the Pompeiian examples.

Pavements.

The floors of all important buildings were of marble

or mosaic. Marble was used in large panels of various colors in circles, squares and simple geometric forms; but as with the wainscoting, most of these pavements have disappeared to provide materials for the floors of Christian basilicas. That of

FIG. 190. DETAIL, FLOOR, MOSAIC, IN VILLA ITALICA, SEVILLE.

the Pantheon may be in part original, and fragments of the floor of the Basilica Julia have also been preserved. Mosaic floors were paved with minute *tesserae* or

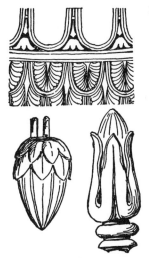

FIG. 193. ORNAMENTS, BRONZE AND GOLD.

roughly squared fragments of colored marble, tile or other material, set in patterns usually of a plain field with a decorative border in the larger rooms, though in smaller rooms all-over patterns were not uncommon (Plate XI, 9, 11, 12). Outside of Rome, in Asia Minor and in other remote provinces as well as in Pompeii, elaborately pictured floors were executed in tesseræ of variously colored marbles. The most famous example from the House of the Faun in Pompeii is now pre-

168

served in the Naples Museum (see page 182). Figure 189 illustrates a floor pattern of "swastikas" from a house in Pompeii. There are some fine examples in the Museum of Constantinople. Fig. 190 shows a detail of the mosaic floor of a Roman villa near Seville, Spain.

Furniture and Utensils.

Whatever furniture was of wood has perished; but the more important and permanent objects in the equip-

FIG. 194. UNDER SIDE OF SILVER VASE, HILDESHEIM TREASURE.

ment of houses were of marble and bronze, and of these, together with the smaller utensils and furnishings in bronze, we have many examples in the various museums. As, however, the great majority of these are from Pompeii, they will be briefly discussed and illustrated in the following chapter on Pompeiian art. Plate X and Figures 191, 192 and Figs. 193, 194 show illustrations

Fig. 191.—Marble Vase, Naples Museum

Fig. 192.—Roman Vase (from Cast in Metropolitan Museum, New York)

of pedestals, candelabra and vases, mostly in the museums of the Vatican and of the Capitol at Rome and in the Museo Nazionale at Naples. Large vases of marble, elaborately sculptured, were used in the decoration of villas, presumably in the gardens, serving most probably as vases for the planting of flowers, vines and small trees or shrubs. In these, Roman decorative art reached a high degree of excellence and supplied models which the Renaissance artists of Italy and later of France imitated with success but hardly surpassed. The Museum of the Louvre possesses a colossal marble vase with spiral flutings and figures in relief, and other examples are found in the Capitoline and Vatican museums at Rome and the Nazionale at Naples (Figures 191, 192). Convex and concave flutings, acanthus-leaves and guilloches, the vine and grotesques are the most common adornments of these fine vases, the grace of whose outlines is fully equal to the splendor of their decoration.

Goldsmith's Work and Jewelry.

Skill in jewelry was shown by the Etruscans, who may have furnished the greater part of the jewelers even in Imperial times. The character of the later jewelry—bracelets, brooches, pendants and pins—does not differ essentially from that of the earlier Etruscan work except in greater variety of form. The bronze and silver mirrors deserve notice for the beauty of the handles and backs. The famous Hildesheim Treasure, discovered in 1868 at Hildesheim, Germany, comprising gold and silver bowls, platters and other vessels magnificently decorated with figures, vines and orna-

A HISTORY OF ORNAMENT

ments in relief, reveals the same excellent taste and fine workmanship observable in Roman works in bronze and marble (Plate X and Figure 193).

FIG. 195.

Books Recommended:

As before, ANDERSON and SPIERS, BAUMEISTER, JACOBSTHAL, KACHEL, VULLIAMY. Also, F. ALBERTOLLI: *Fregi trovati negli Scavi del Foro Trajano* (Milan, 1824); *Ornamenti diversi Antonini* (Milan, 1843); *Manuale di varii ornamenti . . . e framenti antichi* (Rome, 1781–1790).—J. BUEHLMANN: *The Architecture of Classical Antiquity and the Renaissance* (New York, 1900).—G. P. CAMPANA: *Antiche Opere in Plastica* (Rome, 1851).—J. DURM: *Baukunst der Etrusker; Baukunst der Römer* (Darmstadt, 1885).—G. EBE: *Die Schmuckformen*

168

ROMAN ORNAMENT, II

der Monumentalbauten (Leipzig, 1896).—H. D'ESPOUY: *Fragments de l'architecture antique* (Paris, ˆ1896–1905).—P. GUSMAN: *L'Art décoratif de Rome* (Paris, 1908).— S. HESSELBACH: *Vergleichende Darstellung der antiken Ornamentik,* etc. (Würzburg, 1849).—J. DE MARTA: *L'Art Etrusque; Archéologie etrusque et romaine* (Paris, n. d.).—STRACK: *Baudenkmäler Roms.* (Berlin, 1891).—C. H. TATHAM: *Etchings* (London, 1810).—TAYLOR AND CRESY, *Antiquities of Rome* (London, 1824).—THIERRY: *Klassische Ornamente.*—C. UHDE: *Architecturformen des Klassischen Altertums* (Berlin, n. d.); also an edition in English (New York, 1909).

Consult also various volumes of the engravings of PIRANESI (to be found only in the larger libraries); the volumes of *L'Art pour Tous* (Paris, 1863—) ; and the printed transactions of various archæological societies, for valuable material.

CHAPTER XI

The decorative art of Pompeii was a provincial phase of Roman art differing from that of the capital in certain aspects, precisely as in Dalmatia, in Syria and in North Africa, local conditions modified the detailed forms of decorative expression while the Roman impress was nevertheless over all. It is pervaded by a spirit of Grecian delicacy and refinement, due to the strong Greek element in the population of Southern Italy; but there are details on the other hand which smack of the Etruscan. The importance of Pompeiian art is due to its wonderfully complete preservation by burial under the *scoriæ* after the eruption of Vesuvius in 79 A.D. Its progressive excavation since 1748 has laid bare the aspect, life and art of a provincial South Italian city of the first century, while all other Roman cities (except Herculanum, still buried) have suffered complete transformation by successive rebuildings through eighteen centuries.

Two facts must be kept in mind in all study of Pompeiian art: first, that the majority of houses and many of the temples and public buildings were, at the time of the eruption, newly built to replace those destroyed by the earthquake of 63 A.D.; and that in consequence

170

of the earthquake they were mostly low buildings, unlike the more lofty and monumental architecture of
most other cities; secondly, that they represent the
relatively early Roman art of the first century, previous
to the time of Domitian, and not of the later and more
splendid Imperial age. Yet in the matter of decoration
there is less difference of style than one would expect
from the work of the same age in the Capital (*e.g.,* the

FIG. 196. IONIC CAP, CORNER VOLUTES.

House of Livia and the frescoes in the Museo delle
Terme) or even of a later period as seen in the Villa
of Hadrian.

The ornament of Pompeii will be discussed under
four heads: (1) Architectural detail; (2) Mural decoration; (3) Mosaic; (4) Furniture and utensils. It will
be seen that in all these divisions, while the motives are
essentially Roman, there is a freedom, a lightness of
touch and delicacy of treatment, which suggest Greek
workmanship, and which are probably due to the persistent strain of Hellenic blood in the population of all
Southern Italy.

Architectural Detail.

The Orders were handled with great freedom, whether executed in cut-stone, or, as more frequently, in rubble or brick finished in stucco. The Doric order was often of the Greek rather than of the Roman type; the Ionic capital usually had doubled corner-volutes and a very slight projection or width as compared with both Greek and Roman types (Fig. 196), and the Corinthian

FIG. 197. POMPEIIAN MOLDINGS.

capital was considerably varied, both in the number and character of its leaves. The Roman type of acanthus is not found, a more bluntly crinkled leaf being preferred. The Doric columns had no bases, those of the other orders often lacked plinths; the moldings differed from the Roman, in having profiles more varied and delicate, with an almost feminine refinement (Fig. 197). The entablatures have for the most part perished. The few fragments that remain intact show the same characteristics in varying from the fashions of Rome and in refinement of detail. A common Pompeiian feature was the filling-up of the lower part

172

of the flutings of stuccoed columns, to prevent the chipping and marring of the fragile arrises; sometimes a convex "flute" or bead inserted in this portion protected without quite filling the fluting, and this has become a common decorative device of modern architecture.

All this Pompeiian architecture of rubble and stucco was embellished with color, of which traces still remain. Even capitals were painted and the carved and molded

FIG. 198. CARVED POMPEIIAN RINCEAU.

details were adorned in like manner. One house is known as the *Casa dei capitelli colorati,* the House of Painted Capitals, because of the perfect preservation of the color on its stucco or cement capitals; but it was originally but one of hundreds so adorned. Figure 198 illustrates the elegance of detail in a carved rinceau in stone.

Mural Decoration.

In this field the Pompeiian remains are unrivaled. The chief means of decoration was by painting on stucco; the use of rich marbles, whether for construction or wall-incrustation, although increasingly common in Rome for at least a half century before the destruction of Pompeii, was not common in the provincial town. The surprising thing is that within less than sixteen years after the destructive earthquake of A.D. 63, this town should have been rebuilt with such elaboration of elegance in its painted decorations as the remains have exhibited. Many of the paintings have been transferred to the Royal Museum at Naples, but the wealth of decoration still remaining in place is astonishing, in quality as well as quantity. Some of the more recently excavated houses—that of Queen Margherita, of the Vettii, and others, equal or surpass the splendors of the Museum (Figures 199, 200).

Four well-marked periods or styles (for doubtless they overlap independently of period-limits) are recognized. The first, supposed to be Etruscan or Cumæan, and dating as far back as 100 B.C., is that of walls simply divided into panels of different colors with occasional painted imitations of marble wainscot. The second, called the Greek, supposed to have been introduced about 80 B.C., is distinguished by the earliest use of pictures copied from Greek originals, or reminiscences of them, the subjects being mostly taken from Greek mythology. A very simple type of painted architectural embellishment accompanies many of these pictured decorations: painted columns, bases and entablatures serving to mark off the wall-divisions. The third and fourth styles are Roman or Pompeiian; both are found in the houses rebuilt after the earthquake, and both are characterized by a light and fantastic archi-

FIG. 198.—POMPEIIAN WALL DECORATION; THIRD STYLE

FIG. 200.—POMPEIIAN WALL DECORATION; FOURTH OR FLORID STYLE

tecture painted in a conventional perspective, with slender columns as of gold, with extraordinary entablatures, pediments and balconies, giving vistas of the clear sky above, and enclosing pictures of varied subjects, sometimes of large size, or simpler colored panels in the centers of which float airy figures of nymphs, cupids and other mythological beings, In the Fourth or Florid style this "dream" architecture is still more complex, attenuated and fantastic than in the Third, and the simpler and more obvious wall-decorations of friezes and arabesques play a smaller part in the scheme.

In the painted details, apart from pictures and the architecture, there is a great variety of conventional patterns for bands of ornament; a remarkably elegant treatment of the rinceau motive, in varied colors on black or red (Plate XI, 6) ; and a corresponding interpretation of carved pilaster–arabesques in painted arabesques of yellow and other colors on a red, green or dark background (Plate XI, 1–6). Much of this decoration has the character of mere artisanship, but it is extremely clever artisanship, and one has no right to call for the higher qualities of art in the decorations of ordinary houses.

The technic of the painting has been much discussed; but it is now quite generally believed to have been executed in true fresco on the wet plaster, at least in the majority of examples; and then touched up and many of the details worked over, in the finer examples with encaustic painting. In this last process the pigments were mixed in melted wax on a hot metal palette and applied with a hot iron instrument instead of a brush.[1]

Stucco Relief.

This form of mural decoration, as applied both to walls and ceilings, has already been touched upon (see *ante,* page 158). A comparison of the examples from Rome and Pompeii respectively, discloses no fundamental difference of style or even quality between the work in the two cities. The most notable examples in Pompeii are those in the two chief baths—the Thermæ of the Forum and of Stabii. In these we have a rinceau frieze, delicate panel-moldings, ideal or mythological figures, Tritons, winged figures, dolphins and the like, and free-hand arabesques, all treated with an animation of design, a freedom from mechanical repetition and hardness, and a delicacy of handling, worthy of Greece and of the Capital, and surprising to find in a relatively small provincial city (Figure 201; Plate XI, 7, 10). This and the Roman stucco-work ought to be fruitfully suggestive to modern decorators, for its effects are full of charm, and yet not unduly costly or difficult to produce.

Besides these interior decorations in low relief, there should be mentioned the decorations of the exteriors of buildings by stucco details molded upon a rough core of rubble or brick, and also the use of stucco for columns and capitals in place of stone. It is easy to criticize adversely this substitution of a fragile for a monumental

[1] In the Metropolitan Museum of Art at New York there are several sections of wall from a villa at Boscoreale, with decorations of the Third Period,—mostly landscapes of buildings and farms.

Fig. 201.—Pompeiian Stucco Relief; from the Stabian Baths

material in exterior architecture; but given a scarcity of marble and of good building stone with an abundance of soft tufa and of *"pozzolana"* for the making of cement-stucco; given also the necessity of a rapid rebuilding of almost an entire town after the earthquake of 63, and it would be hard to imagine a more artistic and satisfactory result than the Pompeiians produced in a few short years with rubble, stucco and paint.

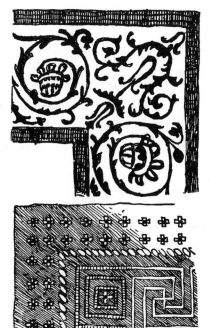

Mosaic.

Mosaic floors were almost all of Opus Grecanicum, laid in small tesseræ of

FIG. 202. MOSAIC FLOOR PATTERNS.

marble and other stone or even tile, in patterns which frequently suggest rug-designs. Each floor has a border and either an all-over patterned field (see Fig. 189), a central medallion, or a spangled field (Fig. 202; Plate XI, 9, 11, 12). The swastika appears in some of these. The chained dog with the inscription *Cave Canem* ("beware the dog") was a common decoration of the *prothyrum* or vestibule. The finer houses boasted elaborate pictures in color, made with very small tesseræ,

181

A HISTORY OF ORNAMENT

and in some cases, no doubt, copying parts or the whole of celebrated Greek pictures. *Genre* pictures and animal subjects were common. The greatest and finest of

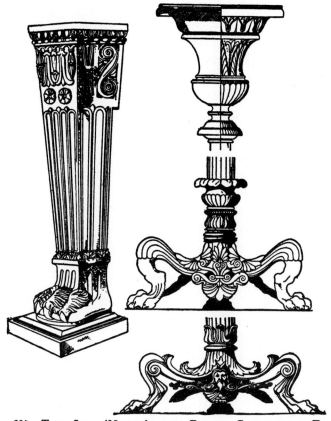

FIG. 205. TABLE-LEG (MARBLE) AND BRONZE CANDELABRUM DETAILS. NAPLES MUSEUM.

all mosaic pictures was found in the House of the Faun and transferred to the Naples Museum; it represents presumably the Battle of Issus, in a panel measuring

182

over 9 by 17 feet, and probably reproduces some celebrated Greek painting in Alexandria, from which city,
after Pompey's victory in 69 B.C., a strong Hellenic influence was exerted on Roman art. The portrait of
Alexander is unmistakable; the light and shade, fore-
shortening, drawing and color are remarkable and the
execution extraordinarily fine.

Mosaic was employed on walls as well as floors, though
sparingly. A singular freak or novelty of design was
the occasional combination of stucco-relief and mosaic.
Another use of mosaic was in the decoration of the
entire visible surface of various edicules, such as shrines
and niche-fountains (Figure 203, p. 185), upon which
the most brilliant colors of blue, red and green were
applied by the use of glass tesserae, and varied effectively
sometimes by scallop-shells inserted in bands or lines.

Furniture and Utensils.

The excavations at Pompeii and Herculanum have
thrown a light on the more intimate details of Roman
life not elsewhere to be obtained; not only by the paintings of scenes from daily life and by the *sgraffiti* or
scribblings on walls, but even more by the great wealth
of utensils, implements and furniture of metal and
marble exhumed from the ruins and for the most part
transferred to the Naples Museum. Everything of
wood and cloth was destroyed by the eruption, but
marble and bronze and even iron were preserved by
their burial in the volcanic ashes, and we have set before
us the marble tables that adorned the atrium and peristyle, the fountains and marble vases or basins, the

bronze couch-heads and frames, the candelabra and tripods of bronze, the braziers, water-heaters, mirrors, lamps, hair pins, *fibulæ* or clasps, and innumerable other objects of metal. Here again the Greek refinement appears in all the details. Grotesques are sculptured with consummate skill (Fig. 204); especially noticeable are the lion's paws terminating in human or in beasts' heads (Plate X, 11, 12) and the winged monsters on table-supports. The lightness and grace of the bases and fluted standards of tripods and candelabra suggest that from them in part came the inspiration for the fantastically slender columns of the wall-paintings (Fig. 205). It is interesting to compare these slender candelabra and tripods with the massively splendid forms of Roman candelabra in bronze and in marble in the Vatican (see Plate X). The Pompeiian tombs and altars compared with the Roman show a somewhat similar contrast in the detail, though less strongly marked; there is more reserve, less monumental boldness in the composition and in the detail.

Books Recommended:

MAU, trans. by KELSEY: *Pompeii* (New York, 1902).— MAZOIS: *Les ruines de Pompéii* (Paris, 1824).—NICCOLINI: *Le case ed i monumenti di Pompeii* (Naples, 1854–96).—PRESUHN: *Die neueste Ausgrabungen zu Pompeii* (Leipzig, 1882).— ZAHN: *Ornemens de Pompéii* (Berlin, 1828); *Ornamente aller Klassischen Kunstepochen* (Berlin, 1860).

FIG. 203.—MOSAIC FOUNTAIN, IN COURT OF
CASA GRANDE

FIG. 204.—MARBLE TABLE SUPPORTS; HOUSE OF CORNELIUS RUFUS

CHAPTER XII

It would be hard to point to two successive styles of architecture and ornament further apart in spirit and detail than those of Imperial Rome and Early Christian Rome, yet they form no exception to the rule of style-development by gradual transition. This transition is for us obscured first by the widespread destruction of early churches in the East during the Moslem conquests and in the West during the persecutions under Diocletian, and also by the fact that the beginnings of Christian symbolic art in Europe were made in the catacombs and not above ground, and were thus humble and inconspicuous. But the Christian artists were Romans, working upon the basis of Roman art traditions which, up to the legalization of Christianity by Constantine in 312 A.D., were applied alike to secular and religious buildings. It was the predominance after that date of religious art employing a wholly new symbolism that most effectively differentiated the Christian from the pagan Imperial style.

Christian art began, then, nowhere as a consciously new art, but everywhere in Syria, Asia Minor, Egypt, Italy and Greece—as a phase of the existing local art. In the Eastern empire, with Constantinople as its center,

187

A HISTORY OF ORNAMENT

religious architecture and decoration diverged rapidly under Greek influence from the style of the West to become what we call the Byzantine. In Italy, with Rome as its center, they took on the development commonly called the Early Christian, or Latin, or—from the resemblance of the churches to the secular basilicas of the Empire—the Basilican style.

Early Christian Art Sepulchral.

The beginnings of Christian art are not, however, to be looked for in architecture. Until the edict of Constantine legalizing Christianity, its rites were, at least in the West, practised in private, largely in secret, and the language of symbols took on increased importance where persecution so often followed open speech. Upon the walls of the catacombs, which served not merely as places of sepulture but also as meeting-places for worship, were painted scriptural scenes and symbolic compositions: the Good Shepherd as a young man

FIG. 206. SARCOPHAGUS END, RAVENNA.

carrying a lamb on his shoulder, in evident reminiscence of the classic Herakles Kriophoros; the fish, the letters of

188

FIG. 207.—DETAIL, SAN LORENZO FUORI LE MURA

FIG. 210.—APSE MOSAIC, SAN CLEMENTE

which word in Greek (ἰχθύς) form an acrostic of the
Greek words for "Jesus Christ, Son of God, Savior";
the vine, in allusion to Christ's saying, "I am the Vine,"
and other like representations. Later many other forms
were added: the Labarum—the standard borne by Constantine's army after his victory of the Milvian Bridge,
in both forms ✺ and ☧ ; the letters I H S, the first
three letters of the Greek ΙΗΣΟΥΣ, later taken to signify
both Iesus Hominum Salvator and In Hoc Signo
(vinces), the words heard or seen by Constantine in his
vision at the Milvian Bridge; the cyress-tree, symbolic
of the cemetery and hence of death and burial and
finally baptism, which was regarded as the burial of
the sinful nature; [1] the emblems of the four evangelists
—the ox for Matthew, the lion for Mark, the head of a
man for Luke, the eagle for John; angels and cherubs,
funereal wreaths and festoons and finally the cross itself,
equal-armed after the Greek fashion, or with a long
standard after the Latin. Sheep to represent the flock
of the Church; the Paschal cup, the peacock and other
emblems of various significations were little by little
added to the list, and appear both in Latin and Byzantine art. It is somewhat remarkable that the cross does
not appear until late; hardly at all before the latter part
of the fifth or the early sixth century. Many of the
Christian emblems were already familiar forms in
Roman pagan art. Angels were but Roman winged
genii endowed with a new significance; the vine, originally a Bacchic emblem, became a Christ-symbol; the
wreath and festoon were transferred from the service

[1] Romans vii, 4.

of Roman sacrifices to that of Christian burial. Most of these forms were used at first with purely symbolic intent, having significance only for the initiated. In time, however, the symbolic intent, as always in the evolution of decorative art, because subordinate to the decorative: the symbol became a common ornament, multiplied and endlessly varied in the decoration not merely of sarcophagi (Fig. 206) and funereal chapels, but of churches, baptisteries, oratories and tombs. All the resources of mosaic, painting and carving were enlisted in their representation. Figure sculpture alone remained for centuries undeveloped, largely in consequence of the hatred of pagan idolatry with which it was so generally associated in the popular mind.

Architectural Ornament.

Early Christian art in the West made little of architecture. Two types of building predominated, the basilican church and the baptistery. The first was a simple three-aisled hall with a wooden roof, a semicirculiar apse for the clergy at the further end, and a transverse porch or narthex across the entrance-front. The two rows of columns which separated the broad central aisle or nave from the side-aisles, supported each a clearstory wall rising above the roofs of the side-aisles and carrying the lofty central roof: these walls were pierced with windows to light the nave. In the larger basilicas there were double side-aisles, and in some instances a transverse aisle, called the transept, as high and nearly as wide as the nave, crossed it directly in front of the apse. The arch forming the front of the apse

BASILICAN ORNAMENT

was generally called the triumphal arch, though in transeptal basilicas the name is applied to the great arch by which the nave enters the transept. Excepting the half-dome over the apse, no vaulting was employed in these churches. The columns were taken from pagan ruins, and so indifferent were the churchmen to architectural regularity that the columns of the same row often display a great variety of sizes and even different orders of capitals (Figure 207). This was partly due to the poverty of the churches during the gloomy centuries following the fall of Rome, but all the evidence points to a strangely prevalent indifference to architecture as an art, which the three great basilicas of St. Peter, St. Paul and Sta.[2] Maria Maggiore (all three originally built before the final fall of Rome) only emphasize by contrast. The builders of basilicas were chiefly engrossed with the applied decorations of their churches. Even in this field, Roman art remained almost stationary for centuries, depending largely upon Byzantine artists for a part of this decoration.

Elements of Latin Ornament.

The architectural ornament consisted of the following elements: (a) pavements of colored marble and hard stone, in a combination of *opus sectile* and *opus Alexandrinum;*[3] (b) marble sheathing or wainscot on the lower walls; (c) mosaic on the apse and its arch, on the, triumphal transept arch, and on the clearstory walls; rarely, in late examples, on the exterior of the front or

[2] Hereafter S. and Sta. will be used for *San, Santo* and *Santa.*
[3] *Sectile* = cut to shape; *Alexandrinum* = of small geometric units.

193

narthex and on cloister arcades; (*d*) the ornamentation
of the fixed furniture of the church; and (*e*), the decoration by painting or otherwise of the wooden ceilings of
nave and aisles.

A.   Floor Pavements.

Dates and periods are hard to fix and signify little in
this field of design, as the style remained practically un-

FIG. 208. FLOOR MOSAIC, SAN CLEMENTE, ROME.

changed for centuries.   The nave floor was commonly
divided into rectangular panels by broad bands of
colored marble in which were set guilloche patterns (Fig.
208) in opus sectile combined with Alexandrinum.
The panels were filled with field patterns of Alexandrinum surrounding discs or slabs of solid color
(see Plate XIII, 12).   Porphyry, verd-antique, ser-

pentine, and white and yellow marble were the usual materials employed, and the resulting effects were rich and yet sober, indestructible, and soft in color-harmony. The round disks were cut from antique columns sawed into slices, and all the ruins of antiquity were a quarry for paving materials.

This form of floor-decoration is probably the most effective ever devised. The contrast of the solid dark red or green of the disks with the sparkle of the minute patterns of Alexandrinum and the sweeping curves of the huge guilloches surrounding them, produce a decorative *ensemble* in every way admirable. Splendid examples survive in the churches of Sta. Maria in Trastevere, Sta. Maria Maggiore, San Lorenzo, San Marco and San Clemente. Floors of this description were in vogue throughout the entire Middle Ages, in Rome and its neighborhood and even in remote Italy, as in the floor of the Byzantine St. Mark's Church at Venice, dating from the 11th century.

B. Marble Wainscoting.

This system of wall decoration, often called *incrustation,* was inherited from ancient Rome, but was used more extensively in the Eastern than in the Western churches. The Roman basilicas have moreover been so often remodeled that nearly every vestige of their incrustations has disappeared. Exceptions are found in Sta. Agnese and in Sta. Sabina; in the latter the arch-spandrels are inlaid with formal conventional patterns. Usually the practice was followed of symmetrically pairing slabs having similar veinings, as is shown in Fig.

195

A HISTORY OF ORNAMENT

Fig. 209. Byzantine Wainscot.

209, a Byzantine example from Constantinople. This practice is common to the Basilican and Byzantine styles.

C. Mosaic.

In this art, at least in that branch of it in which small cubes or *tesseræ* of glass are employed to form pictures and patterns on walls and vaults (*opus Grecanicum*), it is impossible to distinguish sharply between the Byzantine and Basilican or Latin styles.   Greeks from Constantinople doubtless were often employed to execute mosaics in Rome, and were probably the originators of this form of Christian art. By means of minute tesseræ of glass "paste," pictures and patterns can be formed of any desired combination and gradation of colors, gold and silver effects being produced by gold- or silver-leaf imprisoned between two layers of glass paste fused together. The deep blues, from lapis-lazuli to a soft green-blue, the rich reds, soft yellows and greens and brilliant gold and silver of this sort of mosaic made possible a splendor of color far transcending any form of painting, and unrivaled in depth and intensity except by the later invention of stained glass. Its magnificence appealed strongly to the taste of the early Christian centuries, and its adaptation to pictorial representation fitted it to express that symbolism which the mental habit of the times demanded. Accordingly there is more of picturing than of pure ornament, which is confined chiefly to narrow borders, often simulating jewels set in gold. It remained for the Byzantines to develop the possibilities of mosaic in the field of pure ornament.

The most important mosaics were in, or on, the apse-vaults, and represented such subjects as the Kingdom of God by the symbolism of the Shepherd and twelve sheep, or some like composition. Similar subjects, with angels, adorned the spandrels by the apse arch, and the triumphal transept-arch. The clearstory often bore pictures of saints, angels and apostles, and Biblical scenes. Among the finest of all Latin mosaics are those of the apses of Sta. Pudenziana and Sta. Maria in Trastevere, the apse and triumphal arch of St. Paul without the Walls (S. Paolo fuori le mura) recovered from the ruins of the original basilica and incorporated in the modern reconstruction; of Sta. Prassede and Sta. Sabina, all at Rome; and of the two San Apollinare churches at Ravenna (sixth century). Of later date is the superb rinceau decoration in the apse-head of San Clemente (1096–1104): an exceptional example of conventional ornament in mosaic in a basilica (Figure 210). Apart from such applications of the rinceau, there were few distinctive ornament motives in the mosaic decora-

Fig. 211. Early Christian Mosaic Borders.

tions. Fig. 211 shows two examples of mosaic borders, *a* from the palace of St. John Lateran, a mosaic of the eighth century; *b* from the façade of Santa Maria in Trastevere, both in Rome.

D. Ecclesiastical Furniture.

The chief elements in the fixed furniture of the churches were the *ciborium* or baldaquin—the canopy over the altar and tomb of the saint; the altar itself; the choir-enclosure; and the two pulpits or *ambones*, affected respectively to the reading of the Gospels and of the Epistles, the former being adorned with a columnar candelabrum. The seats for the clergy were originally simple steps of marble set around the apse, and the bishop's throne was apparently of very simple design. Later the clergy-seats were removed from the apse or *bema* and the altar placed there in their stead, though the ciborium remained in its original position to mark the tomb of the martyr or saint. All this fixed furniture was of marble, usually built up of flat slabs inlaid with opus Alexandrinum. The ciborium was a structure of four columns with a pyramidal roof; the altar a simple rectangular box or table of marble; the choir-enclosure a

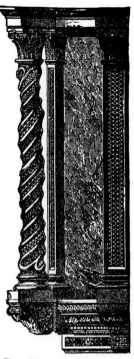

Fig. 212.   Ara Coeli, Rome.

paneled marble parapet about three feet high; the ambones, elevated reading-desks on either side of the choir reached by flights of steep stairs. The decoration of these simple forms was often very rich, especially of the pulpits and altar frontals (Fig. 212). It consisted of inlaid patterns of opus Alexandrinum combined with disks and guilloches of *sectile,* in principle like the floor-mosaics, but finer in scale and execution. In the later work, the geometrical units of the Alexandrine mosaic— triangles, squares, circular segments, etc.—were often of glass paste, producing much more brilliant effects than

A HISTORY OF ORNAMENT

the marble and porphyry units of the earlier works. It appears to have been first used in the spiral flutings of the gospel or Easter column. This brilliant form of Alexandrine work, whatever its origin, became especially common in Southern Italy, and was practised there and in Rome as late as the thirteenth century. It is found in the cloisters of Monreale (twelfth century),

FIG. 213. MOSAIC DETAILS, PULPIT IN SAN LORENZO FUORI.

in Sicily, and in those of San Paolo *fuori* and St. John Lateran at Rome (thirteenth century). Rome became the center of an important school of *marmorarii* and of a great industry in marble mosaic, and its artists traveled far to execute orders for church furniture and cloister-arcades. The family of the Cosmati (from Cosmatus or Cosmas, grandson of the founder of the school), were especially noted for several generations, and their name is often applied to the combination of *sectile* and *Alexandrinum* which they used and developed (Figs. 212, 213 from Ara Coeli and San Lorenzo Rome. See Chapter XIV).

In the cloisters above mentioned, in the Easter columns, and frequently also in the ambones (Fig. 212), twisted shafts or spiral flutings were used. The introduction of this form of column, theoretically inappropriate for a support, into Italian art, may be traced to the rich but ugly twisted column now in St. Peter's at Rome, brought in the sixth century from Jerusalem, where it was believed to have been a part of the "Gate Beautiful" where St. Peter healed the lame man (Acts iii, 2–10). It belongs probably to the decline of Roman Imperial art, much later than St. Peter's time.

E. Ceilings.

Not one of the ceilings of the earlier basilicas remains to us in its original form. It is unlikely that in churches resplendent with marble and mosaic the ceilings were as bare and barnlike as are to-day most of those which have not been entirely remodeled in comparatively recent times. We are, however, left to speculation as to their precise treatment. The painted open-trussed ceilings of several medieval churches of the eleventh and twelfth centuries (Messina,[4] Monreale, San Miniato near Florence) show a somewhat similar treatment though belonging to different styles, which points to the existence of a strong ancient tradition (see Chapter XIV). It is likely also that in some cases the trusses were concealed by a decorative ceiling of wood, paneled in coffers with rosettes, after the fashion of many Greek and Roman ceilings, and richly painted and gilded. But no such ceilings remain to our day. It may be,

[4] Destroyed in the earthquake of 1909.

however, that the splendid ceiling of Sta. Maria Maggiore is a reproduction or imitation of the original of the fifth century.

Vaulted ceilings were chiefly confined to baptisteries and tombs. The earliest of these are the dome over the central space and the annular vault over the encircling aisle of Sta. Costanza at Rome, erected by Constantine presumably as the tomb of his daughter Constantia, but from early times used as a baptistery. The decorations of the dome have perished, but among the well-preserved mosaics of the aisle-vault are vintage scenes (Figure 215), apparently pagan, but here transferred to the service of Christian symbolism; and geometrical patterns combined with small figure subjects. But in nearly all domical and vaulted buildings after the fourth century the Latin and Byzantine styles are one and the same, and the ornament of such buildings will be taken up in the chapter on Byzantine art.

From the preceding paragraphs it may be rightly inferred that the Early Christian builders were singularly lacking in architectural inventiveness. There is not a single structural form, not an architectural innovation, not an ornament of purely architectural character, that can be credited to their initiative. Their art was stationary and unprogressive, and contrasts surprisingly with the rapid progress and splendor of achievement of the contemporary Byzantine art in the Eastern Empire.

Books Recommended:

BUNSEN: *Die Basiliken des christlichen Roms* (Munich, n. d.). —ESSENWEIN: *Ausgänge der klassichen Baukunst* (in *Handbuch der Architektur*, Darmstadt, 1886).—A. L. FROTHING-

FIG. 214.—DETAIL FROM CLOISTER, ST. JOHN LATERAN

FIG. 215.—MOSAIC IN VAULT OF STA. COSTANZA

BASILICAN ORNAMENT

HAM: *Monuments of Christian Rome* (New York, 1908).—
GERSPACH: *La Mosaïque* (Paris, 1889).—GUTENSOHN AND
KNAPP: *Denkmale der christlichen Religion* (Rome, 1822–27).
—HÜBSCH: *Monuments de l'architecture chrétienne* (Paris,
1866).—PORTHEIM: *Uber dem dekorativen Stil in der altchristlichen Kunst* (Stuttgart, 1886).—VON QUAST: *Die altchristlichen Bauwerke zu Ravenna.*—DE ROSSI: *La Roma Soter-
ranea christiana* (Rome, 1864–77).—N. H. J. WESTLAKE:
*History of Design in Mural Painting, from the Earliest Times
to the 12th Century* (London, 1915).

CHAPTER XIII

In striking contrast to the architectural poverty of the
Latin or Western ornament of the early church stands
the architectural richness of the decorative art which
grew up in the East Roman or Byzantine empire, and
which was founded upon and largely dominated by the
architecture. With the decline and fall of Rome, the
lamp of civilization passed to Constantine's eastern
capital on the Bosphorus and into the hands of the
Byzantine Greeks of Thrace, Macedonia, Asia Minor
and Syria. These Greeks, largely Asiatic, borrowing
freely and impartially from classic Greek, Roman and
Asiatic sources, developed with singular rapidity in the
fifth and sixth centuries new types of vaulted construction and a system of decoration of remarkable originality and beauty, in which the Oriental love of brilliant
color and surface ornament was blended with the Occi-
dental appreciation of logical construction and pure
form. This Byzantine art culminated under Justinian
(527–565) ; invaded Italy, especially after the Byzantine
conquest of Ravenna; and spread through the entire
extent of the Byzantine empire. The decline that set
in soon after the brilliant reign of Justinian was a slow
decline, so that we find this art still productive in the

eleventh and twelfth centuries. Indeed, St. Mark's at Venice, one of its most brilliant works, dates from 1047, while offshoots from the parent stem throve for centuries in the ecclesiastical buildings of Russia and Armenia, and later in the impressive mosques of the Ottoman Turks.

Leading Characteristics.

The Byzantine system of design and decoration was in fundamental principle like the Roman in its use of a decorative skin or veneer of marble, mosaic, or other fine material upon a structural mass or core of brick, concrete or like coarser material. The chief difference, structurally, was in the use of the dome on pendentives in place of groined vaulting;

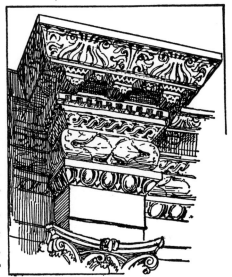

Fig. 216. Detail from Spalato.

and decoratively, in an entirely new and original treatment of detail. For the classic Roman play of light and shade by means of relief carving and architectural features the Byzantines substituted a system of decoration in color and surface-etching, reducing all surfaces as nearly as possible to unbroken planes or curves, suppressing all avoidable projections and recessings. Marble incrustations and pavements were used with even greater splendor than in Rome, and all vaults covered with superb mosaics, or, when means were lacking for the more splendid adornment, with pictures in fresco on plaster.

Architectural Ornament.

Such details of architecture as were inherited from classic Roman precedent were subjected to a flatten-

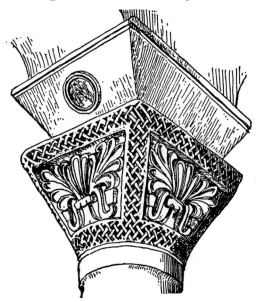

FIG. 217. IMPOST CAP, S. VITALE.

ing process by which they lost all their strong reliefs, high lights and deep shadows. This process had begun as far back as 300 A.D. in the Palace of Diocletian at Spalato (Fig. 216), in another part of which one also observes arches carried directly on columns, as in Byzantine buildings. In the Spalato entablature, by changes of profile and proportion the architrave has been exaggerated, the frieze reduced to a mere molding, the corona to a fillet, and the general profile of the cornice almost to a 45° splay. In Hagia Sophia, the masterpiece of Byzantine art, we find a similar treat-

FIG. 218. CORINTHIANESQUE CAP, S. APOLLINARE NUOVO, RAVENNA.

ment of cornices and moldings, while capitals, shafts, archivolts and all other features depart in an equally striking degree from Roman models (Plate XII, 1, 2).

Impost Blocks.

The Byzantines invented a new feature, the *impostblock*, to replace the bits of entablature which the

Romans in their vaulted buildings interposed between the capital and the spring of the vaulting. The Byzantine impost-block, shaped like the inverted frustum of a pyramid (Fig. 217; Plate XII, 3) was decorated with monograms, crosses, lambs or other symbols, or sur-

FIG. 219. "BASKET" CAP, S. APOLLINARE NUOVO, RAVENNA.

face-carving. The capital proper sometimes retained a semblance of the Corinthian (Fig. 218) or Ionic type; but was in other cases greatly simplified in mass and covered with lace-like or basket-like patterns, sometimes deeply undercut—the basket type Fig. 219; Figure 232, page 221. These occur alike in Ravenna, Parenzo, Constantinople, Salonica, Venice and Syria. In the magnificent capitals of the great columns of Hagia Sophia the impost-block is dispensed with (Plates XII,

2; XIII, 2), and the vigorous but graceful mass of the capital, with its corner volutes and surface carving of flat acanthus-leaves, performs adequately its true function of carrying the heavy arches that rest upon it. A frequently occurring type with central and corner ridges (Fig. 219) may have been suggested by uncut or roughed-out Corinthian caps, blocked-out in this way for the subsequent detailed cutting of the

FIG. 220. ABOVE, CARVED SPANDREL FROM HAGIA SOPHIA; BELOW, FRIEZE FROM ST. SERGIUS.

central rosettes and volutes and the corner volutes, caulicoli and leaves.[1]

Shafts.

Shafts are of polished marble, granite or porphyry, sometimes, as in Hagia Sophia, ringed with a number of astragals or annulets, a treatment detrimental to the best effect.

Spandrels and Soffits.

The soffits were decorated either with mosaic, as in S. Vitale at Ravenna and the upper arcades of Hagia

[1] This ingenious and plausible suggestion seems to have originated with the late Professor W. R. Ware.

Sophia, or with marble, which was sometimes carved in bands of lace-like patterns as in the lower arcades of Hagia Sophia. The archivolt was marked by small moldings (Plate XII, 2). Spandrels were commonly incrusted with marble without other ornament, as in St. Mark's; sometimes mosaic or fresco was used in either pictorial or arabesque patterns (Plate XIII, 2), or surface-carving was executed on the marble incrustation (Fig. 220). The nave of Hagia Sophia shows both of the last two treatments.

Carving.

In all Byzantine decorative carving, figure-sculpture, high relief and indeed true relief of any kind are singularly lacking. In their place the Byzantine artists de-

FIG. 221. FRIEZE, ST. JOHN STUDIOS, CONSTANTINOPLE.

veloped a system of carving by incision, the entire pattern lying in one plane, so designed that the background formed a series of isolated pits or depressions, the total effect being rich and highly decorative in spite of its flatness. The patterns were chiefly based on the acanthus and rinceau (Figs. 220, 221, 222); but the leaves and stems were flattened, the lobes made pointed, the pipes suppressed, the calyx-flowers and caulicoli of the rinceau obliterated, and the points of the leaves so disposed as to touch the concave sides of the stems of their neighbors, or to meet each other point to point, forming innumerable triangular or quadrilateral pits or spots of background. The leaves were channeled with V-section channels, and the whole produced an effect as of stone lace work applied to a flat background (Figs. 224, 226). The origin of this peculiar treatment of classic motives has been variously explained. Viollet-le-Duc credits

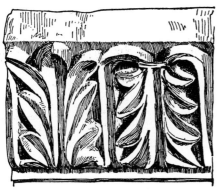 

FIG. 222.   ACANTHUS ANTHEMIONS.   FIG. 223.

it to Syrian, and chiefly to Jewish influence. Early Christian and pre-Christian tombs in Palestine show a somewhat similar style of dry and flat surface-carving, with frequent use of the vine-motive which is also common in Byzantine ornament. In Central Syria interesting remains from the third to sixth centuries also display kinship with Byzantine work (Fig. 240). On the other hand, the same tendencies are visible in the palace at Spalato (see *ante,* Fig. 216) in Dalmatia, and to some extent in works of Constantine's time. The

213

most probable explanation of the genesis of the style, so far as its decorative art is concerned, is found in the influence of the Asiatic Greeks, who would most naturally combine the Asiatic love of surface decoration in minutely detailed all-over patterns, with the traditional motives of Greek classic and Roman art. It was the rise and preëminence of Constantinople in the sixth cen-

FIG. 224. ANTHEMION FRIEZE, ST. MARK'S, VENICE.

tury under Justinian, that gave to this nascent style its first great impulse. The artificers in mosaic, ivory-carving, enamel and other arts from Constantinople, many of whom had, during the preceding century, found their chief employment in Italy and other foreign countries, were now abundantly and constantly employed in their home Capital. Under Justinian's strenuous and splendor-loving rule, the arts of design were developed with an almost feverish activity. The flat surface-carving harmonized better with the flat color-decoration in marble and mosaic than the more vigorous relief of the

214

Roman and Greek prototypes; and architectural light-and-shade was treated in a wholly new spirit, and the old types of capital and entablature gradually disappeared.

Moldings.

The profiles were weak; effect was sought by enrichment rather than pro-filing; and splay faces covered with acanthus-leaves frequently occur (Fig. 222 and Plate XII, 1, 2, 4). The most characteristic molding was the so-called *billet molding,* cut into small blocks or dentils, often in two rows in which the blocks of one are opposite the spaces of the other, as appears in the lower part of 1 in Plate XII. This molding

FIG. 225. CROSSES AND ANTHEMIONS.

was especially used for framing the slabs of marble veneer, and contributed strongly to the general effect of a sparkling play of minute spots of light and shade which the Byzantine artists loved.

Bands and Borders.

The fret, anthemion, vine and rinceau of classic art all appear in Byzantine borders and friezes, but in

215

modified forms, often exhibiting a singular reversion towards earlier, long-forgotten types in Greek pottery. The artists of the sixth to twelfth centuries could hardly have known or even seen any antique Greek vases, and it is hard to explain how and why this reversion took place; it most probably came about through Roman versions of the anthemion and other vase ornaments, sur-

FIG. 226. ACANTHUS LEAVES (above); and RINCEAU
FROM BISHOP'S.

viving in Roman carvings and mosaics (compare Fig. 225 with Fig. 135). What makes this reversion the more interesting is that most of these Byzantine anthemions are really acanthus leaves in disguise, as may be seen by comparing them with unmistakable acanthus leaves like those in Figs. 218 and 221. The Byzantine carvers, by flattening the leaf and altering its lobes, gradually worked it into a quasi-anthemion form, and then under a similar decorative impulse did

216

Fig. 229

Fig. 231   Fig. 230

Fig. 232

Fig. 229 Peacock Panel, Torcello   Fig. 230 Interlace (Italian).
Fig. 231 Perforated Panel, S. Vitale   Fig. 232 Capital, St. Mark's.

with it much as the Greek pottery-painters had done with the anthemion and palmette, nearly or quite a thousand years earlier.

The Rinceau.

This has already been alluded to. The friezes from St. Sergius (Fig. 220) and St. John Studios (Emir Akhor Jami) at Constantinople (Fig. 221), are fine examples of the typical Byzantine continuous rinceau-movement uninterrupted by calyx-flowers, and the merging of stem and caulicolus into one flat, flowing leaf design; while in Fig. 226, *b* it is seen in its most degenerate form, in a carved slab from the Bishop's Palace at Ferentino. The *vine* also occurs frequently, especially in Italy, singularly recalling painted vine-patterns on Greek vases (Fig. 227).

Symbols.

Symbolism played an important part in the carved decoration as well as the mosaics of the Byzantines. The *vine,* already alluded to, is often represented as springing from the Paschal cup or chalice (Plate XII, 5) ; the *cross* often studded with jewels and always with spreading ends (Figs. 225, *a, b;* 228 and Plate

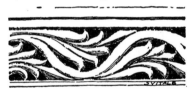

FIG. 227. VINE BORDER, S. VITALE.

XII, 3, 9) ; the *cypress-tree,* symbol of the grave, and hence of the mystic burial of baptism (see *ante,* page 189), and in this sense carved on baptismal fonts and plutei and elsewhere in baptisteries (Fig. 228) in a form

FIG. 228. DETAIL OF CROSS IN FIG. 225.

singularly like an anthemion; the peacock, as the symbol of the soul (Figure 229; Plate XII, 9)—these are the most frequently recurring symbols. An effective decoration for square or circular panels was devised by making the four arms of the cross frame four acanthus-anthemions, as in Fig. 225, *a* from Hagia Sophia.

In later work, especially in Italy where Lombard influence may account for it, monsters and grotesques sometimes appear. It is curious to note how often peacocks (as in Figure 229; Plate XII, 9), lions or monsters, even griffins, as in the example from Sta. Maria Pomposa (Figure 235) are placed symmetrically at the base of a cross or tree, recalling a favorite device of Greek and Roman art, derived originally from Assyrian and Hittite prototypes.[2]

Guilloches and Interlace.

FIG. 230A.

The Byzantine artists expanded the applications of the Greek guilloche-motive into a whole system of interlaced patterns, in which squares, lozenges and circles, large and small, are combined with great variety and ingenuity. The more elab-

[2] See Figure 34 and cf. Goblet d'Alviella, "The Migration of Symbols," pages 122–140.

orate examples belong to the later developments. Some of the most complex designs are found in Armenia, where they almost rival the Celtic interlaces (see page 271). Whether these are due to Celtic manuscripts carried into Armenia, or whether the Celtic interlaces were themselves descended from Byzantine sources is not clear (Fig. 230A; Figures 230, 231; Plate XII, 10).

Perforated panels were a special delight of the Italo-Byzantine designers; they are found chiefly at Ravenna, serving as parapet-panels. Figure 231 shows a detail of one of the most splendid of these remarkable works (see also Plate XII, 9).

Floors and Incrustations.

The rich and varied marbles of the East supplied abundant materials for decorative pavements and wall-veneers. In principle these resemble those of the Latin buildings; guilloche-patterns or borders frame large circles or rectangles of marble, porphyry and verd-antique in the floors; while thin slabs of veined marble set so as to form symmetrical veining-patterns, encrust the walls up to the spring of the main arches and vaults (Fig. 209; Plate XII, 1). The monotony of their smooth surfaces was broken by the billet-moldings with which the slabs and bands were framed. The composition of this wall-paneling was not always good; the apse of Hagia Sophia, for example, is a jumble of panels with little or no organic system in their arrangement. The general effect, however, of this veneering in veined marbles is always rich and yet sober; and in St. Mark's at Venice it reached the highest perfection of internal harmony.

Mosaic.

The crowning splendor of Byzantine decoration was

in its mosaics. These at first differed in no wise from the Latin (see page 196), which were, indeed, probably executed in many cases by Byzantine artists. But the domes and vaults of the East gave special opportunities for the application of this noble form of decoration, and these were freely availed of. Conventional ornament was made to play a far more important rôle in the Byzantine than in the basilican churches,

Fig. 233. From Hagia Sophia.

though figure-subjects and pictures still form the chief decoration. Hagia Sophia and the Kahrié Mosque (once a Byzantine church called Moné tes Choras) at Constantinople and the two churches of San Apollinare, the Episcopal palace and San Vitale at Ravenna offer the finest examples of this art, the cubes or tesseræ of glass being very small, espe-

Fig. 234. Sarcophagus End, Ravenna.

FIG. 235.—FROM STA. MARIA POMPOSA

FIG. 236.—MOSAIC, TOMB OF GALLA
PLACIDIA

FIG. 237.—IVORY THRONE OF BISHOP MAXIMIAN, RAVENNA

cially in the first-named. One of the earliest examples of the application of glass mosaic of this type to vaulting is the tomb of Galla Placidia, the daughter of Theodosius, at Ravenna; the barrel-vaults of the cross arms and the rude dome of the central lantern being adorned with remarkably effective pictures and patterns, some on a blue and some on a gold ground (Figure 230). The gold ground predominates in Hagia Sophia and in some other examples and imparts a richness of effect not otherwise attainable (Plate XIII).

In many Byzantine mosaic pictures there appear representations of shrines, niches and other architectural subjects derived from sarcophagi, church furniture and minor structures of which no trace has survived. Similar forms are seen in manuscript illuminations and in ivory carvings and sarcophagi (Fig. 236).

Church Furniture.

Few examples remain of this branch of decorative design for which the Byzantines were so celebrated. The accounts of the furniture of Hagia Sophia given by Paul the Silentiary describe an almost incredible splendor of jewels, gold and silver. The most important work of this sort in metal now extant is the "Pala d'Oro" or silver-and-gold altar-piece of St. Mark's in Venice, by Constantinople artists of the twelfth century (but much altered in more recent times). Plate XII, 8, figures the end of an Italo-Byzantine silver chest in Florence. Of works in marble there exists in the basilica of S. Apollinare in Classe at Ravenna a Byzantine baldaquin or ciborium, and in Venice the much later ciborium of St. Mark's, besides a fine octagonal canopy and pulpit in the north aisle. In the cathedral of Ravenna the ivory throne of Bishop Maximianus is carefully preserved (sixth century, Figure 237). Ivory carving, indeed, was one of the special arts of Byzantine civilization; book-covers, diptychs and triptychs in this material exist in museums and private collections. Ivory was a precious material in the Middle Ages, and the art displayed in these small works combined the pictorial composition of the manuscript illuminators with the technic and the ornament of the marble-carvers, but with more freedom in the relief. The cross, pictorial scenes and grapevine borders of the throne of Maximianus just referred to, are precisely in the style of the diptychs, though on a larger scale.

In many of the minor works of church equipment and furniture enamel was used with or without the accompaniment of gems in elaborate settings, to impart rich color to the object decorated. The field of each color was slightly hollowed out in the metal—silver, gold or copper—and in this shallow pool the separate colors were fused in the furnace. This process, called *champlevé* enameling, was carried in the path of Byzantine trade to France where, at Limoges, an important center of this art-industry was developed in the twelfth to fourteenth centuries. Fig. 238 represents the Crown of Charlemagne, a fine example of late Byzantine goldsmith's work of the ninth century. There are in various libraries highly ornate book-covers in gold, enamel and precious stones of the ninth to twelfth centuries.

Textile Ornament.

The arts of weaving and embroidery were highly developed by the Byzantine civilization, which delighted

FIG. 238. THE CROWN OF CHARLEMAGNE.

in splendor of official apparel. Byzantine stuffs, fabrics and embroideries are found in many museums, mostly those of the later phases of the art (ninth to twelfth centuries). Fig. 239 shows an example from the Museum of Bamberg.

Manuscript Illumination.

Christianity has been called the religion of a book. In no other religion has the written word played so important a part. Long before the final fixing of the canon of the New Testament, individual books—gospels, epistles, writings by the early Fathers—were being

227

multiplied by skilful scribes and widely circulated by missionaries. The development of monasticism stimulated the production of books and led to the establishment of schools of calligraphists and miniaturists or illuminators. With increasing veneration for the sacred writings there came increasing splendor in the manuscripts, which were embellished by pictures, illuminated initials and decorative borders. In this new art the Byzantine Greeks showed the highest skill, and the result was the final domination of the Byzantine taste and style in this field, as in the closely allied art of mosaic picturing and ornament.

The initial letters of chapters or books were made into ornamental designs covering a considerable portion of the page, and painted with brilliant red, blue, green and gold, often with accompaniments of an architectural character with or without figures. Illustrations of scriptural scenes and allegorical compositions were often introduced, covering an entire page. In these the drawing and coloring followed the formulas that governed the design of like figures in mosaic and fresco decorations of the churches; formulas that became hieratic and were finally written down in inflexible rules that have survived to modern times in the monasteries of Mt. Athos,[3] and in the *icons* of the Russian churches. This stiff and conventional style of painting was the parent of Italian religious painting in the Middle Ages; and indeed of all Christian medieval painting, architectural as well as in manuscripts. For the Byzantine manuscripts were scattered through the monasteries and

[3] Cf. Crowninshield, "Mural Painting."

Carvings from Churches at Mokheta and Chouamta; Georgia.

FIG. 241.—GEORGIAN AND ARMENIAN CARVING

FIG. 239. BYZANTINE FABRIC, BAMBERG.

churches of Western as well as Eastern Europe, and formed the models from which both the Celtic and Scandinavian schools of manuscript decoration took their early inspiration. In these interlace, which is a subordinate element in the Eastern models, became a dominant feature, though it made use of the North-

ern myths, even those of pagan origin, to supply motives for elaborate interlaces in borders and initials.

Syrian Christian Ornament.

In Syria, Christian art took on a special form in the absence of the brick, timber, marble and glass on which Latin and Byzantine art so largely depended for artistic expression. The buildings of central Syria show a

FIG. 240. SYRIAN CARVING.

231

dry, restricted style of stone carving, akin in its flatness to the Byzantine, making much use of geometric patterns and retaining classic details only in forms so changed as to be little more than travesties of the originals, as at Kelat Seman, Rouheiha, Tourmanin, etc. In certain cities, however, Byzantine artists introduced marble and mosaic, as in the famous Golden Church at Antioch, no longer extant. The Moslem conquest under Omar (638) put an end to the life of Syrian Christian art and resulted in the destruction of most of the Christian churches. (Figure 240, from Tourmanin and Bakouza.)

Russian, Georgian and Armenian Ornament.

The Eastern Church, in the Balkan peninsula, and in what is now the Russian Empire, including Georgia and Russian Armenia, highly interesting phases of Byzantine art. Aside from the singular architecture of the Russian churches with high pinnacled lanterns, this art is especially rich in manuscript illumination, enameled and jeweled silver- and goldsmith's work, and surface carving. In this last department of design intricate interlaces suggest the reacting influence of the Celtic manuscripts; although it is possible that both may hark back to a common derivation from the simpler interlaces of early Byzantine art in Constantinople. They frequently betray also the influence of Moslem art and have a strongly Oriental character throughout.

Figure 241 exhibits a number of examples of this architectural carving from Mokheta and Chouamta in Georgia and Gelathi in Armenia.

BYZANTINE ORNAMENT

Books Recommended:

BYZANTINE

As before, Essenwein, Gerspach, Hübsch, Von Quast. Also, Bayet: *L'Art byzantin* (Paris, n. d.).—H. C. Butler: *Architecture and other Arts in Northern Central Syria* (New York, 1903).—A. Dehli: *Selections of Byzantine Ornament* (New York, 1890).—Diehl: *Manuel de l'art byzantin* (Paris, 1910).—G. G. Gagarin: *Sbornik bisantiskikh i drevnerusskikh ornamentor* (St. Petersburg [Petrograd], 1887).—Moscow Museum of Art: *Histoire de l'ornement russe du Xme au XVIme siècle d'après les manuscrits* (Paris, 1870).—Ongania: *La basilica di San Marco* (Venice, 1881–88).—R. P. Pullan: *On the Decoration of Basilicas and Byzantine Churches* (Papers of the R. I. B. A.; London, 1875–76).—Salzenberg: *Die altchristlichen Baudeukmale von Constantinopel* (Berlin, 1854).— N. Simakov: *L'Ornement russe* (St. Petersburg [Petrograd], 1882).—Texier and Pullan: *Byzantine Architecture* (London, 1865).—Viollet-le-Duc: *L'Art russe* (Paris, 1877).— De Vogüé: *Syrie Centrale* (Paris, 1865–77).

CHAPTER XIV

1. ITALIAN AND FRENCH

A strictly chronological treatment of ornament history might be held to require taking up at this point the beginnings of Mohammedan ornament; but a due regard for continuity prescribes rather the following of the current of European Christian art through the Middle Ages before taking up the diverging art of the Moslems, which will therefore be reserved for another volume.

The name Romanesque has been so widely applied to the various phases of European art in its transition from the Latin and Byzantine phases to the so-called Gothic, that it will be retained in this discussion. It is, indeed, not an inappropriate term, since the art of Italy and Western Europe from about the ninth to the thirteenth century sprang from roots easily traced back to primary sources in the art of classic Rome.

The Romanesque Period.

Throughout all Europe, except in parts of the Byzantine Empire, the centuries from the fall of Rome to the twelfth constituted a period of chaos, upheaval, and gradual evolution. War, famine, and pestilence re-

Fig. 243.—Altar Front, Ferentino

Fig. 244. Detail from Front of San Michele, Lucca

Fig. 245.—False Window, San Stefano, Bologna

peatedly devastated Italy; the Arabs and Moors overran Sicily and Spain and threatened France; there was
commotion and turmoil among the German and Scandinavian tribes, who poured over the lands occupied by the
older civilizations. Out of this chaos Christian institutions were slowly emerging, and it was the Church
which first reared its majestic form, appearing as the
one universal and invincible fact, everywhere claiming
supreme authority and divine power. Of its two chief
manifestations, the papacy and the monastic system, the
last was nearer the people, visible and tangible, and in
the confusion of warring authorities it gained steadily
in favor and influence. Uneasy souls gave or bequeathed to the monasteries treasures of land and
money; peace-loving souls fled to them as asylums from
war and oppression, and the great monastic brother-
hoods multiplied their chapters, grew rich, built churches
and cherished such arts and such learning as the Church
demanded or favored. Architecture, decorative religious sculpture and carving, manuscript illumination
and other decorative arts flourished in the monasteries
as they grew in wealth and the centuries brought increased peace and order.

As, in the preceding ages, there was a marked difference between the art of Eastern and Western Christendom, so in this Romanesque period Italian art differed in important ways from that of France and western Europe. That of Germany stood midway between
the two, the Italian Lombard influence predominating.
But in all these styles Byzantine influence is discernible,
exerted through the medium of those artistic products

for which Constantinople was famous, manuscripts, ivory-carvings, ecclesiastical goldsmith's work and embroideries. Mosaic, however, was never in demand in the West; form rather than color dominates Romanesque art, and the resources of the abbeys and parishes were bestowed upon large and spacious edifices rather than upon such costly adornments as that of mosaic.

Italian Romanesque Ornament.

Italy being not a state but a group of states and provinces, there appear at least five more or less distinct styles in her early medieval art: the Basilican or Latin in Rome and its neighborhood; the Byzantine in Venice, Ravenna and on the East coast generally; the Tuscan in Etruria (Tuscany) from Pisa to Florence and even Siena; in the South, especially in Sicily, the Siculo-Arabic, a compound of Arabic, Byzantine, Latin and Norman elements; and in the North the Lombard, in which the Germanic spirit of the race which overran northern Italy in the seventh century expressed itself in new forms and combinations.

But while these may be properly called distinct styles, they so frequently overlap and mingle that it is not always easy, nor indeed reasonable, to classify a given building definitely in one of these categories. The unity of the Church, the migrations of monks and other ecclesiastics and especially of builders and carvers, contributed to a constant blurring of the boundary lines of these styles.

The Basilican and Byzantine styles have been already discussed, but in many examples from the other styles

ROMANESQUE ORNAMENT

their influence is clearly seen in various details. Moreover, these two styles in their later manifestations underwent developments and changes, from the influence of Western art, which differentiate them from their earlier phases. Basilicas of the Latin type continued to be built until the thirteenth century, and the art of the mosaicist in *opus Alexandrinum* was developed in great splendor by successive generations of the Cosma family and their apprentices, in altars, pulpits, and other architectural applications, so that this sort of inlaid geometric mosaic is commonly known as Cosmati work. Roman artists carried it into southern Italy and Sicily, where it mingled with the Siculo-Arabic work. The examples referred to in Chapter XII, and illustrated in Figs. 211–213, may be compared with the altar-front from Ferentino in Figure 243 and the columns from Monreale in Figure 249. In Florence especially, examples of the persistence of this art may be seen in various details of the cathedral and Giotto's campanile (Figure 394).

Tuscan Romanesque.

In Pisa, Lucca, Pistoia and the neighborhood there was developed in the 11th–13th centuries an ecclesiastical style based on the basilican plan but dressed in an architectural apparel of black and white marble in stripes, adorned with purely decorative arcades; recessed arches springing from pilasters against the lower-story walls, and superposed tiers of free arches on columns in the upper stories of the front. Inlaid patterns, chiefly geometric, adorned the tympana and

239

A HISTORY OF ORNAMENT

spandrels of the lower arches (Fig. 242). Carving was sparingly used, but the capitals were carefully carved on classic models, and the shafts sometimes carved with rinceaux of equally classic character (Cathedral and Baptistery of Pisa, eleventh century). In Lucca the Cathedral and the later church of S. Mi-

FIG. 242. INLAID PATTERNS, PISA CATHEDRAL.

chele (Figure 244) show rich inlays of black on white, with fantastic grotesques, due perhaps to Lombard influence which is also seen in some of the columns, and in the lions or monsters which serve as bases to columns in many churches. Some of the carving at Lucca suggests Byzantine influence. The use of striping in dark marble and of inlay is seen as far east as in Bologna. Figure 245 shows a window of the Baptistery of S. Stefano, where Byzantine influence appears in the interlaces of the perforated panels set in the striped wall. The richly carved lintels of doors in the church of S. Giusto, Lucca (Figure 246), show the mixture of influences which impinged on art in Tuscany.

In Florence and San Miniato, paneling in black and white takes the place of striping—a less correct treat-

FIG. 246.—LINTEL, SAN GIUSTO, LUCCA

FIG. 247.—DETAIL, PAVEMENT OF BAPTISTERY, FLORENCE

ment structurally though more decorative. In some churches, especially in the Baptistery at Florence and in San Miniato, the pavements show inlaid patterns in black and white which could hardly be surpassed for decorative beauty (Figure 247). Altar and altar-rail at S. Miniato are treated with inlays of the same sort.

The style was occasionally imitated in remote cities, as at Troja in southeast Italy, where the cathedral is decorated with recessed arcades after the Pisan manner.

The Siculo-Arabic Style.

The Arab conquest of Sicily and the subsequent expulsion of the Mohammedans by the Crusaders, with the establishment of a Norman kingdom, and the persistence of Byzantine traditions, all combined to develop a singularly mixed but effective style of decoration. The Arabic pointed arch, inlaid marble wainscot with a serrated parapet-cresting after the fashion of Cairo, Byzantine glass-mosaic on the upper walls and occasional vaults, are conspicuous in such edifices as the cathedrals of Monreale (Figure 248), the Martorana and Palatine chapels at Palermo, and others. Latin or "Cosmati" mosaics inlaid in twisted shafts adorn the cloisters of Monreale (Figure 249; see also Figure 214), and some of the pulpits and altars. The open-timber ceilings are richly painted and gilded; Cufic inscriptions

FIG. 250. CUFIC DECORATION, PALERMO.

FIG. 251. DETAIL FROM BRONZE DOORS, MONREALE CATHEDRAL.

appear in these (Fig. 250) and Arabic geometric interlace in the pavements. The bronze doors are by North Italian artists (Fig. 251), and here and there even Lombard details occur. Color appears everywhere, in Oriental profusion. Except in the capitals, many of which are antique, carving is little used, but some of the cloister capitals at Monreale are fine examples of decorative sculpture, showing both Norman and Byzantine influences (Figure 248).[1] It was a brilliant, confused, and short-lived style.

Lombard.

This style was not confined to Lombardy; it prevailed through Emilia and as far east as Verona, and south even into Calabria and Apulia. The Lombards, a Germanic race by origin, introduced into Italian art an entirely new note of solemnity and somber humor, expressed in the rugged massiveness of their churches and the grotesques in their carving. They contributed to architecture decorative forms and devices which spread

[1] The spiral and zigzag flutings shown in Figure 249 were originally filled with Cosmati-work of inlaid mosaics.

244

into western Romanesque art. Among these were the arcade cornice (Fig. 252), long pilaster strips—flat, semi-cylindrical, or spirally twisted; the round or wheel-window (Figure 253), the col-umn resting on a monster's back; the splayed doorway adorned with many columns in the jambs and with successively recessed or stepped arches above the door-lintel (Figure 254). The open arcade under the eaves of many Lombard churches is a part of the architecture rather than ornament.

FIG. 252. ARCADED CORN-ICE, S. MARTINO, PALAIA.

Many of these features are common in the French and Germanic Romanesque, though they originated in Italy. There was a constant interchange between the Benedictine monasteries of these countries; the Crusades brought Western hordes into Italy, and such commerce as there was aided the dissemination of architectural ideas as well as of commodities. Moreover the *mæstri comacini,* the skilled masons and carvers organized into guilds of traveling artisans, were almost wholly recruited from the North Italian country, and they carried their art into remote regions of Italy and into other lands.

Grotesques.

The medieval "bestiaries," of which copies have come down to our day, prove the symbolic significance of many of the grotesque sculptures, each beast and part of a beast having a specific meaning, so that each combination of heterogeneous parts to form a grotesque monster, signified a particular combination of definite ideas, as in a symbolic language. But the medieval

sculptors of Lombardy, with imaginations saturated with the medieval superstitions which peopled air, earth and sea with countless invisible beings, mostly malefic, loving to blast and blight every perfect and beautiful thing, but which could be diverted by charms, incantations and symbols, and even by marring in appearance the seeming perfection of a human work [2]—these Germanic Italians of the North treated with a species of humor-

FIG. 255. CAP FROM AURONA; SYMBOLS OF EVANGELISTS ON A PULPIT; CENTAUR FROM SAN AMBROGIO, MILAN.

ous decorative art the wild and fantastic symbols and

[2] This superstition survives in a real but attenuated form in the *jettatura* of Italy and the "evil eye" of the Eastern Mediterranean.

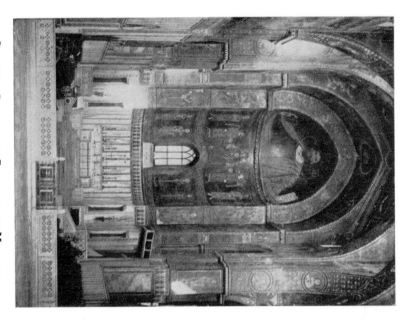

Fig. 248.—Interior of Cathedral of Monreale

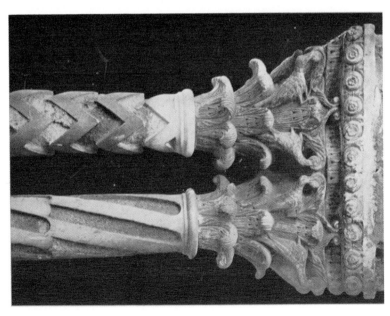

Fig. 249.—Capitals in Cloister of Cathedral, Monreale

talismans which grew out of this superstition (Fig. 255).

Other Forms.

Not a little of the Italian ornament of the Romanesque period is hard to classify under any particular style-name, being the product of local or of conflicting influences. Thus the wheel-windows show considerable variety. The marble perforations of the Cathedral of Troja suggest Oriental prototypes, while the traceries of those of S. Pietro and of Sta. Maria at Toscanella are designed on quite different principles. Certain Italian manuscripts of this period betray the hand or influence of Irish scribes. This variety of style in Italian Romanesque art presents an interesting contrast to the impressive unity of general effect in Western, especially French, work of the same period.

THE FRENCH ROMANESQUE

General Character.

French Romanesque ornament is completely dominated by the monastic architecture. Previous to about 1020 architecture in France was extremely crude, except in Provence, while Roman traditions still imparted a certain elegance to ecclesiastical buildings.[3] By 1000 A. D. the feudal system on the one hand, and the monastic on the other, had attained coherent form, and were dominant over the developments of the nascent civilization. Architecture was chiefly military and monastic, and while the feudal lords built strong castles, the monks

[3] Consult Révoil, "Architecture romane du Midi de la France:" plates.

249

FIG. 256. DETAILS FROM CHURCH OF ST. PAUL-TROIS-CHÂTEAUX.

were learning to build stone churches with vaults. In the absence of antique ruins to serve as quarries of ready-made decorative material, and without either models or trained artisans for the production of mosaic, carving and inlay, the arts of decoration had to be created anew. The art that slowly emerged from this destitution was a struggling art, at first crude in design and execution. To its earliest phase the French give the name of Carolingian art. The architecture was massive, thick-jointed, sparing in ornament except about the doorways, at which the builders' highest art was bestowed. As the eleventh century advances, this art becomes finer, richer, more knowing, still vigorous but better in technic; the accessory arts multiply and grow in perfection. There developed a certain unity of general style throughout France, controlled to a remarkable extent by a rigid logic of construction. More than in any previous style in any land, the forms not merely of the structure proper, but also of its decoration, were determined by the special exigencies of materials and structural science. Although provincial schools appear in

250

the architecture (Provence, Charente, Auvergne, Burgundy, Normandy, Ile-de-France) the decorative details do not vary greatly. True, the Byzantine influence is more clearly traceable in some districts, the classic in others, especially in Provence (Fig. 256), but it requires a closer discrimination to detect these provincial variations in the ornament than in the architecture, in the details than in the composition, and far more than is required to classify Italian ornament of the same period. This is due to the dominance of the great monastic orders, especially of the Benedictines; uniformly skilful artists, they tended to develop a common style wherever they established their abbeys.

Architectural Ornament: Columns and Capitals.

The French Romanesque column is a descendant from the classic column, modified by its new uses as a member of a compound pier or as a jamb-shaft or nook-column in a door or window. Lombard or comacine influences seem to have had a share in its development. The shaft is straight, without entasis or taper (Figure 257); sometimes, in late doorways, richly carved with geometric patterns (Figure 260). The base is of the Attic type, often with corner-leaves (Figure 264). The capitals

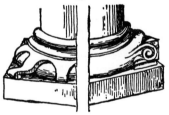

FIG. 264. BASEO WITH SPURS.

are generally of the Corinthian type, but with a heavy abacus added, and the proportions and details modified in innumerable ways (Figure 265; Plate XIV). At

Moissac they have a decidedly Byzantine character. The introduction of grotesques, both human and bestial, gave rise to new types (Figures 259, 261). Occasionally a species of cushion capital is used, especially in Normandy, the upper part square, with a heavy abacus; the lower part scalloped or convex-fluted once or more times on each face. A very beautiful double capital is preserved in the Museum at Toulouse (Plate XIV, 1). Another double cap is Number 2 in the same Plate, from Châlons-sur-Marne. The contrast in style illustrates the difference between the carving of Provence, with strong Byzantine tinge, and that of the Ile-de-France in the North. Some of the earlier work is hewn out with the mason's-ax;

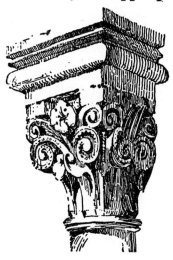

FIG. 265. LATE ROMANESQUE CAPITAL, PARIS.

later the chisel comes into more general use, and the established types are greatly varied by the introduction of figures, jewel-studded bands, and foliage of new types.[4] In Plate XIV, 3, 4, 5, the Corinthian tradition is clearly shown in all the capitals.

Carving; Bands and Panels.

The classic acanthus-leaf, rinceau, and even anthemion appear constantly in various modifications, and in

[4] Consult article "Sculpture" in V.-le-Duc "Dictionnaire Raisonné de l'architecture."

FIG. 253.—WHEEL WINDOW, CATHEDRAL, OF ALTAMURA

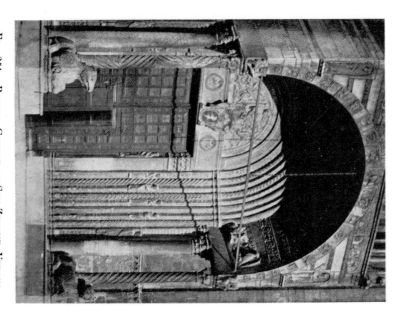

FIG. 254.—PORTAL, CHURCH OF SAN ZENONE, VERONA

Provence the fret is
used as a carved run-
ning ornament, as at
St. Gilles. The acan-
thus-leaf and rinceau
preserve in some cases
an   extraordinarily
classic character, even
in comparatively late
examples, suggesting
direct copying from
antique   fragments
(Avallon, Fig. 267,
St.   Denis,   etc.).
Even late in the
twelfth century the
Roman   tradition
sometimes   appears
very strong in carved
rinceaux, as in Figs.
266, 268. But gen-
erally the classic tra-
dition was gradually

Fig. 266. Carved Rinceau: Upper, from
Mantes; Lower, from Vaison.

lost, and a sort of naturalism began to creep in, though
not yet the direct copying of Nature. The rinceau has
a round stem but no wrapping-leaves; the stem is fluted
or ridged to suggest the bark; the branches spring from
it like grafts, with little ridges around their starting-
places; the leaves are still strongly conventional but not
at all like acanthus-leaves, having rounded lobes and
spoon-like hollows; they are broad and massive, and the

entire design is carved in high relief and sometimes deeply undercut (Figs. 266, 268). The double rinceau sometimes appears, enclosing the large leaves in ovals or in heart-shaped openings (Fig. 269). In almost all cases the rinceau represents the grape-vine and its ecclesiastical symbolism is obvious.

The framed anthemion, so common in Byzantine carving, hardly occurs in French Romanesque friezes or bands. Towards the end of the twelfth century, however, we find in its place, and evidently descended from it, an ornament consisting of broad fluted triple or five-lobed leaves enclosed by branching

Fig. 267. Ac-ANTHUS LEAVES FROM AVALLON.

leaves often adorned with jewels. Sometimes the central leaf of the trilobe is carried up under the framing leaves and curled over it (Figure 262). This motive seems to have come in from Germany, and is frequently found in painted ornament, both on walls and on manuscripts.

In certain regions along the paths of Byzantine and Lombard influence, beasts and human figures are shown twined into the convolutions of the rinceau (Plate XIV). *Arcading* as a decorative external feature never attained in France the

Fig. 268. RINCEAU, AVALLON.

256

importance it achieved in northern Italy. The two most noted examples are the fronts of Notre Dame at Poitiers and of the Cathedral of Angoulême (about 1130). These betray Italian and Byzantine influence; the arches are not free as at Pisa, but attached to (or recessed in) the wall, framing statues, windows or reliefs. Internally, however, wall-arcades occur frequently, especially as decorations of the side-aisle walls under the windows; such arcades are called *arcatures*. In Normandy the arches are sometimes interlaced, and this device was later

Fig. 269. Double Rinceau, Notre Dame, Paris.

adopted in England and is common in Anglo-Norman churches.

Moldings.

With the new types of building a new art of molding-profiles begins to appear. Whether its origin is in the Lombard doorways or is local, its development was controlled by that logic of structure to which allusion has already been made, and which specially distinguishes French Romanesque architectural art. All arches being stepped, and their square edges, as already described, cut into roll-moldings between chamfers, there resulted in doorways and pier-arches an alternation of plane, hollow and convex surfaces which proved extremely effective (Figures 257, 258). Out of this simple treatment was developed a more elaborate system of varying hollows, rolls and flat surfaces, which the English Gothic artists were to carry in later times to the highest perfection (see Chapter XVIII). In contrast with the classic tradition, according to which all important moldings project from the general surface, the medieval builders developed the contrary system of moldings cut into the surface. The exception is in the projecting drip-moldings which defined the extrados of the arch on exterior walls, especially over doorways.

Doorways.

As a general rule the outer step or "order" of a series of stepped doorway-arches was brought down upon an inpost carried by a column set flush with the outer face of the wall, or upon the square pier formed by the wall itself. Sometimes, however, it was returned into the wall, as in Figure 258, or abutted into projecting members, as in Figure 259. Each "order" of the series of diminishing arches was carried by its own distinct supports, whether columns (jamb-shafts) or piers, as in Figures 257, 258. The various orders were either plain, with roll-moldings, as already explained, or carved with enrichments often of great splendor of ef-

Fig. 257 Carennac.

Fig. 258
Porte St Jean, Rouen Cath.

Fig 262

Fig 263.

Fig 260.

Chartres Cath.

Fig 259 From Angoulème Cath

Fig 261 From St. Pierre d'Aulnay

fect. It was upon the church doorways
that the monastic artists lavished their
richest ornaments. In the North, geometric motives were especially prominent, and among these the zigzag was
particularly favored in Normandy (*d*
in Fig. 270), cut into the face of the
arch, or into the soffit, or both; the
"broken-stick" (*"bâtons-rompus"*), the
lozenge and dog-tooth or pyramid (*i*)
are also common. Byzantine influence
is discernible in the billet (*e,* Fig. 270),
and in the flat treatment of figure-re-
liefs in the tympanum as at Carrenac
(Figure 257). Imbrications (*g*),
checkers (*b*), "nail-heads," foliage-
forms and grotesques are also of fre-

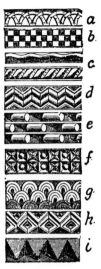

Fig. 270. Ro-
manesque Or-
naments.

quent occurrence. Figures 261, from St. Pierre at
Aulnay, and 258 from Rouen Cathedral (Porte St.
Jean) show the extraordinary richness of some of these
Romanesque doorways. The Rouen example belongs
to the early 13th century and is therefore early Gothic,
but it is still full of the spirit, and shows many of the
details, of the Romanesque.

Horizontal moldings receive but little emphasis in
French Romanesque ornament, and there are no distinctly typical horizontal moldings, except those of the
Attic bases of the columns already mentioned. Horizontal bands, however, are not uncommon, richly carved,
often with anthemions or palmettes (Fig. 271) which
betray the ever-present Byzantine influence. In place

FIG. 271. CARVED BANDS, FROM ST. AUBIN, ANGERS.

of the classic cornice the monastic builders had only the Lombard arcaded cornice, or the more elaborate corbel table. In minor positions the simplest copings with one or two moldings suffice.

Corbel Tables.

These may have originated in the classic modillion-cornice, or they may have been evolved out of the necessity of providing a projecting shelf at the top of the wall. In Provence (Southern France) the first is doubtless the correct explanation, as the corbel-table of the gable over the porch of St. Trophime at Arles has corbels carved with the acanthus in evident reminiscence of classic modillions. In Central and Northern France the corbels are usually grotesques of masks or monsters. In some cases they are found in conjunction with the Lombard arcaded cornice, particularly in Auvergne and in Southern France. *Corbels* for other purposes than the support of a corbel-table were of varied forms, often resembling capitals with a "drop" or "cul-de-lampe" at the bottom, formed either of foliage or of figures or grotesques.

Figure Sculpture.

It was during this period that the French began the development of that wonderful art of decorative sculpture which they carried to so marvelous a height of artistic beauty in the portal-sculptures of their Gothic cathedrals, at Chartres, Amiens and Reims. At first they were contented with reliefs in the portal tympanium (Figure 257) but free statues were later set in the deep jambs of the portals, representing saints and apostles and martyrs: this practice appears to have begun about

FIG. 272. FRENCH ROMANESQUE GROTESQUE.

the middle of the 12th century (Figure 260). Byzantine and classic influences and traditions dominate in the earlier sculpture (Plate XIV, 3, 5); but the French soon impressed upon all their sculpture, whether of statues, reliefs or grotesques, the stamp of their own original genius (Fig. 272; Plate XIV, 7). Both in technical execution and in appropriateness to its architectural setting, these later Romanesque sculptures mark the opening of a new chapter in decorative art.

Painted Decoration.

The scanty remains of the painted decoration in

French Romanesque churches indicate a prevailing simplicity, marked by effective composition with rather crude coloring and execution. The painted ornament was generally restricted to certain well-defined portions of the edifice, such as the apse and chapels. Wall surfaces were marked with conventional masonry joints or simple quarries, spangles or diapers in red ochre and black; sometimes the effect was varied by painted wall-arcades and representations of wall-draperies with conventional folds. Columns were striped or painted with chevrons or zigzags in red, dark green and yellow or gold, and the capitals were enriched in the same colors. Figure painting was rare; when employed it was strongly Byzantine in character, like the contemporary manuscript pictures, as at St. Cénéri, or Ste. Radégonde, Poitiers. Leaf-forms were sometimes used for borders and narrow bands.

Accessory Arts.

In iron-work, tiles and wood-carving the French monastic artists executed works of considerable merit, employing generally forms akin to the architectural ornament or else inspired from Byzantine models; but they

FIG. 273. LEAF PATTERN, TILE, ST. OMER.

by no means equaled the variety and richness of the Italian decorators. Figure 263 shows a door knocker of the 12th century, from a cast in the Trocadéro museum. At Limoges there was a flourishing school of workers in enamel by the *cham-*

plevé process. In this work, as in the other minor arts, the Byzantine influence is prominent. Fig. 273 is a characteristic leaf-detail from the red-and-brown tiling in the cathedral of St. Omer. The tile floors of chancels and chapels of the late Romanesque period were often of great elegance, in simple and effective patterns in buff, red, brown and black.

Books Recommended:

As before, Hübsch. Also: Baum: *Romanesque Architecture in France* (London, 1912).—Cahier and Martin: *Mélanges d'archéologie* (Paris, 1868).—Cattaneo: *L'Architecture en Italie* (Venice, 1890).—Courajod: *Leçons professées,* etc. (Paris, 1903).—Cummings: *A History of Architecture in Italy* (Boston, 1901).—De Dartein: *Etudes sur l'architecture lombarde* (Paris, 1882).—Dehio and Bezold: *Die Kirchliche Baukunst des Abendlandes* (Stuttgart, 1887–1901).—F. M. Hessemer: *Arabische und alt-italienische Bauverzierungen* (Berlin, 1842).—Lecoy de la Marche: *Les manuscrits et la miniature* (Paris, 1886).—E. Molinier: *L'Orfèvrerie civile et religieuse du Ve à la fin du X^esiècle* (Paris, 1899).—*Musée de sculpture comparée du Trocadéro* (Paris, no date).—F. Osten: *Bauwerke in der Lombardei* (Frankfort, n. d.).—H. Révoil: *Architecture romane du Midi de la France* (Paris, 1867).—Rohault de Fleury: *Les Monuments de Pise* (Paris, 1866).—E. E. Viollet-le-Duc: *Dictionnaire raisonné de l'architecture française,* etc. (Paris, 1868).

CHAPTER XV

II. ANGLO-NORMAN, GERMAN, SPANISH AND SCANDINAVIAN

Anglo-Norman Ornament.

Previous to the Norman conquest of England in 1066, the architecture of that country was of the crudest description, and, the ornament of the style, the so-called Saxon, was so rude and scanty as hardly to deserve mention. With the incoming of the new and foreign element, however, there began a remarkable development, both architectural and decorative; and, as is so often the case, the result of the blending was in some respects more brilliant than even the stronger of the parent styles. While the Norman (more properly "Anglo-Norman") architecture derived its chief inspiration from French Norman models, it rapidly diverged from them into a strongly national style in which carved decoration was very liberally employed. This Anglo-Norman ornament is remarkable for its vigor, variety and effectiveness. Its fundamental elements were comparatively few, and chiefly of French origin, but it was more abundant and varied in its details and applications.

Norman Columns.

The bases, of the Attic type, have spur-leaves sometimes but not always; the shafts are usually plain, but sometimes carved with zigzags, spiral flutings, or large quarry-patterns (as at Durham). The capitals are rarely of the Corinthianesque type (Fig. 274; Plate XV, 5), except in late instances under French influence. The prevailing type is the cubic or cushion type (Fig. 275); next the foliated or Corinthianesque, and the least frequent are the grotesque capitals. Sometimes two

FIG. 274. CAPITAL FROM LINCOLN CATHEDRAL.

FIG. 275. CAPITAL FROM ST. PETER'S, NORTHAMPTON.

types are combined side by side, as in Plate XV, 1. The abacus is heavy, molded, sometimes carved with saw-teeth, zigzags or other ornaments. The scalloped cushion type is also very common (Plate XV, 3). *Corbels* are either plain or grotesque.

Doorways, Arches and Moldings.

The doorways are often extremely rich, especially after 1130. The zigzag is the ornament most frequently used; it is carved on each of several arch-steps and sometimes carried down the jambs in lieu of nook-

FIG. 276. ORNAMENTS FROM IFFLEY CHURCH.

shafts, as at Iffley. Zigzags on the face and soffit of an arch are arrayed to produce alternate pyramids and lozenge-shaped holes; alternate zigzags are convex and concave in section. Saw-teeth, star-flavers, pyramid-jewels, moldings (Fig. 276). Round jewels or "nailheads" are applied in hollow moldings, and rosettes or flowers are not uncommon. Another characteristic ornament is the beak-head,—a grotesque bird's head with enormous beak, applied to the voussoirs of an arch, the beak pointed inwards, and sometimes spanning several moldings (Fig. 277). Grotesques occur in arch ornaments, but rarely. The billet-molding also occurs occasionally, but usually with round billets instead of square.

The effect of the crowded ornament of the Anglo-Norman doorways is often extremely rich,

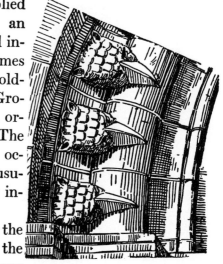

FIG. 277. BEAK-HEAD MOLDING, IFFLEY CHURCH.

the multiplied points of light on projecting details showing brilliantly against the dark shadows. Famous examples of such doorways are those of Iffley Church,
Barfreston Church and the Prior's Door of Ely Cathedral, and many others.

Arcatures are of frequent occurrence, usually with interlaced arches. These are found sometimes even on
the exterior, though more usually employed for interior
walls (Fig. 278).

Other Carved Ornament.

Free figure sculpture is almost unknown, but figures
in relief are sometimes seen, and grotesques, both human
and animal are very frequent. Foli-
age is rare, and when it occurs is
highly conventional and very simple.
The anthemion motive is not uncommon (Fig. 279); it is obviously of
Byzantine derivation by way of the
French Romanesque. Interlace is occasionally met with, probably due to
Celtic influence.

Fig. 278. Inter-
laced Arches.

Painted ornament appears to have been occasionally
used in the chancels and wooden roofs of churches, but
extant examples are very rare. That of the east end of
St. Cross Church, near Winchester, discovered late in the
last century and restored, shows simple conventional patterns in red ocher and black. The ceiling of Peterboro'
reproduces the painted lozenge-pattern of the original
which it replaces. That of Ely is also a modern decoration based on Norman precedents.

269

Fonts; Metalwork.

A few "Saxon" or pre-Norman fonts have been pre-

FIG. 279. CARVED ANGLO-NORMAN AN-
THEMIONS: FROM ST. SAVIOR'S, SOUTH-
WARK (ABOVE); HEREFORD CATHEDRAL (BE-
LOW).

served, all of crude workmanship, the more elaborate among them suggesting an effort to copy Byzantine details. The Norman fonts are of better workmanship, cut in stone or cast in lead, usually in the form of a square or round bowl on a short shaft (or several shafts) and base, and quite frequently adorned with figure subjects, poorly executed. The Byzantine influence is often evident in the Norman fonts, some of which resemble

FIG. 280. CELTIC MSS. INITIALS.

270

Venetian-Byzantine well-curbs. Metal work does not appear to have been carried to an advanced degree of perfection in this period. The celebrated bronze candlestick of Gloucester Cathedral is evidently of foreign, probably of Italian, workmanship. It is of an alloy of bronze and silver. (But see below.)

FIG. 281. CELTIC INTERLACES.

Celtic Ornament.

The artists in the Irish monasteries developed a remarkable skill in certain departments of decorative art, notably and foremost, in manuscript illumination; almost to an equal degree in ecclesiastical metalwork. Interlace of an extraordinary intricacy is a characteristic of their art in both fields. In this they display a close kinship of spirit with

FIG. 282. COVER OR SHRINE FOR ST. PATRICK'S BELL.

271

Scandinavian art, in which the representation of the Great Tree Yggdrasil, whose branches cover Earth, Heaven and the Underworld, are interlaced with the convolutions of the serpent or dragon Nithhoggr. Whether these interlaces originated in the North or were developed from Byzantine interlace it is difficult to decide. Fig. 280 illustrates various forms of Celtic interlace initials; Fig. 281 shows carved interlaces and the

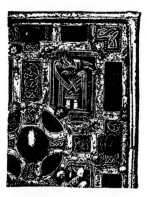

FIG. 283. ONE QUARTER OF COVER OF MOLAISE GOSPELS.

curious spiral ornament called the "trumpet pattern." Fig. 282 is the famous shrine or cover of the iron bell of St. Patrick, decorated with jewels and interlaced filigree of flat silver wires; while Fig. 283 shows one quarter of the *cumdach* or case made for the Molaise Gospels, of silver on bronze with jewels and the grotesque symbolic lion of St. Mark. This is dated about 1020. The bell shrine is later.

The Celtic crosses serving as grave stones—particularly the so-called "high crosses" present the best examples of Irish stone-carving. The cross-arms are connected by a circle, and the angles between them cut into by curved notches; the flat faces and often the sides of the stone are covered with patterns (rarely with figures as at Monasterboice) in low relief; the patterns show the characteristic interlaces, often very complex and elaborate. Such a cross is shown in Plate XV, 16.

ROMANESQUE ORNAMENT

German Romanesque Ornament.

In Germany, as in France and England, architectural decoration may be said to have its real beginning in the eleventh century, the earlier works being crude and almost bare of ornament. The architectural awakening began in Saxony, but its most brilliant and prolific

Fig. 284. Capitals from Gernrode.

achievements were in the Rhine provinces, where a truly splendid style of church architecture grew up in the 11th–13th centuries, in which the ornament is remarkable for its admirable propriety and its force and richness of design. It would be hard to find better capitals in any of the medieval styles than those of these Rhenish minsters, and the carving of grotesques fully equaled that in any other country. The decorative forms are all of foreign origin, French, Lombard and Byzantine, but combined with remarkable skill and wealth of fancy. The medium of transmission of these vari-

273

ous influences is complex; commerce, the interchange between Eastern and Western monasteries, the circulation of Byzantine and Irish manuscripts and Byzantine

 ivories and ecclesiastical work, and other causes, all united in giving form to the German Romanesque types. The Byzantine is the strongest influence in the details of the ornament; the acanthus-anthemion, jeweled bands and shallow surface carving are frequent (Plate XVI,

FIG. 285.   FROM WÜRTTEMBERG. 4, 5, 10, 12, 15). The German capitals vary from strongly Byzantine types to almost Gothic foliage. Thus the cap from Gernrode (Fig. 284) shows Byzantine massiveness with its impost-black and jeweled bands. Fig. 285 shows a capital on an octagonal shaft with molded abacus and a somewhat free and loose treatment of the Byzantine-Romanesque framed anthemion motive. The zigzag occurs occasionally, and grotesques abound, not only in capitals and corbels but also in shafts, bands and other places. The execution of most of the ornament is excellent.

The Lombard influence appears in the grotesques, though these often give evidence of independent German design, but also in such architectural features as the deeply-splayed doorways (Fig. 286, from Heilsbronn), the arcaded cornices, pilaster-strips and open arcades under the eaves of apses and sometimes of façades. At Rosheim, in Alsace, is a church-front of almost pure Italian or Lombard design. The arts of metal were practised with skill. Both wrought-iron and cast bronze were employed for grilles, gates, hanging lamps or crown-lights and for candela-

FIG. 286. PORTAL FROM HEILSBRONN.

bra and church vessels. Gold, silver and enamel were also employed for richer and finer products (of which an early example, perhaps of real Byzantine manufacture, at Aachen was illustrated in Fig. 238). Manuscript illumination reached a high pitch of development in the twelfth and thirteenth centuries, and stained glass in the thirteenth; the former following purely Byzantine models, the latter retaining its Romanesque character in the face of the growing Gothic influence. In all these arts Germany was influenced both from the West and the East, France, Italy and Byzantium contributing to the final result. Examples of some of these various phases of German art are illustrated in Plate XVI.

Spanish Romanesque Ornament.

The Spanish peninsula was the field of successive invasions, conquests and internal struggles through the

FIG. 287. TARRAGONA.   FIG. 288. TARRAGONA (?).

entire Middle Ages, and there was little chance for the development of any independent national style. The few great churches erected in the twelfth and thirteenth centuries show a dominant French influence (Zamorra, Avila, Tarragona, Salamanca, Barcelona, Compostella) ; and while the composition is vigorous and effective and the ornament well disposed, it presents no striking novelty of detail (Figs. 287 and 288 illustrate two

276

capitals which are thoroughly German in style). A remarkable characteristic of this style is its absolute freedom from Moorish details or influence, although the eleventh and twelfth centuries witnessed the culmination

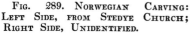

FIG. 289. NORWEGIAN CARVING: LEFT SIDE, FROM STEDYE CHURCH; RIGHT SIDE, UNIDENTIFIED.

FIG. 290. CHOIR SEAT, NORWEGIAN.

of that brilliant art. This exemption was doubtless due to the hostility between the Christians and Moslems.

Scandinavian Ornament.

The decorative art of the north of Europe, in the Scandinavian peninsula especially, took on a special character, the precise origin and relations of which to Byzantine art on the one hand and to Celtic art on the other, are still subjects of controversy. As in Celtic ornament, elaborate and complicated interlace is the dominant characteristic; and as in the Celtic manu-

277

FIG. 291. DETAILS OF CANDELABRUM,
MILAN CATHEDRAL.

scripts, the interlace is based largely on the convolutions of a dragon or serpent, Nithhoggr, with the branches of the great earth-covering . tree Yggdrasil. The most characteristic examples of this art are in the wood-carvings of doors and doorways of ancient churches, some dating from the eleventh or even the tenth century (Fig. 289). As these are of later date than many masterpieces of Irish manuscript ornament, some of which belong to the eighth and possibly to the seventh century, it seems likely that this Scandinavian art is, in part at least, rooted in Irish art, though this doubtless derived its first inspiration from Constantinople and Byzantine church fittings, ivories and Gospels. Fig. 290 shows a Norwegian chair (or rather stall from a choir) of perhaps the twelfth century, in which the character of the earlier art still appears.

Romanesque Metal Work.

It is difficult to assign precise national limits to some of the phases of metal work of the Romanesque period,

FIG. 292. DETAIL, CHANDELIER AT HILDESHEIM.

especially in the line of ecclesiastical gold and silver and silver-gilt copper. Some of this work found in Western churches was undoubtedly from the Constantinople workshops—*e.g.*, the famous Pala d'Oro or jeweled golden altarpiece of St. Mark's, Venice. The Byzantines taught the art to the artisans of Italy, France and Germany, and Figs. 291–293 illustrate some of the most famous examples of this work. Fig. 291 shows two details of the magnificent bronze candlestick in Milan Cathedral. A very similar candlestick, at least as to its base, is among the treasures of Reims Cathedral. Fig. 292 is from a bronze candlestick at Hildesheim. The fine chalice in Fig. 293 is a part of the treasure of a church at Bergen (Norway), and illustrates the use of filigree with jewels, which was a characteristic Byzantine form of the goldsmith's art. A very similar chalice is, or was, in the treasury of Reims Cathedral.

FIG. 293. GOLD CUP, BERGEN.

The architectural styles, thus grouped under the general name of Romanesque, gradually passed over into what are called the Gothic styles. The transition was not sudden, but the change though gradual, was a real one: not alone a change of details or of structural principles, but of spirit and character. The Gothic styles

ROMANESQUE ORNAMENT

expressed the new order which came in with the final establishment of settled institutions, religious, political and social, throughout all Western Christendom.

Books Recommended:

As before, DEHIO and BEZOLD, HÜBSCH. Also, BOND: *Introduction to English Church Architecture* (London, 1913); *Cathedrals of England and Wales* (London, 1912).—DAHLERUP, HOLM AND STORK: *Tegninger af aeldre Nordisk Architektur* (Stockholm).—FÖRSTER: *Denkmäler deutscher Baukunst* (Leipzig, 1855–69).—J. T. GILBERT: *Facsimiles of National Manuscripts of Ireland* (Dublin, 1871).—A. HARTEL: *Architectural Details and Ornaments of Church Buildings*, etc. (New York, 1904).—HASAK: *Die romanische und die gotische Baukunst* (Stuttgart, 1899).—T. KUTSCHMANN: *Romanesque Architecture and Ornament in Germany* (Text in German; New York, 1906).—C. MÖLLINGER: *Die deutsch-romanische Architektur* (Leipzig, 1891).—H. OTTE: *Geschichte der romanischen Baukunst in Deutschland* (Leipzig, 1874).—T. RICKMAN: *An Attempt to Discriminate the Styles*, etc. (London, 1817).—E. SHARPE: *Churches of the Nene Valley; Ornaments of the Transitional Period; The Seven Periods of English Architecture* (London, various dates).—E. SULLIVAN: *The Book of Kells* (New York, 1914).—W. R. TYMMS: *The History, Theory and Practice of Illuminating* (London, 1861).

For Spanish Romanesque, consult the fine work of LAMPEREZ Y ROMEA, *Historia de la arquitectura cristiana española*, etc., also the incomplete series entitled *Monumentos Arquitectonicos de España*, to be found in a few of the larger libraries.

CHAPTER XVI

GOTHIC ORNAMENT: STRUCTURAL

Gothic architecture was the result of the development which took place in the effort to solve the problem of constructing a vaulted cruciform church of stone, with a clearstory to light the central aisle or nave. All the special forms and details of this architecture are more or less directly incidental to this development: vault-ribbing, buttresses and pinnacles, clustered shafts, pointed arches, moldings and tracery, were all evolved in this process of working out the above problem. The greater part of the ornament of the medieval churches, chapels and even secular buildings, consisted of the adornment of these structural features. Whatever decoration was not structural, either in function or origin, was symbolic or pictorial. The sculpture and the stained glass of the great cathedrals constituted an illustrated Bible which even the most illiterate could in a measure understand.

This style-development took place first of all in France. Other countries borrowed from France both the general composition and the details of their Gothic architecture. England alone among them retained a large measure of independence, developing her own Gothic style freely along national lines from germs brought over from France, grafting upon the foreign plant their own original additions. Germany copied French models much more closely in some cases, while manifesting in others an originality verging on caprice. Spain and Portugal borrowed from all three, though mostly from France; Belgium was hardly more than a province of France in her architecture; while the Italians developed no truly Gothic style, but grafted Gothic decorative details, much altered, on structures in which the Gothic principles, both of construction and composition, were wholly ignored.

Periods.

It is convenient to divide the history of the style in all the above countries except Italy into three periods—those of development, culmination and decline, or Early,

Fig. 294. Gothic Capitals: *a*, Early French, from the Sainte Chapelle; *b*, 14th Century Cap from Transept of Notre Dame; *c*, Flamboyant, from North Spire of Chartres.

Developed, and Florid. These correspond to the so-called Early French, Rayonnant and Flamboyant phases of Gothic architecture in France, and the Lancet, Decorated and Perpendicular in England; these names being derived from the form and tracery of the windows.

In the English styles these phases belong roughly to the thirteenth, fourteenth and fifteenth centuries, respecttively: in France they appear from twenty to fifty years earlier: in Germany somewhat later. The ornament of the Early Period (in France 1160 to 1240 or 1250) is the simplest and most vigorous, the imitation of natural forms least literal. In the Developed Period design and execution are finer, ornament more profuse and more naturalistic, and window tracery (and in England vault-ribbing also) became more important elements in the decorative scheme. In the Florid Period the styles diverge considerably in the different countries, but in all, the ornament is more complex and often overloaded, and also often more thin, wiry and dry, technical cleverness

and minute detail taking the place of restraint and vigor of artistic design. The ornament oscillates between the extremes of realism and conventionalism. This sequence is illustrated in the three capitals of Fig. 294.

Structural Ornament.

Every important structural feature was either made ornamental in itself, like the clustered shafts, capitals, triforium-arcades, window-traceries, roof-balustrades and water-spouts; or adorned with carved adjuncts and de-

FIG. 295. DECORATIVE GABLE OVER A WINDOW, COLOGNE.

tails, like the crockets, finials, gablets and tabernacles of pinnacles and buttresses, or the foliage and flowers on enriched moldings (See Plate XVII). In the Developed and Florid Periods, by the operation of a never-failing law of decorative evolution, certain forms and features originally structural came to be used as pure ornament. Thus gables, originally used only at the ends of gabled roofs, came to be used as purely decorative features, adorned with surface or openwork tracery, over doors and windows where no such roofs existed (Fig. 295); in England the vaultribs, serving in earlier buildings as a framework upon which to build the fillings, became finally a mere patterning in relief on

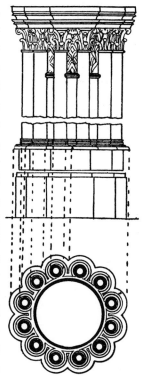

Fig. 296. Clustered Gothic Pier.

the vault-surface; in Germany the spire, at first a steep roof over a bell tower, became a gigantic ornament of open tracery and not a roof at all.[1]

Piers, Shafts and Columns.

Except in some of the earlier French and later Belgian and Dutch churches, all the piers were clustered,

[1] See pages 134, 135, and 137 *note* for other examples of this law of development, and comments upon it.

slender shafts being grouped around a central core, sometimes joined to it, sometimes quite separate. These shafts were usually circular, but sometimes pear-shaped, springing from bases at a common level, except in the later examples and carrying elaborate foliated capitals (Fig. 296). Sometimes, in England espe-

Fig. 297. Romanesque and Gothic Capitals; *a*, from Bayeux Cathedral, *b*, from St. Martin des Champs, Paris.

cially, the shafts are belted at intervals with molded bands. Vaulting shafts are often sprung from carved corbels high up, instead of bases on the ground, or set on the caps of the main piers. Gothic shafts are never carved, but are sometimes painted.

Capitals display a a great variety of designs, usually employing foliage as their chief adornment. The earlier French capitals generally recall the Corinthian type by their bell-shaped core, square abacus with the corners cut off, and volute-like corner crockets, but the abacus is always massive in proportion to the cap and shaft, and the development of the type from the Romanesque is evident (Fig. 297). Later capitals have the foliage more complex and more naturalistic in detail (Fig. 294 *b*); the abacus is octagonal or round; in England the plain molded bell-capital without foliage occurs frequently, and the Corinthian type is lost in the convex wreaths or bunches of foliage in the foliated caps. In the Florid Period capitals are often omitted, and when

FIG. 298. GOTHIC BASES: EARLY TYPE, FROM HALBERSTADT; LATE TYPE, FROM ROUEN.

used are often poor in design; they vary between extreme naturalism and capricious convention (Figure 294*c*).

Bases show a very interesting progressive development. The simple Attic type of the Romanesque styles survives for a while but first loses its corner spurs, then changes gradually, the plinth taking on a constantly increasing importance until it becomes a high pedestal, with the moldings above it much reduced and simplified. The lower torus also becomes higher and larger, assuming the later phases an ogee or pear-like profile. The corners of the plinth were cut off in many Romanesque bases; in the Gothic the plinth (*i.e.*, each member of a complex base) is almost always frankly an octagon or semi-octagon in plan (Fig. 298). In the later period of the style it is often in two stages, constituting a pedestal rather than a simple base.

Moldings.

The simple roll molding of the Romanesque styles is replaced by increasingly complex profiles, in which pear-shaped sections frequently alternate with deep hollows, producing effective contrasts of multiplied narrow lines of light and shadow. In the first two periods the pro-

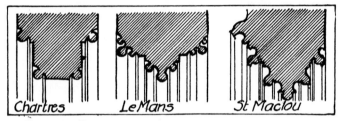

Fig. 299. French Pier-Arch Moldings of Three Periods.

files are sharp and vigorous, and in the pier-arches the grouping of rounds and hollows conforms more or less closely to the stepped profile of the arch-construction. In the Florid Period the steppings of the arch-section generally disappear in a generally splayed effect. The profiles in this period are less vigorous than in the preceding, the hollows being broad and shallow, the convex moldings smaller, and fine fillets are multiplied, giving at times a thin and wiry appearance to the grouped profiles (Fig. 299).

Enriched moldings are more frequent in English than in French work, though they occur in all the periods in France (especially in late work), England, Germany

288

and Spain. Convex moldings are rarely enriched, but the hollows between them are adorned with leaves, crockets, ball-flowers, and in early English work with pyramid-flowers or "dogtooth" ornaments. In place of a cornice or corbel-table, the wall (especially in France) was often crowned with a high, deep cavetto

FIG. 300. CORNICE-MOLDING, NOTRE DAME, PARIS.

filled with standing leaves (Fig. 300). In the Florid Period, the French sometimes filled the broad hollows between the finer members of a molding-group with exquisitely carved naturalistic vines. This treatment occurs in English examples (*e.g.* the portals of Southwell Chapter House) in the Decorated Period. In the following (Perpendicular) Period in England the hollows were more often enriched with widely spaced square rosettes.

FIG. 301. CARVED VAULT BOSS: FRENCH.

In both France and Germany moldings of different profiles were made to cross and intersect in work of the latest phase of the Gothic, the intricate cutting of their intersections giving occasion for that display of technical cleverness which characterizes that period.

Vaulting.

Gothic vaulting is based upon the principle of a framework of *ribs* supporting the *fillings* of masonry of small stones. The rib framework is simple in the early work of all countries, the only ornament being the moldings of the ribs and sometimes a carved keystone or boss at their intersections (Figure 301). In France this simplicity persists nearly to the end (Fig. 302). In

FIG. 302. VAULTING, APSIDAL CHAPEL, BEAUVAIS.

England the ribs were multiplied by the addition of *tiercerons* (Figure 303) and of subordinate connecting ribs or *liernes,* and combined into highly ornamental patterns ("star" and "net" vaults), with carved bosses at each intersection. This patterning developed finally into "fan vaulting," in which the ribs were purely decorative moldings cut in the stones of the inverted semiconoids of the vaulting (Figure 304, *b;* a sumptuously ornate form of stone ceiling, but without that

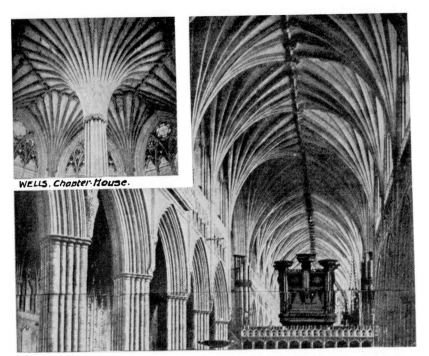

WELLS. Chapter·House.

EXETER CATHEDRAL.

LINCOLN CATHEDRAL; Half of Tower Vault

FIG. 303

FIG. 304A.—INTERIOR, WINCHESTER CATHEDRAL: LIERNE VAULTING

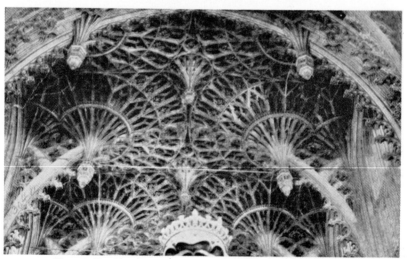

FIG. 304B.—FAN VAULT, HENRY VII'S CHAPEL, WESTMINSTER

clear expression of structure which marked the earlier vaulting.

In Germany and Spain the vault-ribs were, as early as the latter part of the Developed Period, built to fit predetermined conventional patterns, in which the lines were not always, as they always were in England, true plane curves. The builders in these two countries delighted in *tours-de-force,* displays of cleverness in creating and solving difficult problems of vault-rib construction; but the results are neither so rich nor so pleasing as in England.

Window Tracery.

This was one of the most decorative and characteristic features of Gothic architecture. Its development may be followed from the Romanesque coupling of windows under a discharging arch through successive stages in which the separating pier became a column or a slender chamfered or molded pier of cut stone, while the spandrel above was perforated with a circle; then treated like a thick plate of stone with decoratively cusped or foiled openings cut

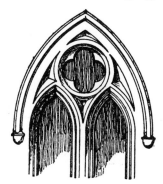

Fig. 305 *a.* Plate Tracery, Etton Church.

through it (*plate tracery* Fig. 305 *a*). Then the window was further divided into three, four, or more lights by slender molded or shafted mullions, and the space between their pointed-arched heads and the main window-arch filled with circles or geometric patterns of stone work, the interest of the design being now transferred from the shapes of the openings to the shapes of the stone work (*bar tracery,* Fig. 305 *b*). Towards the end of the middle Period the circular arcs and circles of this type of tracery (which was carried to the highest perfection in the great East and West windows of Eng-

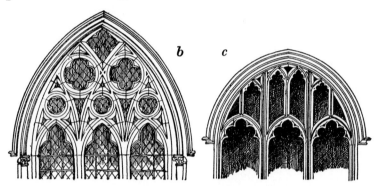

FIG. 305 *b*. BAR TRACERY, MEOPHAM CHURCH; *c*, PERPENDICULAR TRACERY, NORTHFLEET.

land and the great wheel-windows of France) reverse curves were introduced, giving a swaying movement to the lines. In France this is continued through the next period, giving it the name of Flamboyant from the flame-like forms of the very intricate tracery patterns used both in arched and circular windows. In England on the contrary there supervened, from about 1375, a rapid change, leading to the Perpendicular style of tracery; huge windows being filled with a very mechanical, though structurally excellent, system of vertical bars, sometimes crossed by transoms on small flattened arches (Fig. 305 c). In Germany there was less uniformity, but a general resemblance to the French flamboyant forms. These various developments are illustrated in Fig. 305 and Plate XXI.

Noticeable in all developed Gothic tracery is the introduction of *cusps,* separating or enclosing *foils,* also the branching of the moldings, so arranged that the main mullions and circles have a section composed of the aggregate of all the subordinate arch—or mullion—mold-

FIG. 306. VARIETIES OF CUSPS.

ings which came together in them. The several component groups of moldings are called *orders.* Cusps may consist of only the inmost molding widened into a point, or of a molding or complete order branching off so as to form a small triangular opening (Fig. 306). Sometimes one of the outer moldings of the arch of a door or window was pointed with cusps terminating in small finials (Plate XVII, 2, shows this treatment applied to a flying buttress-arch in Germany).

Wall and Gable Tracery.

During the course of the Developed Period the decorative richness of the window-tracery led to the repetition of like forms on certain wall-surfaces, upon which they formed ornamental panels framed in the lines of the

tracery in relief; a practice especially common in English Perpendicular and German Florid Gothic work, but found in all countries (see Plate XVII). In France it also became an increasingly frequent practice to erect over doorways and windows false gables—*i.e.*

FIG. 307. RAYONNANT GOTHIC BALUSTRADE.

tracery in relief; a practice especially common in English Perpendicular and German Florid Gothic work, but found in all countries (see Plate XVII). In France it also became an increasingly frequent practice to erect over doorways and windows false gables—*i.e.* gables having no roof behind them but employed as ornaments—filled with openwork tracery similar in character to that in the arched heads of the windows. Such gables were especially elegant in design in the Flamboyant churches of France (Figure 359).

Balustrades.

These were at first composed of small columns carrying round or pointed arches under the capstone or rail. Later the geometric forms of open tracery were applied,

FIG. 308. FLAMBOYANT FRENCH BALUSTRADE; CHÂTEAU OF JOSSELYN.

296

circles, triangles and quadrilaterals with closed or open cusps predominating. Such balustrades are used at the lower edges of roofs as well as for balconies, tower-parapets and (rarely) stairways (Fig. 307, Plate XVII, 14, 17). They became as complex as other features in the Florid Period (Fig. 308) especially in Germany, where they often formed veritable geometric puzzles.

Pinnacles, Crockets and Finials.

These are as characteristic of the Gothic styles as is the tracery. The buttresses—both the clearstory wall-buttresses and the outer buttresses external to the side-aisles—were commonly terminated by a tall slender pyramid, square or octagonal in plan, rising from gablets crowning two or four faces of the buttress-top, or from minor pinnacles at the corners (Plate XVII, 1, 2, 5). These pinnacles were adorned along the hips or edges with *crockets* (Plate XVII, 4)—outward-curling leaf-like or flame-like protuberances richly carved; —and terminated in a *finial,* composed usually of a central stem ending in a ball or bud and branching out below this into four or more crockets, forming a remarkably effective terminal flower or ornament (Plate XVII, 6, 11).

Crockets (Fig. 295) are also used to fret the salient edges of the saddleback copings of gables; along the hips of spires; as ornaments to the outer drip-moldings of arches, especially in the Florid Period; and (rarely) between the clustered shafts in doorways and triforiums. Finials, of like character with those on pinnacles, are the usual termination of the summits of gables, and of ogee-

A HISTORY OF ORNAMENT

arches in late Gothic design (Plate XVIII, 5). In early work the crockets, alike those of the finials and of gable-edges or spire-angles, invariably curl outwards,

a   b

FIG. 309. CROCKETS: a, EARLY FRENCH; b, FLAMBOYANT.

like the curled-up volutes of fern in the Spring (Fig. 309 a). Later they took on more elaborate foliage-forms with complex, wavy outlines, often in the last period of the style losing all decision and character in their mass and detail (Fig. 309 b).

FIG. 310. GOTHIC CRESTING.

Crestings of stone, of cast-lead, of terra-cotta were employed to decorate the ridges of most of the roofs, on which the covering was usually of lead, copper or slate. They were customarily of rather simple design, ending against finials of metal of a more elaborate sort (Fig. 310).

Tabernacles.

Not strictly structural in themselves, these were em-

FIG. 311.—TABERNACLE CANOPY, HOUSE OF JACQUES
COEUR, BOURGES

FIG. 312.—GARGOYLE, NOTRE DAME, PARIS

bellishments of structural features or parts, chiefly of buttresses and of the jambs of deep doorways. They consist of a niche or recessed arch to hold a statue, a corbel to support it, and a decorative gable or canopy over it, the canopy often running up into an elaborate spire. The decorative function of the whole was that of breaking up the bare mass of a vertical strip or buttress, or of a wall, or of the doorway jambs with a deep shadow and the brilliant lights of the statue, and to emphasize the vertical movement of the lines of the whole composition. The canopy was made increasingly elaborate as the style progressed, and in late examples was composed of a bewildering intricacy of minute arches, pinnacles and traceries, the whole forming an extraordinarily rich decoration (Figure 311).

Corbels were of frequent occurrence in all the Gothic styles, as supports for statues, for vaulting-ribs, for vaulting-shafts and for columns; they were not used, as in Romanesque buildings, to support a cornice or corbel-table. They were almost invariably carved with foliage, after the general fashion of the capitals, though sometimes in England made very long vertically (*e.g.* Lichfield Nave). Grotesque heads and human figures appear in the third period; they are rare in the two preceding. A late French corbel and crocket are shown in Plate XVIII, 13, 14.

Gargoyles.

Gothic eaves-spouts and those also which projected from the buttresses were invariably carved into the semblance of long-necked, vomiting monsters, called gargoyles (Plate XVII, 1). Remarkable skill was displayed in the composition and anatomy of these grotesque monsters. They are among the most striking examples of the decorative-symbolic treatment of purely utilitarian members (Figure 312).

Books Recommended:

As before, BOND, DEHIO AND BEZOLD, HARTEL, VIOLLET-LE-DUC. Also, G. L. ADAMS: *Recueil de sculptures gothiques* (Paris, 1856).—BAUDOT: *La Sculpture française au moyen-age et à la renaissance* (Paris, 1884).—ENLART: *Manuel d'archéologie française* (Paris, 1902).—A. L. FROTHINGHAM: *A History of Architecture*, vol. iii, iv (New York, 1915).—L. GONSE: *L'Art gothique* (Paris, n. d.).—HASAK: *Die romanische und die gotische Baukunst; Der Kirchenbau; Einzelheiten des Kirchenbaues* (Stuttgart, 1903).—A. HAUSER: *Stillehre der architektonischen Formen des Mittelalters* (Vienna, 1899).—K. A. HEIDELOFF: *Ornamentik des Mittelalters* (Nuremberg, 1838–55).—T. G. JACKSON: *Gothic Architecture* (London, 1915).—KLINGENBERG: *Die ornamentale Baukunst*, etc. (Leipzig, n. d.).—C. MARTIN: *L'Art gothique en France* (Paris, 1915).—C. MOORE: *Development and Character of Gothic Architecture* (New York, 1899).—NESFIELD: *Specimens of Mediæval Architecture* (London, 1862).—PARKER: *Introduction to Gothic Architecture; Glossary of Terms in Gothic Architecture; Companion to Glossary* (London, 1861–66).—A. N. W. PUGIN: *Glossary of Ecclesiastical Ornament and Costume* (London, 1868).—M. SCHMIDT: *Meisterwerke der dekorativen Sculptur, XI–XVI Jahrhundert* (Stuttgart, 1894–95. This is a German edition of the work listed after Chapter XIV under the title *Musée de Sculpture Comparée du Trocadéro*).—E. SCHMÜZER: *Gothische Ornamente* (Berlin, 1892).—G. G. UNGEWITTER (tr. by Monicke): *Gothic Model Book* (London, 1862); *Sammlung mittelalterlicher Ornamentik* (Leipzig, 1866).

CHAPTER XVII

Decorative Carving and Sculpture: Foliage.

The tradition of the classic acanthus and of its Byzantine modifications, clearly evident in all Romanesque carved foliage, gradually disappeared in Gothic art. In the second half of the 12th century the French carvers began to turn for inspiration and suggestion to the common vegetation about them, and developed an entirely new category of foliage-forms. This change was due to the formation of guilds of free or non-monastic masons and carvers who traveled from one site to another to ply their art, untrammeled by the monastic traditions. They were the counterpart in France of the *maestri comacini* of Italy, and their appearance was synchronous with the cathedral-building movement in France, to which was chiefly due the impulse toward progress and innovation which produced the Gothic style. As Viollet-le-Duc has pointed out,[1] these artists first conventionalized the simple forms of the earliest sprouting Spring herbage, thick and crisp, suggestive of the new life and energy of Nature. The crocket, descended no doubt from the Corinthian corner-volute, was carved like a thick flattened shoot bearing a globular bunch of uncurling leaves (Fig. 309). Like the Cor-

[1] Article "Sculpture" in "Dictionnaire raisonné" (vol. viii).

A HISTORY OF ORNAMENT

inthian volute, it was the dominant feature of capitals, as in Fig. 313; see also Plate XVIII, 1, 2, 3. The other leaves were massive and concave in modeling, and all the foliage was made to grow out of the capital

Fig. 313. Capital, St. Martin-des-Champs, Paris.

or other member which bore it (Fig. 314). As the carver's skill increased, the stiffness of the early conventionalism disappeared, and a beautiful type of foliage was evolved, still conventional and thoroughly architectural, but with grace and delicacy of detail, and varied by a closer study of particular plant-types (Plate XVIII, 1). This study led to an increasing naturalism, to a more and more realistic copying of more com-

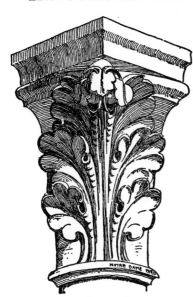

FIG. 314. CORNER LEAF FROM NOTRE DAME, PARIS.

plex and more mature leaf-types from shrubs and trees, and these were wreathed about the architecture instead of seeming to grow out of it (Figs. 294 *b* and 315). By the end of the 14th century this tendency was being carried to extremes, though with remarkable technical beauty of execution, and thereafter the design oscillates between dry conventionalism and excessively minute realism (Figs. 294 *c* and 316). In England the first stage of development is hardly at all represented. The crocket from Wells Cathedral (Fig. 317) is an exception in its resemblance to early French models. The early English capitals, crockets and corbels of the 13th century show instead an extraordinarily beautiful handling of minute curl-

FIG. 315. FRENCH RAYONNANT CAPITAL.

305

FIG. 316. CAPITALS, CHAPTER HOUSE OF
SOUTHWELL CATHEDRAL.

ing trefoils, often highly intricate and of marvelous execution (Fig. 318). The naturalistic stage is seen in
innumerable late thirteenth and early fourteenth century churches, in which, as in France, the flowers and

FIG. 317. CROCKET,
WELLS CATHEDRAL.

foliage are *applied* to the architecture
in wreaths and bunches, as in the remarkable doorways of Southwell
chapter-house (*cir.* 1294; Fig. 315).
Foliage is scanty in Perpendicular
work, and the mechanical form of the
Tudor rose (Fig. 319) is the most
characteristic floral adornment. In
Germany there is no systematic development of foliage design, though
there is much very beautiful foliage; it is, however, in
great measure copied or imitated from French models.

306

Figure Sculpture.

Figure sculpture applied to the decoration of buildings had become almost a lost art during the Dark Ages,

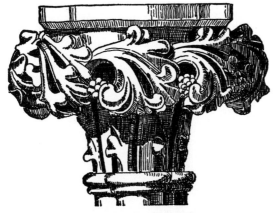

FIG. 318. CAPITAL, SALISBURY CATHEDRAL.

and the monastic builders of the eleventh century and the first half of the twelfth had only partially and sporadically renewed it. We have already seen, however, that in occasional instances the French sculptors had displayed great skill in such works as the porches of St. Trophime and St. Gilles at Arles (Plate XIV), and the west portal of Chartres (Figure 260), and the widespread use of grotesques had developed both technical and artistic ability in the use of the chisel.

In the cathedral and church architecture of the Gothic period—1160 to 1500—and particularly during

FIG. 319. TUDOR FLOWER.

307

the thirteenth and fourteenth centuries, the free development of art which succeeded the monastic period brought into being an entirely new phase of decorative figure-sculpture. The French cathedrals were people's churches quite as truly as bishops' churches, and their builders made them into picture-Bibles in stone. The portals were especially rich in plastic representations of saints and angels, kings, prophets and martyrs, and the

 figures were modeled with fine regard for their architectural setting. The deep jambs and the central door-pier were adorned with standing figures, often of heroic size, sometimes of great beauty. The great tympana over the doorways bore reliefs of Christ or the Virgin enthroned amid scenes of life of the Virgin,

FIG. 320. PART OF "GALLERY OF KINGS," AMIENS CATHEDRAL.

of the Last Judgment or equally solemn subjects (Figure 321). The cavernous arches were studded with concentric ranks of throned and adoring angels. An arcade high up on the façade was filled with figures of crowned kings of France or of Judea (Fig. 320), while from tabernacles on buttresses and rood-screens and transept-fronts angels and saints looked down upon the throngs below. The earlier sculpture is the most architectural in character: as the thirteenth century advanced the treatment was more realistic, with more of positive beauty of pose and feature (Figure 322) reaching its

FIG. 321.—TYM-
PANUM OF PORTE
DE LA VIERGE,
NOTRE DAME

FIG. 321

FIG. 32

FIG. 3

FIG. 322.—RELIEFS FROM PORTAL OF NOTRE DAME
FIG. 323.—TOMB OF ABBOT STEPHEN OF AUBAGINE

culmination in the "Beau Dieu" and other superb features of Reims (Plate XVIII, 10; Figure 323) though the transept porches of Chartres are perhaps, taken all together, the most magnificent examples in medieval art of the perfect balance between architecture and sculpture. The most notable Gothic sculptured portals in France are those of Chartres, Reims and Amiens; outside of France, those of Strassburg, Freiburg and Bâle. The later sculptures were excessively pictorial, small in scale and wonderful in their minute realism and delicate detail, as in the choir-screens of Amiens and Chartres.

Outside of France figure sculpture was far less abundant and less skilful: that of Lichfield and of Wells for instance, though decoratively effective, has only inferior merit as sculpture. The "Angel Choir" of Lincoln (Figure 362) is charming from both points of view, but is an exceptional work. It is in the porches and rood-screens of the fourteenth century that the best English figure-sculpture is found. The figure-sculpture of Germany is hardly of importance, except at Strassburg and Freiburg, and the marvelously minute and realistic figure-work of the fifteenth and early sixteenth centuries, especially in pulpits, screens and the like. That of Spain and of the Low Countries is relatively unimportant.

Minor Architecture.

Choir screens, stalls and thrones, pulpits, tombs (Figure 323), shrines, altars and fonts were designed with the fundamental features of monumental architecture, but with greater richness and greater freedom and minuteness of detail (Plate XVIII, 16). As the tendency toward minute ornamentation grew, through the fourteenth and fifteenth centuries, and as such minute decoration was better adapted for works of less monumental scale than for the churches themselves, these minor works became more and more the characteristic masterpieces of the stone-carver's art. The intricacy of the canopy-work with its bewildering network of arches, cusps and pinnacles is only equaled by the perfection and delicacy of the execution. Verbal descriptions can give little idea of the marvelous detail of some of these works, and even the illustrations fail to convey a complete impression to which the works themselves give rise. The most beautiful of these works are generally the French, though the Germans at times press them closely (see Figure 339), and some even of the French works, as the rood-screens at Bourg-en-Bresse and Alby, are attributed to German artists (Figure 325).

Wood-Carving.

Choir-stalls offered a specially rich field for the wood-carver's chisel. Each seat was provided with a high back usually terminating in a projecting canopy, which

in turn was finished with gablets, pinnacles and a high and complex spire. The arms separating the seats were richly carved, and the hinged seat, when folded back, dis-

FIG. 326. A MISERERE, BEVERLEY CATHEDRAL.

FIG. 324.—TYMPANUM, CENTRAL DOORS OF NOTRE DAME, PARIS:
THE LAST JUDGMENT

FIG. 325.—ROOD SCREEN, ALBY CATHEDRAL

closed a grotesque cor-
bel, called the "mise-
rere" (Fig. 326). In
the later Gothic the
choir stalls were extra-
ordinarily elaborate.
Other specimens of
wood carving are found
in the pew-ends of Eng-
lish churches, with
elaborate finials (Fig.
327); in the bosses and
hammer beams of Eng-
lish wooden ceilings
(see Fig. 374); in
chests and furniture for
the sacristy, and in the
details of half-timbered
houses in England,
France and Germany;
as well as in domestic
furniture (chests, ta-
bles and chairs), espe-
cially of the 15th and
16th centuries. The
details are all derived
from the contemporary
stone architecture and
carving, though modi-
fied to suit the material.

FIG. 327. PEW END, WINTHORPE
CHURCH.

Metal Work.

Iron was costly in the Middle Ages, and, except for clamps and *chainages,* and in Italy for tie-rods in the

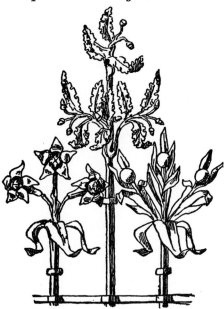

vaulting, was rarely used for primary construction. Its chief uses were for nails and bolts, for hinges and door-fittings, for gates and grilles, and for locks, latches, keys, armor and arms. Cast-iron was rarely employed, although a late Gothic example is shown in Plate XVIII, 17. The medieval wrought iron, especially of France, Italy, Germany and Flanders, shows marvelous skill in forging, decorative effects being produced by splitting, twisting, welding and riveting the bars by scroll-work, rosettes, and *repoussé* or hammered work in sheet metal (Fig. 328; Figures 329, 330).

FIG. 328. CRESTING OF IRON GRILLE, ST. SERNIN, TOULOUSE.

Lead was used for crestings and for covering spires and dormers. Bronze, brass, copper and silver were handled with skill in the movable furnishings of the church, candelabra, pyxes, monstrances, chalices, croziers, pastoral staves and the like. Enamel and jewels

FIG. 329.—IRON SCREEN, BOURGES CATHEDRAL

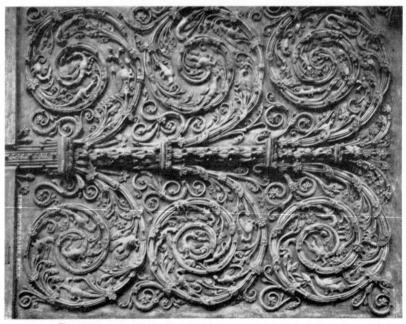

FIG. 330.—IRON FALSE HINGE (*Penture*); NOTRE DAME, PARIS

were employed to heighten the richness of these objects. The goldsmith's and silversmith's art derived most of its origins from Byzantine art, but departed rapidly from it and developed a style wholly Western and Gothic.

Textile Ornament.

The remains of medieval embroideries, laces and tapestries are not abundant. There was little richness of dress or textile furnishings except in ecclesiastical dress and among the few who were rich and powerful in Church and State, and to a remarkable extent the ecclesiastical robes and embroideries have disappeared, though they were undoubtedly often of great beauty and even magnificence. Those preserved to this day are mostly of the fifteenth century, except a respectable number of Spanish and Sicilian embroideries and silk damasks of the thirteenth to fifteenth centuries which show a strongly Oriental inspiration.

Tiles.

Fine pottery was an almost unknown art in western Europe in the Middle Ages except among the Mohammedans of Spain and Sicily. Ceramic tiles were, however, used in floors, especially about the altar in France,

Fig. 331. French Tile Patterns.

319

A HISTORY OF ORNAMENT

and examples of their simple but effective patterning are
seen in Fig. 331.

Manuscript Decoration.

This art, derived originally from Byzantine, elaborated in Ireland, England and France in the Roman-

FIG. 332. LATE GOTHIC MANUSCRIPT ORNAMENTS.

esque period, reached a very high state of perfection in
the fourteenth and fifteenth centuries, developing into
different schools of design in France, Flanders, England, Germany, Spain and Italy. Three different
classes of design are to be distinguished: pictorial decoration (the so-called miniatures), initials, and borders.
The first belongs to the art of painting, though it always displayed a highly decorative character; the other
two belong to the domain of pure ornament. They
drew largely upon the contemporary art of stained glass,

Fig. 335.—*a.* Jesse Window, Chartres
b. Upper Part of a Canopy Window, Cologne
c. Canopy Window, York

both for the color scheme and the details, but with much freer handling and frequent use'of foliage and of free abstract design in flourishes, scrolls and interlaces. Gold was used with fine effect though sparingly. The name of Jean Fouquet stands conspicuous in the brilliant French school of the late fifteenth century. The most notable production of the Flemish school was the Grimani Breviary, now in Venice; but every considerable collection of manuscripts possesses beautiful examples of the various schools in breviaries, books of hours, psalm-books, chant-books and secular works— chronicles, histories and editions of the classics. Fig.

FIG. 333. A FRENCH MEDALLION WINDOW.

A HISTORY OF ORNAMENT

332 illustrates a few details of this brilliant and fascinating phase of medieval design; other examples are shown in Plate XX.

Stained Glass.

Of all the arts allied to Gothic architecture, that of

FIG. 336. GERMAN GRISAILLE. ABOVE, FROM COLOGNE; BELOW, FROM ALTENBURG.

the stained glass windows is the most characteristic as a special product of the style. From timid beginnings in the Romanesque buildings [1] it developed rapidly as the size and splendor of the traceried windows increased. The depth and brilliancy of color attained by the glass-makers of the thirteenth century provided a new decorative resource for the church-builders and window-designers; a richness and intensity of blues, reds, yellows and greens rivaling the splendor of mosaic. The mechani-

[1] The Germans claim an active production of mosaic glass as early as 1000 A.D. at Tegernsee (Meyer, "Ornamentale Formenlehre").

324

cal imperfections of the early glass made it only the more sparkling, while the heavy leading employed gave a suitable foil to the glowing colors by its black lines which tended to harmonize as well as separate otherwise crude juxtapositions of color.

The early windows were arranged in medallions, each containing a picture in mosaic, as it were, made up of small units of color separated by the lines of the leading (Fig. 337). The spandrels between the medallions were filled with quarry-work or foliage in *grisaille* (lines of a semi-opaque brown pigment fused onto the glass at a comparatively low tem-

FIG. 337. LEADING OF AN EARLY FRENCH WINDOW: THE MARRIAGE AT CANA.

perature). A border of leaves or other conventional units framed the whole. A few such windows have come down from the 12th century (the earliest stained glass extant is at St. Denis, said to be of 1108), and they continued to be used through the greater part of the thirteenth century. "Jesse-tree" windows and medallion windows entirely composed of foliage, conventional ornament and grisaille were also common through this century (Fig. 335). The invention of the yellow stain (stannic oxide) led then to the making of "canopy" windows, with large figures standing under elaborate traceried canopies of yellow glass (Figures 335, from York Cathedral). Ribbons with inscriptions were increasingly used, the coloring was less pure and intense, the composition more involved, with much painted detail. With the 15th century there was a further decline in richness of color; much white or nearly transparent glass is used, and the treatment is more pictorial and less decorative. With the advent of the Renaissance the art in western Europe passed into eclipse, except for occasional artists in France, in Flanders and in Germany. In Italy, where windows had usually been of moderate size in medieval times, the art of decorative stained glass had not

FIG. 338. EARLY FRENCH FIGURE WINDOW: CHARTRES.

flourished; but with the Renaissance it received a sudden impulse, and some beautiful works were produced, by Ghiberti among the first. The most splendid medieval glass is to be found in France, Chartres Cathedral and the Sainte Chapelle being especially rich; the transepts of Notre Dame, Paris, and the clearstory of Tours Cathedral also supplying notable examples. Unhappily, the superb glass which was once the glory of Reims Cathedral has been completely destroyed by the German bombardment. In England the icono-

Fig. 339.—Detail from Pulpit, Strassburg
Cathedral

Fig. 340.—Church of St. Maclou, Rouen

clasm of the Puritans and the havoc of Wyatt in the early nineteenth century have left but scanty remains of the old glass. Canterbury and York possess fine glass and there are a few good pieces still left in Salisbury Cathedral. Very late examples are to be seen in King's College Chapel, Cambridge, and in St. Jacques at Liège. The best German glass is in the Cathedrals of Cologne, Altenburg and Strassburg (Fig. 336). Figs. 337 and 338 illustrate the leading of the early glass,—a most important element in the decorative effect of the window.

With the later years of the fifteenth century the Gothic style approached its extinction by the rapidly-spreading art of the Renaissance. But while it had reached the final limit of structural development, and architecture was sensibly declining, the arts of ornament were still at the highest point of richness and of technical perfection (Figures 339, 340). This splendor of minute decoration, of complex tracery, realistic pictorial sculpture, sumptuous embroidery and showy furniture was, however, the final coruscation of an expiring flame. The decorative details of the style long resisted the invasion of the Renaissance style from Italy, in France, England, Germany and Spain. But the new style was more than a fashion; it was but one symptom of a fundamental change of spirit of the artistic point of view, of civilization and ideals, and by the middle of the sixteenth century Gothic art had passed away.

A HISTORY OF ORNAMENT

Books Recommended:

As before, DEHIO AND BEZOLD, ENLART, GONSE, HASAK, MARTIN. Also, H. ADAMS: *Mont St. Michel and Chartres* (N. Y. and Boston, 1913).—DECLOUX AND DOURY: *La Sainte Chapel du palais* (Paris, 1865).—F. H. EGGERT: *Sammlung gothischer Verzierungen* (Munich, 1865).—E. HERDTL: *Flachenverzierungen des Mittelalters und der Renaissance* (Hannover, 1875).—A RACINET: *L'Ornement polychrome* (Paris, 1869–87).—J. ROSENTHAL: *L'Art du livre au Moyen-age et dans les temps modernes* (Munich, 1901).—H. SHAW: *Alphabets, Numerals and Devices of the Middle Ages* (London, 1845).—V. TEIRICH: *Eingelegte Marmor-Ornamente des Mittelalters und der Renaissance* (Vienna, 1875).—VIOLLET-LE-DUC: *Articles* "Peinture" and "Vitrail" in the *Dictionnaire raisonné*, etc., previously cited (Paris, 1868).—J. B. WARING: *Examples of Weaving and Embroidery* (London, 1880).

CHAPTER XVIII

PARTICULAR SCHOOLS OF GOTHIC ORNAMENT

I. FRENCH AND ENGLISH

In the general discussion of Gothic ornament in the last two chapters, while the chief attention was given to the developments in France, many references were made to the diverging practice of the English, German and Spanish schools. This chapter and the following will be devoted to a more detailed treatment of the several national styles or sub-styles of Gothic decorative art.

French Gothic Ornament.

The Gothic style in France may be considered as lasting from the beginning of Notre Dame at Paris in 1163, to the accession of Francis I in 1515. It is customary to divide this period into three divisions or periods, the Early French, from 1163 to 1250 or thereabout; the Rayonnant, 1250 to 1375, and the Flamboyant, 1375 to 1515. These are somewhat arbitrary divisions, as the progress from one stage and phase of development to another, whether in window-tracey, carving or stained glass, was continuous and gradual. Through all this development French Gothic ornament was marked by certain characteristics which distinguish it from the English and other national styles.

331

A HISTORY OF ORNAMENT

Carving.

The carving of *foliage* underwent a progressive development which has already been described (pp. 303–306),

FIG. 341. CARVED BAND, FRONT OF SENS CATHEDRAL.

from the simple and strongly conventional early type (Fig. 341), to the highly naturalistic and detailed foliage of the Rayonnant period, and thence through the decline of the Flamboyant. But in all these stages it was marked by a vigor of design, a crispness of execution, and a strongly architectural character hardly equaled elsewhere.

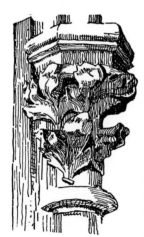

FIG. 342. CAPITAL FROM SAINTE CHAPELLE.

Capitals were tall and bell-shaped at first, with high square or octagonal abaci (Figs. 297, 313, 342; Plate XVIII, 1, 2, 3); later the foliage, which in the earlier stages of the style seemed to grow out of the shaft and was strongly

332

Fig. 351.—Detail from Choir Screen, Amiens Cathedral

Fig. 350.—Grotesque, Chartres Cathedral

conventional, was made more naturalistic and applied to or wreathed around the bell in less organic fashion, as in the splendid caps of the nave-piers of the Cathedral of Reims

FIG. 343. DETAIL FROM CORNICE, NOTRE DAME, PARIS.

(Plate XVIII, 7). In the Flamboyant period capitals are often dispensed with altogether between the piers and pier-arches.

Moldings.

Until that period foliage was occasionally employed in the hollows of moldings, especially in cornices formed by rows of standing leaves or crockets occupying the

FIG. 344. CORNICE MOLDING, FROM NORREY.

high hollow or cavetto between convex moldings above and below (Figs. 343–346). In the series shown in these figures we may trace the progress of the treatment from conventional through naturalistic carving to the weaker conventionalism of the later Gothic. In the Flamboyant period elaborate vines were carved in highly

FIG. 345. OAK LEAF MOLDING, SAINTE CHAPELLE, PARIS.

naturalistic fashion in the hollow moldings, as in the example from the porch of Troyes Cathedral in Plate XVIII, 15. A more conventional rendering of foliage is seen in the example from St. Urbain at Troyes in the

FIG. 346. LATE GOTHIC MOLDING, CHOIR ENCLOSURE, NOTRE DAME, PARIS.

same Plate, No. 18. Foliage was throughout all these periods employed with admirable effect in crockets, finials, vaulting-bosses and the like (Fig. 347). Surface-carving is seldom employed. The *rinceau* survives in early work in occasional pilaster-like vertical bands and horizontal lintels (Fig. 348), but passes out of use very early in the thirteenth century.

FIG. 347. BOSS FROM VAULT OF SAINTE CHAPELLE.

Figure Sculpture.

FIG. 348. CARVED VERTICAL RINCEAU, NOTRE DAME, PARIS.

The free figure-sculpture of the great portals of cathedrals has already been alluded to (page 307). The throned angels in the portal arches, the standing figures of apostles, martyrs and saints in the deep jambs (Figure 352), the reliefs on the pedestal courses of the jambs (Fig. 349) constitute a combination of deeply significant and artistically appropriate sculpture never elsewhere equaled, before or since (see

337

ante, page 308 and Figure 323; also Figs. 320, 349).
Grotesques often mingle effectively with carved
foliage, as in Figure 350 from Chartres Cathedral.
Very striking and nobly decorative also are the
colossal angels standing in the pinnacled tabernacles

surmounting the but-
tresses of Reims Cathe-
dral.

The culmination of
minute realism, alike in
statues and reliefs,
came in the fifteenth
and early sixteenth
centuries, in choir-en-
closures like those in
Amiens Cathedral
(Figure 351) and
Chartres, and in choir-
screens and tombs, as

FIG. 349. RELIEFS FROM BASE OF
PORTAL, NOTRE DAME.

in the famous examples in the Brou church at Bourg-
en-Bresse. In no other country did figure-sculpture
play so important a part in the decorative system.
Equally appropriate and decorative with these architectural sculptures was the minor decorative figure-
work in wood and ivory, as evidenced, for example, in
the beautiful ivory triptych from the Municipal Library
of Amiens, of which Figure 353 illustrates the central
panel.

Tracery.

In the Early French period the tracery was at first

Fig. 352.—Two Figures from
Portal, Amiens Cathedral

Fig. 353.—Ivory Triptych, in Amiens Library
French, XVth Century

extremely simple. The Cathedral of Chartres shows the finest examples of plate tracery in its western rose window (Fig. 354) and the tops of the clearstory windows of the nave. In the windows of St. Denis, Notre Dame at Paris, Reims and the nave of Amiens we have the simpler types of bar-tracery (1225–1240; Fig. 355). In the Sainte Chapelle at Paris, the choir of

Fig. 354. Half of West Rose, Chartres.

Amiens and the external chapels of Notre Dame at Paris, bar-tracery takes on a greater geometrical elaboration; very possibly under the influence of English examples (see page 360); and throughout the

Fig. 355. Early Tracery, Reims Cathedral.

Rayonnant period, both in the splendid rose windows of the transepts, as in those of Notre Dame and of Reims (Plate XVIII, 9), and in the side windows, especially of the clearstories, there is a great variety of rich geometrical patterning. While the English during the thirteenth and early fourteenth centuries unquestionably surpassed the French in the richness and variety of their bar-tracery, the French rose windows of the same period are un-

341

equaled elsewhere in their kind; and it is they that give the name Rayonnant (= radiating) to the period, on account of their radiating or wheel-like design. The illustration in Plate XVIII, 12, from the fine model of a portion of the church of St. Urbain, Troyes (about 1260), in the Trocadéro Museum, Paris, shows the more slender and open type of the French geometric bar-tracery of the thirteenth century which developed out of the simpler early types.

Cusping is an important element in these designs (Plate XVII, 10, 15; Plate XVIII, 5, 9, 12), both the closed and the open cusp being employed. An unusual treatment is the cusped fringe on the intrados of the outer arch in the portals of Amiens (about 1280).

As the style developed, tracery-design became more and more important as mere ornament, in openwork gables and tracery cut in relief on solid walls as a mere surface decoration. Plate XVII, 10, shows a detail from the transept of the Cathedral of Meaux; *ib.* 15, a detail from the south transept of Notre Dame, Paris, showing a bit of the great rose window and the wall-tracery on the spandrel. *Balustrades,* which in the first period were hardly more than rows of colonnettes or narrow arches supporting a rail (Plate XVII, 14, 17), were in the two following periods composed of openwork tracery of great beauty (see *ante,* Figs. 307, 308).

Flamboyant Tracery.

By the middle of the fourteenth century the increasing taste for minute and fanciful decorative detail began

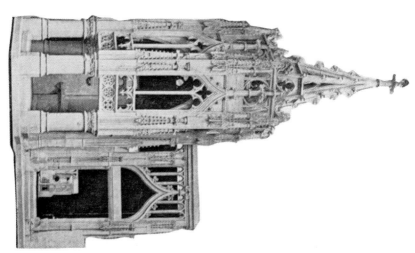

FIG. 356.—LANTERNE DES MORTS, AVIOTH, BRITTANY

FIG. 357.—FLAMBOYANT DETAIL, CHURCH OF ST. JACQUES, REIMS

to affect the design of window-tracery, by the substitution of flowing and waving lines for the simpler geometric combinations of circles, pointed arches and cusps which had hitherto satisfied all requirements for over a century. The "ogee" arch was substituted for the arch formed by simple circular arcs, and the flame-like forms which result from dividing a circle through the center by a wave-line, became almost the dominant motive in the tracery-design. The resulting style of design, though less logical structurally than the earlier geometric types of tracery, was more flexible and capable of a greater variety of combinations. It dominated the entire architecture of France from 1375 to 1515, and covered the exteriors of churches with an extraordinary wealth of traceries, both of openwork and of blind or wall-tracery (Figures 340, 356, 357; Figs. 358, 359). It was especially effective in the rose windows, as in the front of St. Ouen, Rouen, the fronts of Rouen Cathedral, the Sainte Chapelle, Paris, Tours, Amiens, and Reims Cathedrals, and the transepts of Beauvais. In several cases these Flamboyant roses were inserted in earlier façades (Amiens, Sainte Chapelle). The front of Rouen Cathedral, long unfinished, but completed within recent years, is the most elaborate and splendid example of this Flamboyant design; next to it stands the exquisite little church of St. Maclou at Rouen; while the north spire of Chartres Cathedral, and the charming little church at Louviers (Figure 359), are others among many examples of the marvelous richness and delicacy of which the style was capable.

The origin of this change in tracery design is generally now ascribed to English influence. A considerable part of northern France was in English hands in the fourteenth century, and (as will be later shown) the English had before the middle of that century developed their "flowing" or "curvilinear" tracery. While they soon exchanged this for the more rigid "Perpendicular" tracery, the French developed the suggestion of the wavy line to its utmost possible results of decorative splendor.

Stained Glass.

The development of the art of stained glass was so closely associated with the progress of Gothic architecture that Fergusson, in his "History of Architecture," claims it as the one exclusively distinguishing feature of the Gothic style, which might properly be called "the stained glass style." The Romanesque churches, with their thick walls and small windows, offered little scope or suggestion for pictured windows. The Gothic style, with its concentrated supports and gradual reduction of wall areas, developed a progressive increase in the size and loftiness of its windows, and this progress stimulated the art of pictured and decorative glass by giving it greater opportunities. Indeed, the larger the window, the more necessary became colored glass to reduce the excessive glare; while the more splendid the glass and the deeper and richer its tone, the greater was the tendency to enlarge the windows. The structural progress of the French Gothic style was thus closely associated with the progress of window decoration by colored glass. While the French led in this, as in so many other branches of decorative art, and while more

FIG. 358.—RAYONNANT TRACERY, CARVED, ON A CHURCH DOOR

FIG. 359.—FLAMBOYANT TRACERY, CHURCH OF ST. PIERRE, LOUVIERS

fine glass has survived in France than in any other country (see *ante,* page 326), there was at the same time less fundamental difference in style between the French and other national schools than one might perhaps expect. Figure design, in all three periods, was more nearly universal than either in England or Germany, and the colors were generally—at least in the first period—deeper and richer. In purely decorative effect it may be doubted whether any later glass ever equaled the three lancet windows and the western rose of Chartres Cathedral, the earliest of these dating from the end of the 12th century.[1] It is to be noted that in the borders and decorative details of the early Gothic windows Romanesque forms are persistent, as also in the illumination of manuscripts. See Figs. 334, 337, 338; Figure 335; and Plate XIX.

Painted Decoration.

As in the Romanesque period, it is probable that wall-painting in France was confined to the chapels and to a few important spaces in the general design. Possibly all the capitals and chief moldings may also have been picked out with bright color in the hollows and gilding on the projecting fillets. We know that most of the figure-sculpture was painted, and vestiges of the original color decoration can still be detected in some cases. The vault-fillings were in many cases not painted, their careful jointing showing that they were not meant to be plastered. There were, however, exceptions to this rule,

---

[1] See the admirable account of these windows in Henry Adams' "Mont St. Michel and Chartres," published for the American Institute of Architects, Boston, 1913.

and it is likely that not a few were painted blue with gilt stars. From vestiges of the original painting discovered in the Sainte Chapelle at Paris a complete interior decoration in color was carried out in that chapel about 1860. The result is gorgeous, but the opaque colors of the brilliantly painted walls suffer under the glare of transmitted color through the windows, and this

a   *c*

b

Fig. 360. Early English Carving. *a*, from Church at Stone, Kent; *b*, Lincoln Cathedral; *c*, Ely Cathedral.

probably explains why interior coloration was not more general after the 12th century. The essays in color-decoration by Viollet-le-Duc in the chapels of Notre Dame are far less brilliant, but also less interesting.

In conclusion, it should be noted that the French handling of decorative detail of all kinds was in general more logical, more strictly architectural, than in other countries, with the possible exception of England. Elegance and propriety of design are combined in an eminent degree in nearly all French Gothic ornament.

350

FIG. 361.—EARLY ENGLISH CAPITALS, FROM CASTS IN METROPOLITAN MUSEUM, NEW YORK

FIG. 362.—DETAIL OF ANGEL CHOIR, LINCOLN CATHEDRAL

English Gothic Ornament.

The English work of the first two periods, as compared with the French, shows a general predominance of decorative over structural conceptions, but without sacrifice of structural propriety. It displays less of severe logic, but often more of charm; less vigor, but often greater delicacy and richness. English cathedral interiors, while far less lofty and majestic than the French, are generally more ornate, richer in the play of light and shade, often more beautiful. All the details are on a

FIG. 363. DECORATED CAPITAL: BEVERLEY CATHEDRAL.

smaller scale, and remarkable effects are produced by multiplied repetition. The moldings are finer and more numerous, the shaft-clusterings more complex, the carved ornament more varied and abundant (Plate XX, 1–; Figures 362, 363, 364). On the other hand, the exteriors were far less ornate than the French; the figure-

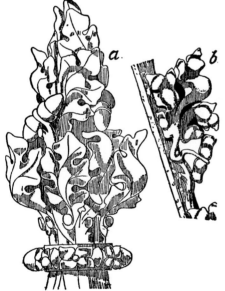

FIG. 364. a, FINIAL, WELLS CHAPTER HOUSE. b, CROCKET, BEVERLEY.

353

sculpture was greatly inferior, both in amount and quality.

Carving.

Its variety is equaled by its richness, in the first two periods, *cir,* 1200–1375. The foliage was at first of minute trilobes, perhaps of the *herba sacra* or water-arum, with globular leaflets beautifully curled and deeply undercut in dense clusters in capitals, corbels, crockets, hollow

FIG. 365. ENGLISH MOLDING ENRICHMENTS.

FIG. 366. SPANDREL, CHURCH AT STONE, KENT.

354

moldings and spandrels, the leaves growing, as it were,
out of the shafts or moldings (Fig. 360; Figure 361).
Later the foliage became highly naturalistic, wreathed

FIG. 367. ABOVE, TRIFORIUM, WESTMINSTER ABBEY; BELOW, DETAIL OF
DIAPERING OF MAIN ARCADE.

in bunches about the capitals (Fig. 363; also *ante* Fig.
316), or forming vines in the arch-moldings of doorways, as in that of the chapter-house of Southwell or
those of Lichfield Cathedral. The oak and maple occur most frequently (Fig. 364 *a*); later sea-weed and

other intricate forms appear (Fig. 364 *b*); and finally there appears a mingling of highly conventional forms with naturalistic vines and flowers. The hollows of moldings are studded with leaves, dogtooth ornaments and ball-flowers, or filled with running vines (Fig. 365), until about 1350, after which molding-enrichments became more rare. Surface carving in panels and on arch-spandrels is much more frequent than in

FIG. 368. PART OF WOODEN SCREEN, MANCHESTER CATHEDRAL.

France (Fig. 366). Diaper patterns occur on flat surfaces, especially spandrels of arcades, as in the nave of Westminster Abbey (Fig. 367).

English figure-sculpture is decidedly inferior to the French; there is nothing like the stupendous porches of the French cathedrals with their wealth of statues and reliefs. The west front of Wells Cathedral is the only example of an English west front adorned profusely with sculpture, and but little remains of the original figures there. Some of the late porches, however, erected in the fourteenth and fifteenth centuries, are

FIG. 368 A. "CURVILINEAR" PANELS IN WOOD.

richly adorned with figures in niches, as at Exeter and Canterbury. Very rich in fig-ure-sculpture were also some of the great 15th-century reredoses of English cathed-rals, as those of Winchester, St. Saviour's at Southwark (cathedral), and some others. Mention has already been made in Chapter XVII of the "Angel Choir" of Lincoln, il-lustrated as to its sculptured triforium-spandrels in Fig-ure 362.

Woodwork of all sorts the English excelled in, especially in the 14th and 15th centuries.

FIG. 369. "POPPY HEAD."

Fig. 370. Plate Tracery, Lillington, Northants.

The wooden choir-screens, choir-stalls, pew-ends, font-covers and the like, were often of great beauty (see *ante,* Fig. 327), with elaborate surface-tracery, canopy-work, and carved grotesques. Very characteristic are the "poppy-head" finials to the pew-ends.

Fig. 368 illustrates part of a carved wooden screen, of which there are many in English parish churches; Fig. 368A, 14th-century surface-paneling in wood; Fig. 369 a poppy-head finial. But the greatest glory in the later woodworkers was the oaken ceilings of halls and churches; these will be discussed later.

Moldings were generally richer, more minute and more varied than the French, more subtile in profile, and more often enriched, as already explained Fig. 365). The English composed their groups of Gothic moldings so as to produce successions of deep undercut hollows contrasting with boldly projecting roll-moldings or bowtels. There was continuous increase in richness and complexity until 1350, after which there is observable a

Fig. 371. East Window, Raunds, Northants.

falling-off in vigor and effectiveness: the hollows are flatter and broader, the rolls and bowtels less vigorous in their contrast with the hollows.   The *bowtel*—a roll-molding with a slightly salient lip or fillet, giving it an almost pear-shaped section—is peculiar to English archi-

FIG. 372. FLOWING OR "CURVILINEAR" TRACERY; *a*, ITHLINGBORO', NORTHANTS; *b*, OVER, CAMBRIDGESHIRE; *c*, LITTLE ADDINGTON, NORTHANTS.

tecture. Another noticeable English feature is the *label* or drip-molding over the pier-arches in church interiors, as well as over exterior arches, doors and windows; the French confined this feature wholly to exteriors.   The English never affected the intricate intersecting moldings of late French and German Gothic art.

Tracery.

In this the English equaled and even surpassed the French architects. There is a more systematic and logical progression from lancet-windows coupled or grouped under a discharging arch (Plate XX, 6), through the stages of plate or perforated tracery (*ib.* 7 and Fig. 370); of molded tracery in the window-head

springing from mullions of slender clustered shafts (8), to the perfection of "Decorated" bar-tracery, with two or three "orders" of moldings and open cusping (9). The "Decorated" period is generally considered to last till the "Perpendicular" period, *i.e.* to about 1375. But the Geometric style of tracery, composed chiefly of circles or wheels and pointed arches, began as early as 1320 or earlier to give way to flowing lines, as in an early example at Wells. This ushered in what is called the

FIG. 373. PERPENDICULAR TRACERY, BEAUCHAMP CHAPEL, WARWICK.

Curvilinear style of tracery, which has already been mentioned as the probable prototype and parent of the French Flamboyant style of tracery. Examples of Flowing or Curvilinear tracery are in Plate XXI, 10, and in Fig. 372. This phase of tracery design was of short duration in England. Instead of developing, as in France, into a style of ornate fantasies, it gave way, somewhat suddenly, to the mechanical rigidity of the

SCHOOLS OF GOTHIC ORNAMENT

Perpendicular style (Plate XXI, 11, and Fig. 373). This last was structurally the most correct form of tracery, though decoratively inferior to the two preceding stages. Thus English tracery passed from a structural origin through a decorative development, to a structural culmination and decline; while in France the progress was throughout to the end in the direction of a purely decorative evolution.

Round windows were less important in England than in France. The transepts of Lincoln show an early "plate" circular window (the "Dean's eye"), and a late curvilinear rose, called "the Bishop's eye." The transept roses of Westminster Abbey (Plate XXI, 13) are almost French in character. The English preferred vast East and West windows to the round windows of France, and made of them sometimes superb compositions, unequaled in their kind elsewhere, as were the French rose windows in theirs. Tracery was carried across wall surfaces to form rich paneling, especially in the Perpendicular period. Openwork gables and balustrades are not important.

Vaults and Ceilings.

In these the English developed phases of art wholly their own. Skilled in shipbuilding and framed structures, they simplified the problem of vault-construction by multiplying the ribs, thus breaking up the twisted surfaces of the fillings into long narrow triangles easy to handle. These additional ribs were called *tiercerons* (Figure 303); they terminated in a horizontal ridge-rib at the summit of the vault. Later, short bridging ribs, called *liernes* were added to the system, forming complex patterns ("star" and "net" vaults), as in Winchester, Norwich, Canterbury Cathedrals, Gloucester choir and Lady-chapel, and many other examples (Figure 304 *a*).

FIG. 374. HAMMER BEAM ROOF, TRUNCH CHURCH.

The decorative idea thenceforth predominated; the tiercerons being given the same curvature throughout, generated surfaces of revolution like inverted semi-conoids of concave profile, their bases meeting at the top, leaving lozenge-shaped voids which were filled up by various decorative devices. The ribs, no longer structural, were simply carved in relief on the conoids, and the whole vault was covered with a patterning of these fine decorative ribs and adorned with rosettes and often long pendants (retro-choir of Peterboro; cloisters of Gloucester; King's College Chapel, Henry VII's chapel at Westminster, etc.). The decorative splendor of the

FIG. 374 A. OPEN-TIMBER CEILING, LAVENHAM CHURCH, SUFFOLK.

English vaulting is of the highest order, and nothing equal to these vaults is found in any other school of Gothic design (Figure 30 *b*).

No less remarkable are the superb oaken ceilings borne on huge arched trusses, of which the highest development is the *hammer-beam* type as illustrated in the

363

roof of Westminster Hall (1395–1525). All the details of these roofs were rich and appropriate to the material, and the ends of the horizontal hammer-beams were frequently adorned with carved heads or sculptured angels, while the glow of discreetly-used color and gilding added to the effect (Figs. 374, 374 A).

The English *stained glass* differed from the French less in fundamental character than in detailed treatment. The English windows were generally lighter in tone than the French, at least after the earliest period when it is likely that there was a strong French influence. The English developed to great splendor the "canopy" window, in which each "light" or vertical division is occupied by a life-size figure of a saint, prince or noble, under a canopy of splendid architecture executed usually in yellow glass, as if to represent gold. An example is illustrated in Figure 335, from York Cathedral.

Unhappily the destruction of "idolatrous" glass by the Puritans and by various "restorers," beginning with Wyatt in the early nineteenth century, has left but little of the old glass to our day, at least compared with the wealth of France in such glass. Some of the finest examples are in Canterbury Cathedral.

Painting.

As in France, but little painted decoration remains from the Middle Ages in England, except in moldings and minor details: but there is no doubt that polychrome decoration was almost universal. A few examples of such decoration are shown in Plate XX.

SCHOOLS OF GOTHIC ORNAMENT

Books Recommended:

As before, DEHIO AND BEZOLD, FROTHINGHAM, MOORE, PARKER, SIMPSON. Also for English Gothic, *Architectural Association Sketch Book* (London).—ATKINSON AND ATKINSON: *Gothic Ornaments selected from various Cathedrals and Churches in England* (London, 1829).—F. BOND: *Gothic Architecture in England; Cathedrals of England and Wales; Wood Carvings in English Churches; Fonts and Font Covers; Screens and Galleries in English Churches; Westminster Abbey; Introduction to English Church Architecture* (Oxford and London, 1905–1913).—BRANDON: *Analysis of Gothic Architecture* (London, 1849); *Open Timber Roofs of the Middle Ages* (London, 1849).—T. T. BURY: *Remains of Ecclesiastical Woodwork* (London, 1847).—J. K. COLLING: *English Mediæval Foliage; Details of Gothic Architecture; Gothic Ornaments* (London, 1848–1856).—E. A. FREEMAN: *An Essay on the Origin and Development of Window Tracery in England* (London, n. d.).—C. MOORE: *The Mediæval Church Architecture of England* (New York, 1912).—PALEY: *A Manual of Gothic Mouldings* (London, 1845).—T. RICKMAN: *An Attempt to Discriminate the Styles* (London, 1817).—E. SHARPE: *Mouldings of the Six Periods; Treatise on the Rise and Progress of Window Tracery in England* (London, 1871).—*Spring Gardens Association Sketch Book* (London).—Consult also monographs on particular churches and cathedrals.

CHAPTER XIX

II. German, Spanish, Italian

German Gothic Ornament.

Cleverness of technical execution and a tendency towards displays of skill rather than purity of design mark the German Gothic work. There is much borrowing from French models and Cologne, the greatest of all Gothic cathedrals, is clearly modeled after Amiens and Beauvais. Most of the German Gothic details of the first two periods are based on French types. In the naturalistic rendering of the leaves of the oak, maple, vine, etc., the German cleverness of technic found free scope, and in the 14th century began to show independence of French models. There is abundant use of the grotesque, in which a very Germanic broad humor often takes the place of the French artistic refinement.

The *moldings* generally resemble the French. In the Florid period intricate intersections of moldings of different profiles seem to have given special delight to the German stone-cutters and wood-carvers because of the technical difficulty of their execution (Figures 339,[1] 375, 381).

[1] It is difficult to distinguish between some of the French, German and Flemish work of the late Gothic period. The Strassburg pulpit may be either a French or a German work.

366

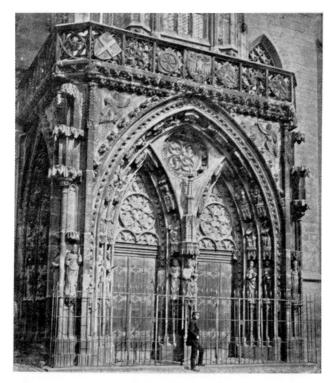

Fig. 375.—Porch of Church of St. Lawrence, Nuremberg

Fig. 383.—Vaulting, Cathedral of Salamanca

Fig. 377.—Freiburg Cathedral, from S. E.

Fig. 376.—Side Portal, Freiburg Cathedral

Tracery.

It was in this the German love of intricate and fantastic design and clever workmanship achieved its highest successes. Such windows as those of Cologne, St. Catherine at Oppenheim, the Frauenkirche, St. Sebaldus and St. Lorenz at Nuremberg, the minster at Ulm and the choir of the Palatine Chapel at Aachen, show skilful geometric design with extraordinarily long, slender mullions. Often the tracery

Fig. 380. Altar-piece or Reredos, Esslingen Church.

is doubled, the outer plane of the window being adorned with purely decorative mullions and tracery, all quite useless, in addition to that which holds the glass (Ulm, Strassburg). In the fifteenth century the design becomes flamboyant, the *vesica* (Fischblase = fish bladder) or palm-leaf form constituting a favorite and much-multiplied detail in the intricate patterning. Quadrilaterals and triangles with curved sides are frequent. Balustrades are often of perplexingly ingenious patterns.

369

Openwork or traceried spires are peculiarly German features, as at Freiburg in Baden, Esslingen, Strassburg, and the modern reproductions of old designs at Cologne, Ulm and Ratisbon (Regensburg). The spire

loses its function as a true roof, but the effect is highly decorative (Figure 377).

Openwork gables and traceried walls are frequent; and the tracery of pinnacles and canopies for tabernacles, shrines (Sac-

FIG. 380 A. CARVED PEW END; GERMAN MIDDLE GOTHIC.

ramentshaüslein) choir-stalls, pulpits and rood-screens is intricate beyond description and executed with consummate skill. Some of the richest screen-work in France (*e.g.* at Alby) is thought to be of German workmanship. *Branch-tracery,* an utterly illogical and monumentally inappropriate naturalistic copying of vine-branches or rustic-work, appears as the last stage of decline in German Gothic art. Figures 378 and 379, from Strassburg, illustrate the richness of the best German late Gothic work.

Stained Glass.

A window from the earlier apse of Cologne cathedral has been preserved in the present structure begun in 1248; in which there are also fine examples of German 14th century glass. Others are to be seen of various dates at Altenburg, Nuremberg (see Fig. 336), Strass-

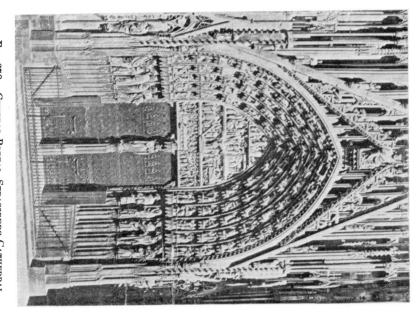

FIG. 378.—CENTRAL PORTAL, STRASSBURG CATHEDRAL

FIG. 379.—SIDE PORTAL, STRASSBURG CATHEDRAL

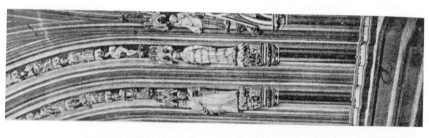

Fig. 382.—Center, Reredos in Carved and Painted Wood, Braunau, Left and Right, Details from Main Portal, Freiburg Cathedral

burg, etc. In principle German glass is like the French, but with much more of grisaille, foliage and geometric patterning, and less of figures until the 15th century, when a pictorial style came in with much painting in place of mosaic or pot-metal coloring, and a very frequent use of figure-subjects.

In the minor arts—wood-carving, metal-work, etc.—the Germans produced much that is interesting, generally marked by the same qualities of fantastic caprice, quaint humor and technical excellence, to which attention has already been called in other departments of art (Figs. 380, 381; Figure 382).

Spanish Gothic Ornament.

Medieval Christian art in Spain was subject to diverse influences, which prevented a homogeneous organic development of style, but helped to impart to it a highly picturesque character. The con-

FIG. 381. GERMAN LATE GOTHIC CARVING.

temporary Moorish art stimulated the tendency towards surface ornamentation, while German, French and even English characteristics occur in not a few cases. The Spanish fondness for unrestrained exuberance of ornament overrode the structural logic of Gothic design and

373

produced, in the fifteenth century especially, compositions of extraordinary and fantastic richness (Figure
384).

Spanish Gothic ornament is especially rich about the
doorways of churches and in the arcades of cloisters and
patios of the 14th and 15th centuries. Tabernacle work,
tracery and cusping of great complexity, and heraldic
escutcheons form the chief resources of such decoration
as is not directly inspired from foreign models.

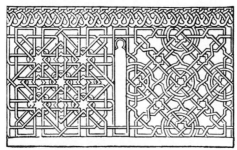

The traceried
spires of Burgos
suggest German
work; the general
decorative details of
the façade suggest
both Amiens and
Ratisbon. The in-

FIG. 386. MUDEJAR DECORATION.

terior decoration of
this and other churches is hard to classify or formulate, it
is so varied and so capricious in character, though almost
always effective (Figure 385). Vault decoration followed in Spain no well-defined principle, but in its use of
multiple ribs resembles the German rather than the English Gothic. The rib-patterns though often designed as
abstract decorations rather than as a structural framework (Figure 383), are nevertheless always true ribs,
not mere moldings carved out of the masonry as in English fan-vaulting. An occasional admixture of Moorish details with the Gothic (Fig. 386) produces what is
called the *Mudejar* style.

Window tracery is of less importance in Spain than

374

Fig. 384.—Patio (Court) of Palace of the Infantado, Guadalajara

Fig. 385.—Interior of Chapel of the Condestabile, Burgos Cathedral

FIG. 387.—DETAIL, FLANK OF FLORENCE CATHEDRAL

in more northern countries because of the small size of windows required in a hot climate; on the other hand, tracery as a surface decoration is carried to the extreme of elaborate complexity.

A striking characteristic frequently met with in Spanish decorative work is the effective way in which the most fanciful and overwrought ornamentation is brought into close contrast with the most severely plain surfaces, and minute detail with grandeur of scale.

Italian Gothic Ornament: the System.

The principles of design that dominated the Gothic styles of western Europe never found acceptance in Italy. The structural logic of the French and English builders and their system of ribbed vaulting, isolated supports and external buttresses were foreign to Italian traditions and ideals. The opportunist methods of the Italian Romanesque builders and the persistent traditions of Roman design, with its pilasters, round arches, cornices and acanthus leaves, were more in accord with Italian taste. When the intercourse between French, German and Italian chapters of the Benedictine and Cistercian orders began to make the splendid church architecture of the West known to the Italians, the result was only a very inadequate attempt to add some of the superficial details of that architecture to buildings constructed after the traditional Romanesque fashion. Pointed arches, steep gables, pinnacles, finials and crockets, and tracery strangely modified or travestied, were applied to buildings wholly Italian in design, without reference to the principles underlying the design and

A HISTORY OF ORNAMENT

use of these details in the West (Figure 387). Each building was conceived of as a walled enclosure—sometimes vaulted, sometimes roofed with wood—upon which to spread decoration, not as an organic structure to be made decorative in itself. The form and outline of a church facade had no necessary relation to the form of

Fig. 389. Detail from Portal of Cathedral, Lucca: Carved Rinceau and Marble Inlay.

the church behind it; it was a screen, a surface to be ornamented like a frontispiece (Figure 388). The flanks might or might not be similarly adorned. The interior provided areas for mural paintings. The materials for exterior decoration were round and pointed windows, gables, pinnacles, pilaster-strips, panels, statues, colored marble, inlays, mosaic, anything that would produce patterns in light and shade, form and color (Plate XXII). The façades of Sienna Cathedral (1284) and Orvieto (1310), and the flanks and east end

378

of the Duomo at Florence (1357–1408) illustrate this conception of the relations of architecture and ornament. The superb campanile at Florence (1334–50) by Giotto, Gaddi and Talenti, is its most perfect embodiment in the admirable harmony of the ornament with the struc-

FIG. 390. CAPITAL FROM A TOMB IN STA. CHIARA, NAPLES.

tural lines and mass (Plate XXII). Polychromy rather than light and shade was the chosen medium of decoration; the use of Gothic forms was a concession to fashion which prevented a truly rational development of style. In the works just mentioned and countless others, black, red, green, yellow and white marbles, in panels, stripes and inlays, are mingled with pseudo-Gothic and half-classic details. The Roman tradition refused to die (Fig. 389), and Corinthian capitals (Fig. 390), the Attic base, round arches with archivolts, acanthus leaves, rinceaux and moldings of Roman profile, are used with no sense of their incongruity with pointed arches, twisted shafts, crockets and tracery.

Architectural Details.

All the Gothic forms are capriciously varied. The most notable single feature is the spirally twisted shaft,

FIG. 391. TOMB IN SAN ANTONIO, PADUA.

frequently used as a mullion in subdivided openings, and as a jamb-shaft in recessed doorways. It is clearly a survival from Romanesque practice (Fig. 391; Plate XXII, 5, 6). Mosaic and inlay the Italians could never give up, and as their Gothic decoration was pre-eminently a decoration of surfaces, inlaid bands and panels of colored marbles in geometric patterns appear perfectly in place alongside of Gothic pinnacles and tracery (Figure 394). The *tracery* was rarely—except in Venice and in a few churches built by foreign artists—designed as a structure to be built up in stone after the true Gothic fashion; it was rather a surface of stone to be

Fig. 388.—Central Portion, Façade of Cathedral of Orvieto

FIG. 392.—TOMB OF CAN SIGNORIO SCALIGER, VERONA

FIG. 392A.—TOMB OF GIOVANNI SCALIGER, VERONA

perforated and carved, as in the Duomo windows and the Or San Michele at Florence (Figure 395). In Venice, however a remarkable and more truly structural type of tracery was developed in the 14th century in secular buildings; first in the majestic arcades of the Doge's Palace, and then in private palace façades, in a style singularly vigorous and original (Fig. 396). The triforium tracery of San Martino (cathedral) at Lucca (1370),

FIG. 396. FAÇADE OF A GOTHIC PALACE, VENICE.

has much of the Western character. That of Milan cathedral (1386—) is presumably of German design.

Minor Works.

In these the Italian decorative genius found its most congenial expression. Tombs, altars, chapels, shrines, ciboria, choir-stalls, fountains and pavements afforded free scope for Italian fancy and love of color. In these inlay and mosaic, Cosmati-work (see *ante* page 200) and surface decoration were perfectly appropriate. The altar of the church of Or San Michele, Florence, by Orcagna (Figure 397); the tombs of the Scaligers in Verona (Figure 392); wall-tombs and canopy-tombs in Venice and elsewhere, are not surpassed by works of like purpose anywhere.

A HISTORY OF ORNAMENT

Decorative Painting.

The remarkable schools of painting which arose and flourished in Florence in the thirteenth and fourteenth centuries and in Sienna in the fourteenth, fall outside the field of a history of ornament, except as to the subordinate details of their mural decorations. The culmination of this school is seen in the frescoes of Giotto (1267–1337), especially in the church of S. Francesco at Assisi, and of his followers, the Gaddi, etc. The decorations of vault-ribs and of borders of pictured panels on walls and vaults show a mingling of classic

FIG. 399. DETAIL FROM THE MANDORLA DOOR. FLORENCE CATHEDRAL.

survivals with geometric details evidently inspired from Cosmati work and geometric inlays (Fig. 398). The persistence of classic rinceaux and acanthus leaves appears often like a foretaste or anticipation of the Renaissance, instead of a lingering reminiscence of traditions never quite lost since the days of the Roman Empire. Carvings like those on the Mandorla door of the Florentine Duomo (*cir.* 1399; Fig. 399) are evidences of the vitality of those traditions, which the foreign Gothic fashion could not wholly drive out. Other painted decorations, as in S. Anastasia, Verona and S. Andrea, Vercilli, and the cloisters of the

384

Fig. 393.—Cathedral of Siena

Fig. 394.—Twisted Column and Inlay, Campanile, Florence

FIG. 395.—CARVED TRACERY, OR SAN MICHELE, FLORENCE

FIG. 398.—DETAIL, PAINTED WALL AND VAULT, SANTA CROCE, FLORENCE

Spanish Chapel of Sta. Maria Novella at Florence, are of a more distinctly Gothic character. The upper chapel of Sta. Maria in the Palazzo Pubblico at Sienna is another noted example.

Wood and Metal.

Choir-stalls and furniture offered abundant opportunity for the decorative skill of the Italian wood-carv-

Fig. 401. Capitals, Doge's Palace, Venice.

ers, who often combined wood-inlay or *intarsia* with their carving. But so many of these medieval wood-carvings were removed to be replaced in the fifteenth and sixteenth centuries with the works of the Renaissance artists, that this phase of Italian medieval art is less impressive than some others. A single example is shown in Figure 400 from Molfetta; it shows a curious survival of earlier tradition in the almost Romanesque aspect of the animal reliefs. There are a number of fine medieval iron grilles in Italian churches, and the grilles surrounding the tombs of the Scaligers (Figure 392) are elegant examples of this form of art.

The foregoing paragraphs have sketched only in the barest outline the Gothic ornament of Italy. The whole country is a vast museum of decorative art of all periods, —for its people, from the days of ancient Rome to our own, have always been decorators first of all, and an encyclopædic volume would be required to treat adequately the history of their achievements in the decorative arts.

Conclusion.

With the closing years of the fourteenth century in Italy, and a century later in western and northern Europe, the Gothic style began to be extinguished by the rapidly-developing and widely-spreading art of the Renaissance. Architecture had already reached the final limit of its structural development under the Gothic system, and was sensibly declining in power and grandeur. But, as we have seen, a splendid decorative flowering accompanied this decline in structural originality, and reached its highest level of richness and technical perfection in the fifteenth century, in France, England, Germany and Spain. This splendor of minute decoration, of complex tracery, realistic pictorial sculp-

FIG. 396.—DETAIL, ALTAR IN OR SAN
MICHELE, FLORENCE

FIG. 399.—DETAIL FROM STALLS,
MOLFETTA CATHEDRAL

ture, sumptuous embroidery and showy furniture was, however, the final coruscation of an expiring flame. In Italy, meanwhile, the new flame of the Renaissance had been kindled and had been growing in brilliancy and spreading as it grew brighter. The Western arts long resisted the Italian invasion; they refused to kindle from this new flame, to copy the new fashion. But the new style was more than a fashion; it was the expression of a fundamental change of spirit, of a new artistic point of view and attitude, of a new civilization and new ideals. The old order was passing away, and by the middle of the sixteenth century Gothic art was dead.

Books Recommended:

As before, ADAMY, DEHIO AND BEZOLD, HASAK, FROTHING-HAM, UNGEWITTER. Also, for the German Gothic, BOISSERÉE: *Histoire et description de la cathédrale de Cologne* (Munich, 1842).—FOERSTER, *Denkmale deutscher Baukunst* (Leipzig, 1855–69).—HARTEL: *Architektonische Details and Ornament der Kirchlichen Baukunst* (Berlin, 1891).—KLINGENBERG: *Die ornamentale Baukunst* (Leipzig, n. d.).—E. AUSM WERTH: *Kunstdenkmäler der christlichen Mittelalters in den Rheinlanden* (Leipzig, 1858).—For the Spanish Gothic, LAMPEREZ Y ROMEA: *Historia de la arquitectura cristiana Española*, etc. (Madrid, 1908–09).—*Monumentos Arquitectonicos de España* (Madrid).—D. ROBERTS: *Sketches in Spain* (London, 1837).—SMITH: *Sketches in Spain* (London, 1883).—G. E. STREET: *Gothic Architecture in Spain* (New Ed., London, 1913).—WARING: *Architectural Studies in Burgos* (London, 1852).—WARING AND MACQUOID: *Examples of Architectural Art in Italy and Spain* (London).

For the Italian Gothic, CUMMINGS: *A History of Architecture in Italy* (Boston, 1901).—GRÜNER: *Terra-Cotta Architecture of North Italy* (London, 1867).—KING: *Study Book of Mediæval Art* (London, 1868).—NESFIELD: *Specimens of*

Mediæval Architecture (London, 1862).—SCHULTZ: *Denkmäler der Kunst des Mittelalters in Unteritalien* (Dresden, n. d.).— G. E. STREET: *Brick and Marble Architecture in the Middle Ages in N. Italy* (London, 1874).—WARING: *The Arts Connected with Architecture in Central Italy* (London, 1858).

LIST OF PLATES

I. Savage Ornament: Polynesian

1. Carved Window-Head, New Zealand (after Pho. in A. M. N. H.).
2. Detail, New Zealand Paddle-Handle (after O. J.).
3. Detail, New Zealand Canoe (after Racinet).
4, 5. Hawaiian Stamped Cloth (after O. J.).
6. Detail, New Zealand Paddle-Handle (after O. J.).
7. Tattooed Mummy-Head, New Zealand (after O. J.).
8. Samoan Grass Cloth, String Decoration (A. M. N. H.).
9. New Zealand Grass Cloth (A. M. N. H.).
10. New Zealand Club (Racinet).
11. Scratched Pattern on a Tongan Club, New Guinea (after A. C. H.).
12. Hawaiian Stamped Cloth (after O. J.).
13. New Zealand Club (after Glazier).
14. From a New Guinea Spatula (after A. C. H.).
15. Detail, Handle of New Zealand Paddle of 21; Faces and Figures.
16. New Zealand Club (A. M. N. H.).
17. Frigate-Bird Ornament, New Guinea (after A. C. H.).
18. Frigate-Bird Scrolls. New Guinea (after A. C. H.).
19. Samoan Fan (A. M. N. H.).
20. New Zealand Stamped Cloth (after O. J.).
21. Blade of New Zealand Ceremonial Paddle (after O. J.).
22. Scratched Ornament on Pipe, New Guinea (after A. C. H.).
23. Carving from New Zealand Canoe (Racinet).
24. Painted Eaves Boards, New Zealand (after Pho. in A. M. N. H.).

PLATE I.   SAVAGE ORNAMENT   POLYNESIAN

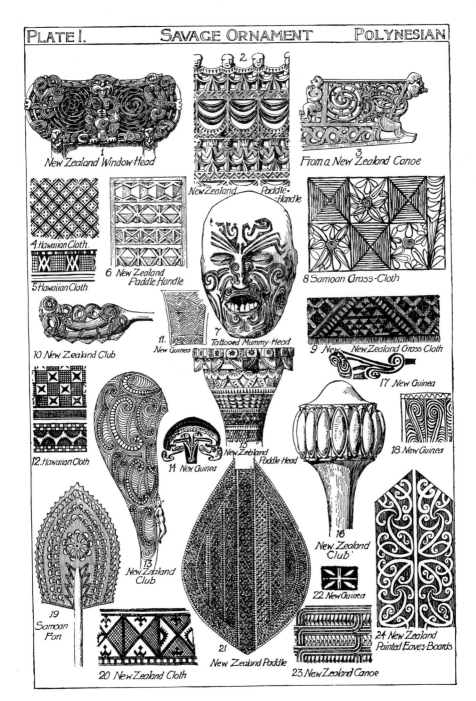

1 New Zealand Window-Head

2 New Zealand Paddle-Handle

3 From a New Zealand Canoe

4 Hawaiian Cloth

5 Hawaiian Cloth

6 New Zealand Paddle-Handle

7 Tattooed Mummy-Head

8 Samoan Grass-Cloth

9 New Zealand Grass-Cloth

10 New Zealand Club

11. New Guinea

12. Hawaiian Cloth

13 New Zealand Club

14 New Guinea

15 New Zealand Paddle-Head

16 New Zealand Club

17 New Guinea

18 New Guinea

19 Samoan Fan

20 New Zealand Cloth

21 New Zealand Paddle

22. New Guinea

23. New Zealand Canoe

24 New Zealand Painted Eaves-Boards

II. Savage Ornament: American

1. Bolivian Cloth.
2. From Temple of Uxmal, Mexico (Racinet).
3. Mexican Terra-Cotta Head.
4. Indian Basketry Patterns.
5. Ancient Mexican Pottery Border.
6. Bolivian Hanging Jar.
7. Sculptured Stele or Pillar, Uxmal.
8. Mexican Jar with Spiral.
9. Mexican Serpent Jar.
10. Neck of Mexican Jar: Pseudo-Anthemions.
11. Mexican Bowl; Spirals and Zigzags.
12. Washoe Basket (after print in *Yale News*).
13. Mexican Duck Jar.
14. Peruvian Gold Disk.
15. Mexican Platter with Grotesque.
16. Peruvian Platter with Snake Ornaments.
17. Carving from a Mexican "Throwing Stick."
18. Peruvian Cloth, Toucan Pattern.
19. Mexican Pipe-Bowl, Carved Stone.
20. Prow of Alaskan War Canoe.
21. Stern of Alaskan War Canoe.

All the above, except 2 and 12, are original sketches from objects in the American Museum of Natural History, New York; 19 by Miss G. K. Hamlin; the rest by the author.

1. Bolivian Cloth

2. From Temple, Uxmal, Mex

3 Mexican Terra-Cotta

4. Indian Basketry

5. Mexican Pottery

6. Bolivian Pot

7. Stele, Uxmal

8. Mexican Jar

9. Mexican Serpent Jar

10. Mexican Jar

11. Mexican Bowl

12. Washoe Basket

13. Mexican Duck Jar

14 Peruvian Gold Disk

15 Mexican Platter

16

17. Mexican (Wood)

18 Peruvian Pottery.

Peru-Cloth

Alaska War Canoe

19. Mexican Pipe (Stone)

20. Prow

21. Stern

III. EGYPTIAN ORNAMENT

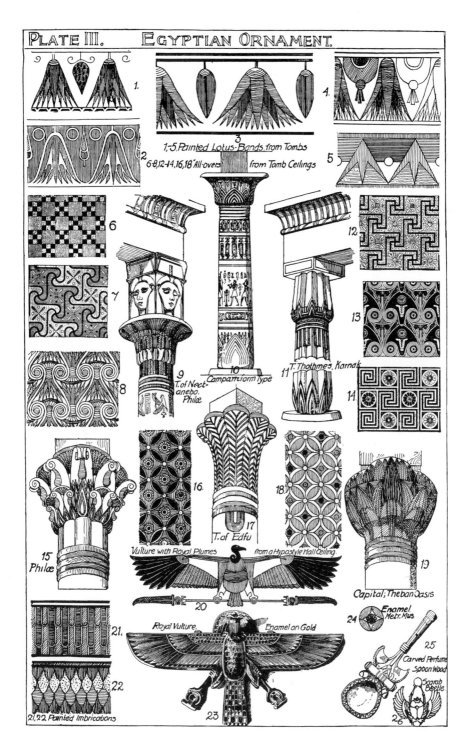

PLATE III. EGYPTIAN ORNAMENT.

1.

4.

3.

1-5. Painted Lotus-Bands from Tombs

2. 6-8,12-14,16,18 'All-overs' from Tomb Ceilings

5.

6.

7.

8.

9. T. of Nect-anebo. Philæ.

10. Campaniform Type.

11. T. Thothmes, Karnak.

12.

13.

14.

15. Philæ.

16.

17. T. of Edfu.

18. from a Hypostyle Hall Ceiling.

Vulture with Royal Plumes

19. Capital; Theban Oasis.

20.

21.

22.

21.22. Painted Imbrications.

Royal Vulture. Enamel on Gold.

23.

24. Enamel Metr. Mus.

25. Carved Perfume Spoon:Wood.

26. Scarab Beetle.

IIIA EGYPTIAN ORNAMENT

1. Various Lotus and Other Borders from Tombs (chiefly after Prisse d'Avennes and Dolmetsch).
2. Campaniform Column, from Ramesseum.
3. Lotus-Bud Clustered Column, Luxor.
4. All-Over Patterns Painted in Tombs (after Dolmetsch, Prisse d'Avennes and Perrot and Chipiez).
5. Ptolemaic Capitals, Hathoric and Floral from Philæ (after Prisse d'Avennes and Owen Jones).
6. Ptolemaic Capitals, Lotus and Palm, from Theban Oasis and Edfu (as above).
7. Feathers as Insignia (after Owen Jones).
8, 9. Imbrications (Dolmetsch).
10. Floral Ornaments (after C. H. Walker).
11. Furniture, in part from Tomb Paintings (after Meyer).
12. Wooden Shrine (Dolmetsch).
13. Detail from Façade of Tomb (after Perrot and Chipiez).
14. Utensils and Jewelry.

Illustrations not otherwise designated are from original drawings by the author.

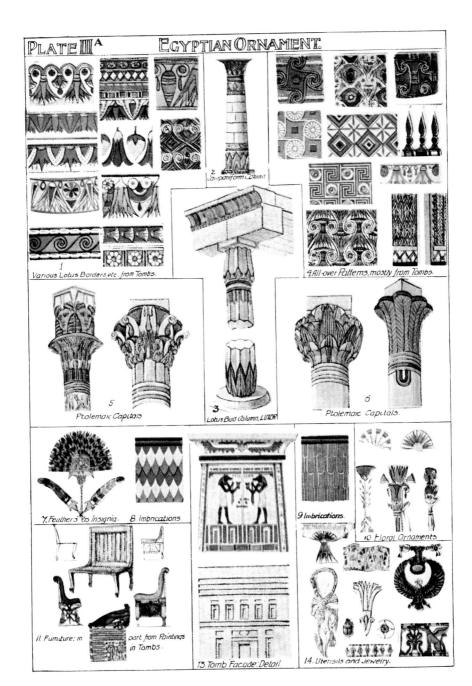

1
Various Lotus Borders, etc., from Tombs.

2
Campaniform Column

4. All-over Patterns, mostly from Tombs.

5
Ptolemaic Capitals

3
Lotus Bud Column, LUXOR

6
Ptolemaic Capitals.

7. Feathers as Insignia.   8. Imbrications

9 Imbrications.

10 Floral Ornaments

11. Furniture; in   part, from Paintings in Tombs.

13. Tomb Facade: Detail

14. Utensils and Jewelry.

IV. Assyrian and Persian Ornament

1. Assyrian Double Palmette Border, Tiles (after P. & C.).
2. Assyrian "Sacred Tree" (after O. J.).
3. Imbrications or Scales: a, Painted; b, Carved (after O. J.).
4. Pavefent Slab, Koyunjik.
5. Pomegranate Border, Nimrond (after O. J.).
6. Assyrian Chair, from a Relief (P. & C.).
7. Assyrian "Portal Guardian" Winged Bull, from Khorsabad (P. & C.).
8. Lotus Rosette from a Pavement, Koyunjik (after O. J.).
9. Column from Susa (after P. & C.).
10. Column from Persepolis (after P. & C.).
11. Lycian Tomb (P. & C.).
12. Detail from Persepolis: Palms and Rosettes (after P. & C.).
13. Details from Staircase Parapet (after Ward).
14. Palmette Tiles from Susa (after P. & C.).
15. Enameled Brick Wall-Facing from Susa (after P. & C.).
16, 17. Details from Rock Tomb, Naksh-i-Rustam.
18. Detail, Architrave, from Persepolis.

PLATE IV. ASSYRIAN AND PERSIAN.

1. Assyrian Palmette Frieze: Tiles

2. Assyrian Sacred Tree.

3. a. Imbrications

5.

6. Scales (carved).

4. Pavement Slab (Koyunjik)

6. Pomegrate Border

6. Assyrian Chair (from a Relief).

7. Portal Guardian (Korsabad.)

8. Lotus Rosette (from Pavement)

Persian Column from Susa.

9.

11. Lycian Tomb.

Persian Column from Persepolis

10.

12. From Persepolis

13.

Stair Parapet, Persepolis

15. Susa: Brick Wall.

16.

17.

16, 17, from Nakshi-Rustam

14. Susa: Tiles.

18. from Persepolis

V. Greek Ornament, Painted: Chiefly on Pottery

1. Anthemions, Black on Red.
2. Dish, Geometric or Dipylon Period (P. & C.).

3, 7. Palmettes, Black and Brown on Red.

4. Framed Anthemions Red on Black.
5. Palmette or Framed Anthemion and "Lotus" Motive: Black and Brown on Red.
6. Hydria, Early Fifth Century (Art Pour Tous).
8. Oblique Anthemions, Black on Red.
9. Anthemions and Fruits.
10. Double Palmette-and-Lotus Band: Red on Black.
11. Anthemion Pattern, from an Apulian Vase in New York.

12, 13. Vine Bands, Red on Black.

14. Ivy Band, Black on Red.

15, 16. Small Vertical Laurel and Ivy Bands.

17. Painted Terra Cotta Antefix (incorrectly labeled as of Marble), Athens.
18. Hydria, Fine Period.
19. Painted Marble Antefix.
20. Framed Anthemions, Red on Black.
21. Foliated Scroll or Rinceau, on a Late Apulian Vase.
22. Anthemions, Black on Red.
23. Vertical Vine Band.

The above illustrations are from various sources: Owen Jones, Kachel, Art Pour Tous, Lau, and original sketches from the object.

PLATE V. GREEK ORNAMENT. PAINTED

1 Anthemions. Black on Red.

2. Dish — Geometric Style.

3. Palmettes etc.-Black & Brown on Red.

4 Anthemions, Framed.-Red on Black.

5. Palmette etc. - Black and Brown on Red.

6. Hydria — Transitional.

7. Palmette -Black and Brown on Red.

8. Oblique Anthemions-Black on Red.

9. Various Vase Ornaments.

10 Double Pal - mette Band

11. Anthemion Decoration on an Apulian Vase (N.Y.)

12. Vine Band. Red on Black.

13 Vine Band

14 Ivy Band.-Bl. on Red

15

16

17 Painted Marble Antefix

18. Wide-Mouthed Hydria

19 Painted Marble Antefix

20 Framed Anthemions

21. Foliated Branching Scrolls-Late (Apulian?) Vase.

22. Anthemions-Bl. on Red

23.

VI. GREEK ORNAMENT, PAINTED: POTTERY AND ARCHITECTURE

1, 2, 3. "Vitruvian" Waves and Scrolls.

4, 5, 9, 10. Various Fret or Meander Bands.

6, 11. Anthemions, Red on Black.

7. Imbrications.

8. Flower Band (Lotuses?).

12. Lotus-Bud Band.

13, 14. Plant and Vine Ornaments.

15. Egg-and-Dart and Laurel Band.

16, 18, 19, 22. Anthemions and Palmettes, Black on Red.

17, 20, 21, 23, 30. Anthemion Bands, Red on Black.

24, 27. Large Anthemion Ornaments, Black on Red.

25, 26. Late Painted Decorations, Apulian.

28, 31, 36. Painted Guilloches on Terra-Cotta Strips and Moldings.

29, 32–35. Polychrome Decorations of Architectural Members.

Nos. 1, 2, 3, 20, 23, 25 are from drawings by the author after Owen Jones and Kachel; 28, 30, 36 from drawings by the late Prof. M. K. Kress of Columbia University; 32 is from Perrot and Chipiez; the rest from the late Prof. W. R. Ware's "Greek Ornament."

Plate VI. GREEK ORNAMENT. PAINTED.

VII. Greek Ornament, Architectural

1. Carved Pediment Rinceau, from one of the "Sidon" Sarcophagi at Constantinople.
2. Marble Antefix, supposedly from the Parthenon.
3. Carved Finial of Choragic Monument of Lysicrates, Athens: Restored.
4. Typical Carved Lotiform Motive, from the Erechtheion.
5. Carved Anthemion on an Ionic Cymatium.
6. Doric Order of the Parthenon.
7. Ionic Capital from the Erechtheion.
8. Moldings from the Erechtheion: Water Leaf, Bead-and-Reel, and Egg-and-Dart.
9. Ionic Order of the Erechtheion.
10. Capital from Eleusis (after Meyer).
11. Anta-Cap from the Erechtheion (Meyer).
12. Greek Corinthian Volutes.
13, 15. Stele Heads from Athens, Fourth Century.
14. Corinthian Capital from the Choragic Monument of Lysicrates: Restored.

All the figures on this Plate are from original drawings by the author except 8 and 11 which are taken by permission from Meyer's "Handbook of Ornament"; and 5, from an unidentified source.

PLATE VII.   GREEK ORNAMENT.   ARCHITECTURAL.

1 Carved Rinceau,   "Sidon" Sarcophagus

4 Carved Lotiform Motive

2. Antefix. Parthenon

3
Finial, Choragic Mont of Lysicrates

5 Fragment of a Cymatium

6

7 Ionic Capital from the Erechtheion.

8. Moldings. Erechtheion.

9.

10. Capital from Eleusis

11 Anta-Cap. from Erechtheion

12
Corinthian Vo-
lutes

Doric Order. Parthenon

Ionic Order Erechtheion

14 Corinthian Capital,
Choragic Mont of Lysicrates

13. Stele-Head, Athens 4th Century

15 Stele-Head. Athens, 4th Century

VIII. Roman Ornament, the Orders

1. Doric Order, Thermæ (Baths) of Diocletian.
2. Composite Order from the Arch of Titus.
3. Ionic Order from the Temple of Fortuna Virilis.
4. Corinthian Order, Temple of Castor and Pollux.
5. Middle Band of Architrave, Temple of Castor and Pollux.
6. Greco-Roman Corinthian Order of Temple of "Vesta" (so-called) at Tivoli.
7. Composite Capital, Thermæ of Caracalla.
8. Unidentified Corinthian Pilaster Capital; Late Greek or Greco-Roman.
9. Enriched Attic Base in Capitoline Museum (after Meyer).
10. Enriched Corinthian Base in Baptistery of Constantine (after Meyer).
11. Enriched Corinthian Base from Temple of Concord (Meyer).

All the figures on this Plate are from original drawings by the author, based on various authorities (7 is after a photograph), except 12 which is taken directly from Meyer's "Handbook of Ornament."

PLATE VIII.

ROMAN·ORNAMENT·
·THE·ORDERS·

1 Doric Order: Thermæ of Diocletian

2 Order of the Arch of Titus: Composite

3 Ionic Order. Temple of 'Fortuna Virilis'

4 Corinthian Order: Temple Castor & Pollux.

5 Middle Band of Architrave; Temple of Castor and Pollux.

6 From 'Vesta Temple, Tivoli.

7 Thermæ of Caracalla

8 Late Greek or Greco Roman

Base in Baptistery   of Constantine

9 Base in Capitoline Museum

10

11 Base from Temple of Concord

IX. ROMAN ORNAMENT, CARVING

1. Tænia Molding, Arch of the Silversmiths.
2, 3. Moldings between Architrave Bands, Temple of Vespasian (from Photographs of French Restorations).
4. Semicircular Panel in Court of Mattei Palace, Rome, with Rinceaux and Rosettes; its source is unknown (after Vulliamy).
5. Detail from Border of a Silver Platter (after Kachel).
6. Rinceau, from Temple of Vespasian.
7. Bucrane, from an Altar (after Tatham).
8. Fragments from Forum of Trajan in Lateran Museum (after a Photograph).
9, 10. Details from so-called "Florentine Tablet" (after Kachel).
11. Enriched Ove, Temple of Vespasian (after an old French Lithograph).
12. Pilaster Fragment in Villa Medici, Rome (from Cast in Columbia University).
13. Oak-Leaf and Rosette Band (Unidentified; after an old French Lithograph).
14. Pilaster Fragment with Double Rinceau, in Palazzo Fano, Rome.

All the above illustrations are from drawings by the author. The sources of 6 and 14 cannot be verified.

PLATE IX. ROMAN ORNAMENT. CARVING

1 Tænia Arch of the Silversmiths

2 Architrave Bead, T. of Vespasian

3 Smaller Bead, from Forum of Vespasian

4. Panel unknown Source, in Court of Mattei Palace, Rome (Marble)

5 Detail from Border of a Silver Platter

6 Rinceau Temple of Vespasian

7 Bucrane from an Altar

8 Fragment from Forum of Trajan

9 Detail Scroll from the Florence Tablet.

10 A Part of the Florence Tablet, in the Uffizi.

11 Enriched Ove. Temple of Vespasian

12 Pilaster Fragment in Villa Medici

13 Oak Leaf and Rosette Band

14 Pilaster Fragment in Pal. Fiano.
(Double Rinceau Type: cp. with 12)

X. Roman Ornament, Minor Arts

1. Cinerary Urn in British Museum (after Glazier).
2. Silver Crater from Hildesheim (Meyer, after Kachel).
3. Silver Patera from Hildesheim (after Kachel).
4. Marble Hydria from Pompeii (after Photograph).
5. Bronze Saucepan, Naples Museum (Meyer).
6. Cinerary Chest and Urn in Vatican Museum (after Piranesi).
7. Bronze-Tripod in Berlin Museum (after Meyer).
8. Marble Support or Stand in Villa Borghese, Rome (after Piranesi).
9. Bronze Tripod, Naples Museum (after Meyer).
10. Candelabrum on Triangular Pedestal in Vatican Museum (after Piranesi).

11, 12. Marble Table Legs, Vatican Museum (after Meyer).

13. Bronze Candelabrum Base, Naples Museum (after engraving in "The Workshop").

All the illustrations on this Plate are from the author's drawings, based on the sources indicated.

PLATE X. ROMAN ORNAMENT. MINOR ARTS.

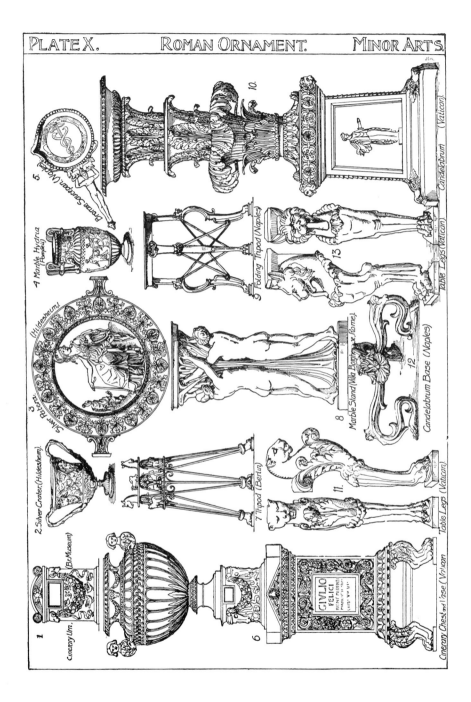

1. Cinerary Urn. (Br. Museum)

2. Silver Crater. (Hildesheim)

3. Silver Patera. (Hildesheim)

4. Marble Hydria (Pompeii)

5. Bronze Saucepan (Naples)

6. Cinerary Chest and Vase (Vatican)

7. Tripod (Berlin)

8. Marble Stand (Villa Borghese, Rome)

9. Folding Tripod (Naples)

10. Candelabrum (Vatican)

11. Table Legs (Vatican)

12. Candelabrum Base (Naples)

13. Table Legs (Vatican)

XI. Pompeiian Ornament

1. Detail from Temple of Isis (R. Paufve after Zahn).
2. From a Painted Wall in Naples Museum (R. Paufve, after Niccolini).
3. From House of Marcus Lucretius (H. W. Haefele, after Niccolini).
4. Painted Border (R. Paufve, after Zahn).
5. From House of the Vestals (Author, after Zahn).
6. Frieze in Temple of Isis (Author, after Zahn).
7. Fragment of Stucco Relief from Excavation Near Villa Farnesina, Rome (Author, after Photograph).
8. From a Wall not now Extant, in Pompeii (H. W. Haefele, after Niccolini).
9. Detail of Pompeiian Floor Mosaic (R. Paufve, after Zahn?).
10. Figure in Stucco Relief, from Excavation Near Villa Farnesina, Rome (Author, after Photograph).
11, 12. Details from Pompeiian Floor Mosaics (H. W. Haefele).

PLATE XI. POMPEIIAN ORNAMENT.

1. Temple of Isis

2. In Naples Museum

3. House of M. Lucretius

4. Painted Border.

5. House of the Vestals

6. Temple of Isis.

7. Stucco (Rome)

8. from a house not now existant

11. Mosaic Border.

9. Floor Mosaic

10. Stucco (Rome).

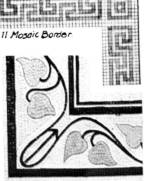

12. Mosaic Border.

XII. BYZANTINE ORNAMENT, CARVED

1. Capital, Impost, Mosaic and Marble Paneling, Hagia Sophia, Constantinople.
2. Spandrel with Surface Carving in Marble, Hagia Sophia, Constantinople.
3. "Basket" Capital and Impost Block, San Vitale, Ravenna.
4. Pier and Cap in Front of St. Mark's, Venice, from St. John of Acre.
5. Inlaid Capital and Impost Block, St. Mark's, Venice.
6, 7. Details from Bronze Doors of the VIth Century, Hagia Sophia, Constantinople.
8. Italo-Byzantine Silver Chest in Museo Nazionale, Florence.
9. Puteal (Perforated Parapet), San Vitale, Ravenna.
10. Panel from Crypt of St. Mark's, Venice; Xth Century.

All the above illustrations are from photographs or photo-prints.

Plate XII. Byzantine Ornament.   Carved.

2 Spandrel. Hagia Sophia

1. Capital. Panels and Mosaic, Hagia Sophia

3.

Cap and Im-   post Block,
San Vitale,   Ravenna

5 Inlaid Cap, St Mark's, Venice

4.

In Front of St Mark's, Venice

6 Doors of Hagia Sophia 7.

8 Silver Chest. Florence.

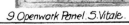

9. Openwork Panel. S. Vitale.

10. Panel. Crypt of St. Mark's.

XIII. BYZANTINE ORNAMENT, MOSAIC

1. Mosaic Detail, Hagia Sophia, Constantinople.
2. Spandrel and Capital, Gallery Arcade of Hagia Sophia, Constantinople.
3, 4. Details of Mosaic from Hagia Sophia, Constantinople.
5. Detail of Mosaic in St. George, Salonika.
6, 7, 8, 10. Details of Mosaic from Hagia Sophia, Constantinople.
9, 11, 14. Mosaic Details from San Lorenzo fuori le Mura, Rome.
12, 13. Details of Floor Mosaic in San Marco, Rome.

Of the above illustrations Nos. 1, 2, 6–10 are from student-drawings by S. Y. Ohta, after Prang and Salzenberg; 11 and 14 from student-drawings by H. J. Burke; 3, 4, 5 and 6 are reproduced by permission from Prang's Plates of Historic Ornament; 12 and 13 are from measured drawings by the author.

PLATE XIII. BYZANTINE ORNAMENT. MOSAIC.

HS. 1.

2.

3 H.S.

Hagia Sophia 4

Hagia Sophia

5 St. George. Salonica

6 Hagia Sophia

1. Hagia Sophia.

8

10 H. Sophia

Hagia Sophia

San Lorenzo Y fuori, Rome.

11. S. Lorenzo f.

12 Floor in S. Marco. Rome.

13. S. Marco. Rome.

14. S. Lorenzo fuori, Rome.

XIV. Romanesque Ornament, French

1. Double Capital from La Dalbade, Toulouse, in the Toulouse Museum.
2. Double Capital from Church of Notre Dame at Châlons-sur-Marne.
3, 5. Details from Central Portal of Church of St. Gilles, near Arles.
4. Capital from Church of St. Pierre-le-Moutier.
6. Carved Rosette, from Portal of Church at Moissac.
7. Carved Tympanum from a House at Reims.
8. Rosette (unidentified).
9. Detail from Porte Ste. Anne, Cathedral of Notre Dame, Paris.
10. Fragment of Frieze from Portal of Church of St. Gilles, near Arles.
11. Carved Monster from Portal of Church at Moissac.

All the illustrations on this Plate are reproduced from photographic post cards of casts in the Museum of Comparative Sculpture of the Trocadéro, Paris.

PLATE XIV.   ROMANESQUE ORNAMENT.   FRENCH.

1. Double Capital, La Dalbade, Toulouse. (In Toulouse Museum)   2. Double Capital, Notre Dame de Chalons-sur-Marne.

Porch of St. Gilles (Arles).   4. Capital from St. Pierre-le-Moutier.   5. Porch of St. Gilles (Arles).

Rosette, Moissac.   7. Tympanum from a House in Reims.   8. Rosette

10. Fragment. Frieze, Porch of St. Gilles (Arles)

Panel, Porte Ste. Anne, N.D. Paris   11. Monster. Moissac.

XV. ANGLO-NORMAN AND CELTIC ORNAMENT

1. Voluted Capitals from Harmston Church, Lincs (after Bond).
2. Grotesque and Scrolls, Shobdon Church, Herefordshire (after Rickman).
3. "Scalloped"-Type Capitals, New Shoreham Church (after Bond).
4. Anglo-Norman Anthemion Ornament (unidentified).
5. Capital, Canterbury Cathedral (after Rickman).
6. Peterboro Choir, Two Bays (illustration by Author in Van Rensselaer, "English Cathedrals").
7. Zigzag Arch-Ornament from Malmesbury Abbey (after Parker).
8. Star-Flower on an Arch in Romsey Abbey (after Rickman).
9. Anglo-Norman Cushion Capital (unidentified; C. U. Student-Drawing).
10. Billet or Checker Molding from Winchester Cathedral (after Parker).
11. Anthemion Ornament from Hereford Cathedral.
12. Initial P, from Book of Kells (after Sullivan).
13. Detail from Celtic Cross at Ruthwell, Ireland (after Champreys).
14. Interlace from Cross at Mugle, Ireland.
15. Interlace Border from an Irish MS. (after Racinet).
16. The South Cross at Aheny, Ireland (after Champreys).

All the above illustrations are from the author's drawings except 9, which is an unidentified student's drawing.

PLATE XV. ANGLO-NORMAN ORNAMENT. CELTIC Oᵗ.

1 Caps Voluted

2 Shobdon. Herefordshire.

3. Caps, Scalloped

4 (Unidentified)

5. Canterbury

6. Peterboro'. Chair.

7 Malmesbury Abbey

8 Romsey Abbey

9. (Unidentified)

10 Winchester.

11 Hereford (?)

12 Initial (P) from Book of Kells

13. From Cross, Ruthwell

14. From Cross, Meigle.

15. From a MS. (Celtic).

16. The South Cross, Ahenŷ

XVI. German Romanesque Ornament

1. Carved Pier in Church at St. Ják, Hungary (from a drawing by Stein).
2. Twelfth Century Capital from Cathedral at Naumburg (C. U. Student-drawing).
3. Twelfth Century Capital from Gelnhausen (from Hauser, "Stillehre . . . des Mittelalters").
4. Double Capital, Minster at Limburg-on-the-Lahn (Hauser, "Stillehre").
5. Detail of Bronze Ornament, Aachen.
6. Rosette from Heiligenberg near Vienna (Meyer's "Handbook" etc.) Gelnhausen.
7. German Romanesque Capital (from an unidentified engraving).
8. Twelfth Century Bronze Knocker (Meyer).
9. Rosette from Cathedral of Bâle (Meyer).
10. Anthemion Band from Church at Hersfeld, Saxony.
11. Acanthus Molding from Münzenberg, Hesse ("Gewerbehalle").
12. Anthemion Band from Fulda, Hesse-Cassel (after Prang).
13. Romanesque Stained Glass from Heiligenkreuz (Hauser, "Stillehre").
14. Carved Band from Liebfrauenkirche, Halberstadt (after "Klingenberg, Mittelalterliche Ornamentik").
15. Anthemion Frieze from South Germany (after Prang).
16. Carving from Tomb in St. Thomas', Strassburg.
17. Carved Band from Anhausen-an-dem-Brienz, S. Germany ("Gewerbehalle").

Illustrations not otherwise attributed are from drawings by the author.

PLATE XVI. GERMAN ROMANESQUE ORNAMENT.

1. Church at Ják. Hungary

2. Capital. XII.th Century

3. Capital. XII Century

4.

5. Bronze, 9.th C., Aachen

6.

Heiligenberg. near Vienna.

7.

8.

9.

Bále. Cath.l

10. From Hersfeld

11. From Münzenberg. Hesse.

12. From Fulda, Hesse-Cassel

13. Glass. Heiligenkreuz.

14. Liebfrauenkirche, Halberstadt.

15. Frieze, South Germany

16. From a Tomb, St. Thomas Church, Strassburg.

17. From South Germany.

XVII. Gothic Structural Ornament

1. Buttress Pinnacle from Notre Dame (Hauser).
2. Flying Arches, Sta. Barbara, Kuttenberg (Hauser).
3. Decorative Gable, Cologne Cathedral; Middle Period Tracery (Hauser).
4. Crocket from St. Urbain, Troyes (Hauser).
5. Buttress Pinnacle, Notre Dame, Paris (C. U. Student Drawing).
6. Early French Finial.
7. French Gothic Vault Rib (Hauser).
8. English Pier Arch Moldings (Hauser).
9. Late Gothic Crocket, Rouen (Hauser).
10. Wall Traceries, Transept of Meaux Cathedral (C. U. Student Drawing).
11. Finial Cathedral of Troyes (Hauser).
12. Half-Plan and Elevation, Clustered Pier, Notre Dame, Paris (C. U. Student Drawing).
13. Pier Cap and Arch Moldings, Chartres Cathedral (Hauser).
14. Early Gothic or Transitional Balustrade (C. U. Student Drawing).
15. Detail from Transept of Notre Dame, Paris (C. U. Student Drawing, after Lassus and V.-le-Duc).
16. Flamboyant Balustrade, Château of Josselyn (C. U. Student Drawing).
17. Early Gothic Balustrade, Notre Dame, Paris (C. U. Student Drawing).

PLATE XVII. GOTHIC ORNAMENT. STRUCTURAL

1. Buttress Pinnacle. N.Dame.

2.

Flying Arches. German: Kuttenberg.

3. Decorative Gable. Cologne.

4. Crocket: St. Urbain. (Troyes)

5. Buttress-Pinnacles. N.Dame. Paris.

6. Early French Finial

7. French Vault-Rib.

8. English Pier-Arch Mouldings

9. Late Gothic Crocket. Rouen.

10. Wall-Traceries. Meaux Cath'l.

11. Finial, Troyes Cath.

12. Plan. 12.

12. Piers of N.Dame. Paris.

13. Chartres Cath'l. Pier-Cap and Arch Moldings

14. Balustrade, Transitional

15. Detail from S. Transept, Notre Dame. Paris

16. Balustrade, Chateau of Josselin Flamboyant

17. Early Gothic Balustrade.

XVIII. Gothic Ornament, Carving

1. Capitals, North Porch of Chartres Cathedral; XIIIth Century.
2. Capitals, Northwest Portal, Laon Cathedral; Early XIIIth Century.
3. Early French Gothic Capital.
4. Pedestal, North Porch, Chartres Cathedral.
5. From St. Urbain, Troyes.
6. Arch Ornament, North Portal, Bourges Cathedral.
7. Nave Piers, Reims Cathedral.
8. Bishop's Throne, Toul Cathedral, Early XIIIth Century.
9. Transept Rose (as before Alteration), Reims Cathedral.
10. The "Beau Dieu," Reims Cathedral.
11. Vault-Boss, from an Apsidal Chapel, Séez Cathedral.
12. Model of Apse of St. Urbain, Troyes; in Trocadéro Museum.
13, 14. Corbel and Crocket, Rouen: Flamboyant.
15. Vine Molding, Window of St. Urbain, Troyes, XIVth Century.
16. "Bahut" in Cluny Museum, XVth Century.
17. Cast-Iron Knocker, from House in Rue du Lion, Troyes (XVth Century).
18. Molding, Porch of Troyes Cathedral (XVth Century).
19. Fragment, Hôtel de la Trémoille, in Court of Ecole des Beaux-Arts.

All the above illustrations are from photo-print post-cards of casts in the Museum of Comparative Sculpture in the Trocadéro, Paris.

PLATE XVIII.   GOTHIC ORNAMENT.   CARVING, FRENCH.

1 Caps. N. Porch. Chartres.

2. Capitals, N.W. Portal, Laon Cathedral.

3 Early Capital St. Leu(?)

4. Chartres: N. Porch.

5. St. Urbain Troyes.

6 Bourges Cath'l. North Portal.

7. Nave Piers, Reims Cath'l.

8. Bishop's Throne. Toul Cathedral.

9 Transept Rose, Reims Cath'l.

The Beau Dieu Reims Cathedral

11 Vault Boss. Abb'y Chapel, Séez.

12. Model of Apse, St. Urbain, Troyes.

13   14

Corbel and Crocket: Rouen(?)

15.

St. Urbain, Troyes.

16. Bahut or Sacristy Chest, 15th C.; Cluny Mus.

17 Cast-Iron Knocker, 15th C.; Hôtel du Lion, Troyes.

18. Cath. Troyes. Porch.

(In Court of Beaux-Arts)

19. Hotel de la Trémoille. Fragment.

XIX. GOTHIC ORNAMENT, STAINED GLASS

1. Border, Window in Bourges Cathedral (Prang).
2. Border, Jesse Window in Chartres Cathedral (H. W. Miller).
3, 4. Figures from Chartres Jesse Window (H. W. Miller).
5. Border, Window in Bourges Cathedral (Author, after Owen Jones).
6. Grisaille, Window in Bourges Cathedral (Owen Jones).
7. Border, Window in Bourges Cathedral (Owen Jones).
8. Border, Window in York Cathedral (Owen Jones).
9. Border from Window in Church of St. Thomas, Strassburg (Author, after Owen Jones).
10. Window Detail from St. Denis (Prang).

PLATE XIX. GOTHIC ORNAMENT. STAINED GLASS.

1 Border. Bourges Cath

2. Border, Jesse window. Chartres Cath., End of XII.th Century

3 and 4 Figures from Jesse Window, Chartres Cathedral.

6 Grisaille. Bourges Cath!.

7. Bourges.

8 Border, York Cath., XIV.th C

5 Border, Bourges   9 St Thomas' Church. Strassburg.   10 St Denis, Early XIII.th C

XX. Gothic Ornament; Painted, Ceramic and MSS. Decoration

Of the above illustrations, Nos. 1 to 7 inclusive and 9, 10, 11 are from Prang's "Plates of Historic Ornament," by permission, Nos. 8 and 12 to 24 inclusive are from Owen Jones, "Grammar of Ornament."

PLATE XX. GOTHIC ORNAMENT. PAINTED.

1. ELY CATHEDRAL

2 BEVERLEY MINSTER.

3. BRUNSWICK CATHEDRAL

4. BRUNSWICK CATHEDRAL.

5. REIMS CATH.

6. SALISBURY CATHEDRAL

7. WINCHESTER CATHEDRAL

8. TILE UNIT

9. JACOBIN CH., TOULOUSE

10. RANWORTH CH., Norfolk.

11. WEST WALTON CH., Norfolk.

12. TILE. UNIT.

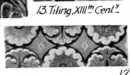

13. Tiling, XIII th Cent y.

14

15

16.

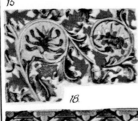

17.

18.

19

20

21.

22.

23.

24.

No's. 14 to 24 inclusive are from Manuscripts: 15 and 18 are of the XIV th Century the others are of the XII th and XIII th Centuries.

XXI. English Gothic Ornament

1. One Bay, Salisbury Cathedral.
2. One Bay, Choir of Lincoln Cathedral.
3. One Bay, Lichfield Cathedral, Nave.
4. Detail from King's College Chapel, Cambridge.
5. Perpendicular Wall Tracery.
6. Lancet Windows, Warmington Church.
7. Plate Tracery, Carlisle Cathedral.
8. Geometric Tracery, Rippington Church.
9. Geometric Tracery, Chapter House, York Cathedral.
10. Curvilinear Tracery, St. Michael's, Warfield.
11. Perpendicular Tracery, Beauchamp Chapel, Warwick.
12. Curvilinear Tracery, Oxford Cathedral.
13. Transept Rose, Westminster Abbey.
14. Capital from Lincoln Cathedral: Early English.
15. Capital from Beverley Cathedral: Decorated.
16. Cresting Ornament, Arundel Church: Perpendicular.
17. "Decorated" Finial.
18. "Decorated" Crocket.
19. "Decorated" Capital, Beverley Cathedral.
20. Carving from Trull Church.
21. One unit of a Diaper Decoration.
22. A "Perpendicular" Doorway and Door Paneling.

Nos. 1, 2, and 3 are reproduced by permission from the Author's drawings in Van Rensselaer's "English Cathedrals" (The Century Co.). No. 4 is from part of an illustration in Simpson's "A History of Architectural Development" (Longmans); 5 is from Speltz, by permission; 6–11 are by the author; 12–15 are from Gwilt's "Encyclopedia"; 17, 18 by the author after Speltz; 20–22 are from drawings by Columbia students, from unidentified sources.

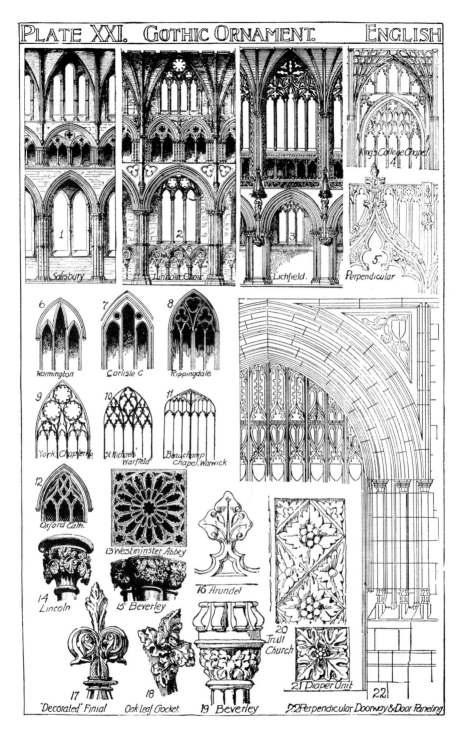

PLATE XXI. GOTHIC ORNAMENT. ENGLISH

1 Salisbury

2 Lincoln Choir

3 Lichfield.

King's College Chapel 4

5 Perpendicular

6 Warmington

7 Carlisle C

8 Rippingdale

9 York, Chapter Ho.

10 St Michael's Warfield

11 Beauchamp Chapel, Warwick

12 Oxford Cath.

13 Westminster Abbey

14 Lincoln

15 Beverley

16 Arundel

17 "Decorated" Finial

18 Oak Leaf Crocket.

19 Beverley

20 Trull Church

21 Diaper Unit

22 Perpendicular Doorway & Door Paneling

XXII. Italian Gothic Ornament

1. Detail, Portal of Cathedral of Messina.
2. Open Tracery, Venetian Style.
3. Central Doorway, Cathedral of Messina.
4. Traceried Window, from a Town Hall.
5. Twisted Columns, from Niche in Façade of Church of Or San Michele, Florence.
6. Detail from Upper Story of Campanile, Florence.
7. Porch of Cathedral of Amalfi.
8. Gothic Detail in Terra-Cotta, Bologna.
9. Capital, Lower Arcade of Doge's Palace, Venice.

All the above illustrations are from photographs or photographic prints except 9, which is from a student's drawing. Nos. 1, 3 and 7 are from photo prints published in the magazine *Stone,* reproduced here by permission.

PLATE XXII. GOTHIC ORNAMENT. ITALIAN.

1. Detail, Doorway, Messina Cathedral.

2. Tracery, Venetian Style

3. Doorway, Messina Cathedral.

4. Window of an Italian Town-Hall.

5. Columns Or San Michele; Flor:

6. Detail, Campanile; Florence

7. Porch, Cathedral of Amalfi.

8. Terra-cotta Detail, Bologna. 9. Capital, Doges Palace, Venice

INDEX

INDEX

Balawat Gates, 64
Bâle Cathedral, 311
Balustrades, Gothic, 296
Bamberg, 227
Baptistery: Florence, 243; of S. Stefano at Bologna, 240
Barcelona, 276
Barfreston Church, 269
Bases: Gothic, 287; Greek, 114, 115; Roman, 142; Romanesque, 251
Basilican Ornament, 187 *sq.*
Basilicas, Christian: Sant' Agnese, 195; San Apollinare at Ravenna, 198, 220, 223, 225; Ara Coeli, 200; San Clemente, 195, 198; St. John Lateran, 198, 200; San Lorenzo fuori le Mura, 200; San Marco, Rome, 195, 198; Santa Maria Maggiore, 193, 201; Santa Maria in Trastevere, 195, 196; St. Paul without the Walls (San Paolo fuori le Mura), 193; St. Peter, 193; Santa Prassede, 198; Santa Pudenziana, 198; Santa Sabina, 198
Basilicas, Pagan: Æmilia, 144; Julia, 163
Bassæ (Phigalæa), 120
Basketry, 22, 27, 28, 78
Baths: of Caracalla, 161; at Pompeii, 161, 178; of Titus, 161, 162
Battle of Issus, Mosaic, 182
"Beau Dieu" of Reims, 311
Beauvais Cathedral, 366
Belgium, 283, 285
Benedictines, 245, 249, 377
Bergen, Golden Chalice at, 279
Biology of Styles, 11
Bologna, Baptistery of S. Stefano, 240
Books Recommended (see end of each chapter).
Bosnia, Jar from, 28
Bourg-en-Bresse, Brou Church, 311, 338
Bowtels, English Gothic, 359
Brazil, Central, 21
Brou Church, 311, 338
Budmer in Bosnia, Jar from, 28

Byzantine Details: Acanthus, 211, 216; Anthemions, 215, 216; Bands and Borders, 215; Carving, 212; Church Furniture, 225; Floors and Incrustations, 219; Guilloches and Interlace, 218; Moldings, 215; Mosaic, 220; MSS. Illumination, 227; Rinceau, 217; Shafts, 211
Byzantine Influences, 237, 240, 243, 244, 249, 252, 255, 261, 264, 265, 270, 273, 274, 275, 277, 279, 319
Byzantine Ornament, 206 *sq.;* Architectural 208; Chief Characteristics of, 207; Textile, 227

C

CALABRIA, 244
Campania, 99, 108
Campanile, Florence, 239, 379
Canopy Windows, 325, 364
Canterbury Cathedral, 329, 362, 364
Capitals: Anglo-Norman, 267; Byzantine, 210, 211; Egyptian, 50; Etruscan, 130; Gothic, 283, 286, 332; Greek, 113; from Neandreia, 66; Persian, 68, 70; Pompeiian, 173; Roman, 140–142, 144, 147; Romanesque, 251, 252, 273
Carolingian Art, 250
Carrenac, Portal of Church, 261
Carved Ornament: Anglo-Norman, 269; Byzantine, 212; English Gothic, 354; French Gothic, 332; French Romanesque, 250; Gothic in General, 332; Greek, 111; Italian Gothic, 384; Italian Romanesque, 240, 245; Roman, 138, 149 *sq.*
Casa dei Capitelli Colorati, 172
Casa di Livia, 162
Castor and Pollux, Temple of, 141
Cathedrals: Alby, 312, 370; Altenburg, 329; Amiens, 262, 311, 338, 341, 342, 345, 366; Bâle, 311; Canterbury, 329, 362, 364; Chartres, 263, 307, 311, 326, 338, 341, 345, 349; Cologne, 329, 366, 369, 370;

INDEX

INDEX

INDEX

INDEX

INDEX

Pattern Defined, 3

Pavements, Decorative (Floors): in Baptistery, Florence, 243; Byzantine, 208; Pompeiian, 181; Roman, 162; Romanesque, 265

Periods: in Egyptian Art, 34; in Gothic Styles, 283, 331; in Greek Art, 91; in Pompeiian Art, 174

Perpendicular Style, 244, 283, 289, 296, 306, 346, 360, 361

Persian: Architectural O., 67; Columns, 68; Ornament Motives, 69; Stepped Parapet, 70

Persistence of Motives, 11

Peruvian Art, 27

Peterboro' Cathedral, 269, 363

Phaistos, Crete, 73, 74

Phenician Ornament, 79, 82, 83

Phigalæa (Bassæ) Apollo Temple, 120

Phrygia, 65, 68

Piers: Egyptian, 49, 51, 52; Gothic, 285

Pine Cone in Assyrian Ornament, 59

Pinnacles in Gothic Architecture, 297

Pisa, 238, 239, 240, 257; Baptistery, 240

Pistoia, 239

Plant Forms: in Egyptian Ornament, 43; in Mycenæan O., 79; in Gothic O. (see Foliage)

Plastic Ornament Defined, 5

Plate Tracery, 293, 360

Poitiers, Notre Dame at, 257; Ste. Radégonde, 264

Polychromy: Greek, 109, 111; Italian, 378, 379, 384

Polynesian Ornament, 25

Pomegranate in Assyrian O., 59

Pompeii, 125, 130, 162, 163, 164

Pompeiian: Architectural Detail, 172; Decorative Art, 170; Furniture and Utensils, 183; Mosaic, 181; Mural Decoration, 173; Periods in Mural Decoration, 174; Stucco Relief, 178

Pomposa, Santa Maria, 220

"Portal Guardians," Assyrian, 62

Portugal, 283

Pottery: American, 27, 28; Apulian, 99, 100, 108, 244; Bolivian, 28; Cretan, 75; Egyptian, 34, 53; Greek, 99; Melian, 74, 86, 99; Mexican, 27; Peruvian, Pueblo, 27, 28; South American, 28; Zuñi, 27

Pottery Decoration, Greek, 99–109

"Powdered" Ornament Defined, 5

Prehistoric and Primitive Ornament, 12

Prehistoric Egyptian Ornament, 35

Priene, 122

Primitive American Ornament, 27

Provence, 249, 251, 252, 255, 262

Pueblo Pottery, 27

Q

Quarry Defined, 5

R

Ratisbon (Regensburg) Cathedral, 370

Ravenna, 206, 210, 211, 220, 223, 224, 238

Rayonnant Style, 283, 331, 332, 341, 342

Reims Cathedral, 262, 278, 279, 280, 326, 335, 338, 341

Rhine Provinces, 273

Rhodes, 77, 86, 99

Rinceau: Byzantine, 217; French Romanesque, 255, 256; French Gothic, 337; Greek, 98, 108, 123; Pompeiian, 177; Roman, 153–155

Roman: Acanthus, 152; Anthemion, 155, 156; Architectural Features, 136; Carved O., 138, 149 sq.; Ceiling Decoration, 155; 156; Conquests of Greece, 93, 124, 132; Conventional O., 138; Decorative System, 133; Figure Sculpture, 156; Floor-Pavements, 162; Furniture and Utensils, 164; Grotesques, 157; Moldings, 139, 153; Mural Painting, 162; Orders of

INDEX

INDEX

St. Cénéri, 264
St. Denis, 255, 325, 341
St. Gilles, near Arles, 255, 307
St. John Lateran, Rome, 198, 200
St. Maclou, Rouen, 345
St. Mark's, Venice, 195, 207, 212, 223, 224, 279
St. Omer, Cathedral, 265
St. Ouen, Rouen, 345
St. Paul without the Walls (San Paolo fuori le Mura), Rome, 198, 200
St. Paul-Trois-Châteaux, 250
St. Pierre, Louviers, 345
St. Saviour's, Southwark, 357
St. Trophime, Arles, 262
St. Urbain, Troyes, 336, 342
Stained Glass, 320, 324; English, 366; French, 346; German, 370
Ste. Radégonde, Poitiers, 264
Stepped Parapet: Assyrian, 59; Persian, 70
Strassburg, Cathedral, 311, 329, 369, 370
Structural Ornament: Defined, 7; Gothic, 283
Stucco Relief: Pompeiian, 178; Roman, 158, 178
Styles: "Biology" of, 11; Historic, 10; Summary of Sequence of, 15; Value of Study of, 14
Summary: of Characteristics of Savage Ornament, 29; of Sequence of Styles, 15
Sun Disk on Egyptian Buildings, 44
Susa, 64, 67, 68
Swastika: in Cypriote Ornament, 84, 85, 86; in Egyptian O., 48; in Greek O., 98; in Pompeiian Mosaics, 181; in Roman O., 164
Syria, 206, 210, 213, 229
Syrian Christian Ornament, 229
System: of Italian Gothic Ornament, 377; Roman Decorative, 133

T

Talenti, Architect of Campanile, 379

Tarragona, 276
Technic Theory of Origins of Ornament, 22
Tegernsee, Earliest Stained Glass, 324 *note*
Temples: of Apollo at Didyme, 114, 115, 122, 124; of Apollo at Phigalæa (Bassæ), 120; of Castor and Pollux, Rome, 140; of Egypt, 43, 51; of Erechtheion, Athens, 118, 120, 122; of Faustina, Rome, 140; of Parthenon, Athens, 115, 119, 124; of Zeus, Athens, 121
Textile Ornament: Byzantine, 227; Gothic, 319
Theories of Origins of Ornament, 20, 22
Tholos: of Atreus, Mycenæ, 77; of Epidauros, 121, 122
Throne of Maximian, 224
Tiercerons, 290, 361
Tiles: Chaldean and Assyrian, 57, 63; Romanesque, 265; Gothic, 319
Tiryns, 74, 75, 77, 78, 92
Titus: Arch of, 136, 156; Baths of, 161
Tombs: of Abbot of Aubazine (ill.), 309; at Doghanlou, 66; of Galla Placidia, Ravenna, 223; "of Midas," 65, 66, 68; Persian, 67; at Sakkarah, 46; of Scaligers, Verona, 383, 388; on Via Latina, 161
Toscanella, Churches at, 249
Totemism, 21
Totem Poles, Alaskan, 22
Totems, New Zealand Female, 24
Toulouse, Capitals in Museum of, 252
Tourmanin, Syria, 231, 232
Tours Cathedral, 326, 345
Tracery, Gothic Window: English, 360; French, 338; German, 369; Italian, 380, 383; Spanish, 374
Trilobe Lotus, 41, 42, 60, 78
Triptych in Amiens Library, 338
Trocadéro Museum, Paris, 264, 342
Troja, 243, 249

INDEX

DATE DUE

Demco, Inc. 38-293